Presented to

_____

Neal

With love,
From

Nancy and Danny Elijah
_____

Date

January, 2012
_____

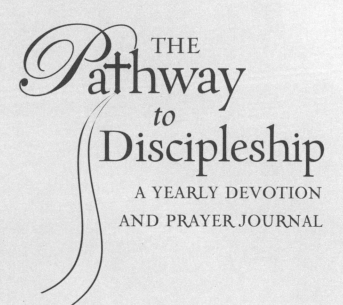

THE Pathway to Discipleship

A YEARLY DEVOTION AND PRAYER JOURNAL

COUNTRYMAN®

A division of Thomas Nelson Publishers
Since 1798

Published in Nashville, Tennessee, by Thomas Nelson. Thomas Nelson is a registered trademark of Thomas Nelson, Inc.

Thomas Nelson, Inc. titles may be purchased in bulk for educational, business, fundraising, or sales promotional use. For information, please email NelsonMinistryServices@ThomasNelson.com.

All Scripture references are from The New King James Version® (NKJV) © 1982 Thomas Nelson, Inc. Used by permission. All rights reserved.

ISBN-13: 978-1-4041-7440-5

Printed in the United States of America

 INTRODUCTION

The Pathway to Discipleship has been created with the contributions of 50 devoted men of God to help you experience a deeper walk with our Savior. This devotion and prayer journal will equip you to guide others in knowing and receiving the salvation God has promised for everyone. Each of the subjects will assist the reader to identify topics that are essential along the pathway to discipleship.

God desires for each of us to daily walk closer to Him. Be fruitful in your calling this year as you read this devotional book and reflect through journaling what you have read. It is our prayer that God will touch your heart and allow His Spirit to guide you to be His disciple.

God's people have only one way to face life—confidently living each day glorifying our heavenly Father. Your daily faithfulness could be life changing for the people God brings into your life. May you be changed and blessed through this book.

Johnny M. Hunt

Dr. Johnny M. Hunt
Pastor, First Baptist Church of Woodstock
Woodstock, Georgia

 CONTENTS

WEEK ..... CONTRIBUTOR	PAGE
WEEK 1 ..... Dr. Johnny Hunt, First Baptist Church, Woodstock, GA	2
WEEK 2 ..... Matt Surber, The Fellowship at Two Rivers, Nashville, TN	7
WEEK 3 ..... Bob Pitman, Bob Pitman Ministries, Muscle Shoals, AL	12
WEEK 4 ..... Allan Taylor, First Baptist Church, Woodstock, GA	17
WEEK 5 ..... Jerry Gillis, The Chapel at Crosspoint, Getzville, NY	22
WEEK 6 ..... Marty Jacumin, Bay Leaf Baptist Church, Raleigh, NC	27
WEEK 7 ..... Mike Whitson, First Baptist Church, Indian Trail, NC	32
WEEK 8 ..... Norman Hunt, Hopewell Baptist Church, Canton, GA	37
WEEK 9 ..... Dennis Nunn, Every Believer a Witness Ministries, Dallas, GA	42
WEEK 10 .... Junior Hill, Junior Hill Ministries, Hartselle, AL	47
WEEK 11 .... Dr. Adam Dooley, Dauphin Way Baptist Church, Mobile, AL	52
WEEK 12 .... Jeff Schreve, First Baptist Church, Texarkana, TX	57
WEEK 13 .... Dr. Grant Ethridge, Liberty Baptist Church, Hampton, VA	62
WEEK 14 .... Eric Thomas, First Baptist Church, Norfolk, VA	67
WEEK 15 .... Dr. R. Philip Roberts, Midwestern Baptist Theological Seminary, Kansas City, MO	72
WEEK 16 .... Paul Purvis, First Baptist Church, Temple Terrace, FL	77
WEEK 17 .... Rick White, The People's Church, Franklin, TN	82
WEEK 18 .... Dr. Ronnie Floyd, Cross Church, Northwest Arkansas	87
WEEK 19 .... Dr. Michael Lewis, First Baptist Church, Plant City, FL	92
WEEK 20 .... Kie Bowman, Hyde Park Baptist Church, Austin, TX	97
WEEK 21 .... Mike Hamlet, First Baptist Church North Spartanburg, Spartanburg, SC	102
WEEK 22 .... Jerry Walls, Southside Baptist Church, Warner Robins, GA	107
WEEK 23 .... Phil Waldrep, Phil Waldrep Ministries, Trinity, AL	112
WEEK 24 .... Dr. Rob Zinn, Immanuel Baptist Church, Highland, CA	117
WEEK 25 .... Dr. Richard Mark Lee, First Baptist Church, McKinney, TX	122
WEEK 26 .... Arden Taylor, Along the Journey, Gray, TN	127

WEEK 27 .... Chris Dixon, Liberty Baptist Church, Dublin, GA 132

WEEK 28 .... Dr. Dwayne Mercer, First Baptist Church, Oviedo, FL 137

WEEK 29 .... Tim Anderson, Clements Baptist Church, Athens, AL 142

WEEK 30 .... Tim Dowdy, Eagle's Landing First Baptist Church, McDonough, GA 147

WEEK 31 .... Vance Pitman, Hope Baptist Church, Las Vegas, NV 152

WEEK 32 .... Dr. James Merritt, Cross Pointe Church, Duluth, GA 157

WEEK 33 .... Jeff Crook, Blackshear Place Baptist Church, Flowery Branch, GA............... 162

WEEK 34 .... Jim Perdue, Crosspointe Baptist Church, Millington, TN 167

WEEK 35 .... Bobby Joiner, Chaplain for NewSong, Leesburg, GA 172

WEEK 36 .... Dan Spencer, First Baptist Church, Thomasville, GA 177

WEEK 37 .... Tim DeTellis, New Missions, Orlando, FL 182

WEEK 38 .... Alex Himaya, The Church at Battle Creek, Broken Arrow, OK..................... 187

WEEK 39 .... Craig Bowers, First Baptist Church, Locust Grove, GA......................... 192

WEEK 40 .... Dr. Danny Wood, Shades Mountain Baptist Church, Birmingham, AL 197

WEEK 41 .... Mark Hoover, New Spring Church, Wichita, KS 202

WEEK 42 .... Dr. Ted Traylor, Olive Baptist Church, Pensacola, FL.......................... 207

WEEK 43 .... Dr. Richard Powell, McGregor Baptist Church, Fort Myers, FL 212

WEEK 44 .... Paul Brooks, First Baptist Church, Raytown, MO 217

WEEK 45 .... Dr. Peter Chin, Global Mission Church, South Korea 222

WEEK 46 .... Dr. Glynn Stone, Mobberly Baptist Church, Longview, TX 227

WEEK 47 .... John Meador, First Baptist Church, Euless, TX 232

WEEK 48 .... Roy Mack, Pinecrest Baptist Church, McDonough, GA 237

WEEK 49 .... Willy Rice, Calvary Baptist Church, Clearwater, FL 242

WEEK 50 .... Brian Fossett, Brian Fossett Ministries, Dalton, GA........................... 247

WEEK 51 .... Dr. Stephen Rummage, Bell Shoals Baptist Church, Brandon, FL................. 252

WEEK 52 .... Dr. Johnny Hunt, First Baptist Church, Woodstock, GA 257

CONTRIBUTORS 263

SCRIPTURE INDEX 265

PRAYER JOURNAL 273

DISCIPLESHIP MOMENTS... 287

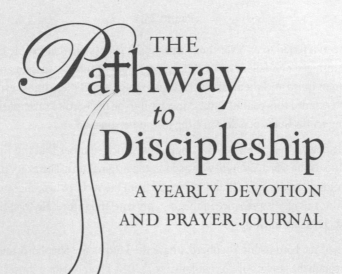

THE Pathway to Discipleship

A YEARLY DEVOTION AND PRAYER JOURNAL

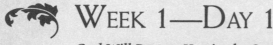

WEEK 1—DAY 1
God Will Protect You in the Storm

The LORD is my shepherd; I shall not want.

Psalm 23:1

Psalm 23 has been referred to as "everybody's psalm." It is possible that people from all walks of life have been encouraged or challenged by this passage of Scripture more than any other. It may very well be the most mentioned and memorized passage in the entire Bible. Almost every funeral service I have attended has included this psalm. Some consider it to be the Lord's Prayer of the Old Testament. It is filled with lasting truths God's people can cling to and personalize.

In the very first line, we see "the LORD" in small caps, which signifies that the Hebrew word *YHWH*, what we understand as the word *Yahweh*, was used in the original text. The exact meaning of the word is unknown, but many scholars agree that it is derived from the verb "to be." The very fact that our Lord is "He who is" reminds us of His presence in the past, present, and future: He was; He is; He will be. The name signifies the eternality of God.

David said he had the Lord as his Shepherd. I have the Lord as my Shepherd, and He has helped me and guided me through the storms of life. On January 7, 2010, I had prostate cancer surgery. As that day approached, I was amazed at how much encouragement I received from others who had had similar experiences. They shared testimonies of success, healing, and God's faithfulness. In the midst of that dark time, God's presence was so reassuring and sweet.

David said, "I shall not want," which means there will be no lacking of what is needed. The Lord literally provided everything I needed for the uncertain path I had to travel. He caused me "to lie down in green pastures" (Psalm 23:2). These pastures were rich with deeper grass than usual—His Word. As I lay there and prayed, He was faithful to speak to my needy soul. He quieted my soul and kept me from being frightened by the unknown. He was faithful to His name, His character, and His promises. And now I can comfort others going through that same dark valley and assure them of our Good Shepherd's faithfulness. Whatever you are facing today, know that He cares and, most of all, that He is with you.

 Lord, encourage me today to take You at Your word and to believe Your promises. In Jesus' powerful name, Amen.

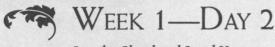 # WEEK 1—DAY 2

Let the Shepherd Lead You

He leads me in the paths of righteousness for His name's sake.

Psalm 23:3

As a shepherd, David knew that if a flock was to flourish and if its owner's name or reputation was to be held in high esteem as a good leader, the sheep had to be continually under the shepherd's meticulous control and guidance. For a shepherd to lead his sheep in the right paths, he needs to be very familiar with the pastures. A good shepherd knows where his flock will thrive and grow, and where the land is barren. As a pastor, I desire to help the Lord's flock feed in the pasture of truth, His Word. I share with the apostle Paul the passionate desire to see the flock mature in Christ (Colossians 1:28, 29).

David said, "He leads me." The Good Shepherd does not *drive* His sheep; instead, He speaks gently so they will hear Him and follow Him. Jesus said in John 10:3, 4, "The sheep hear his voice; and he calls his own sheep by name and leads them out. And when he brings out his own sheep, he goes before them; and the sheep follow him, for they know his voice." As we follow our Shepherd, His chosen paths bring us most directly to our destination. Simply put: our Shepherd guides us along the correct pathway in our daily walk. The only barrier to enjoying the blessing of being led by the Shepherd is a lack of trust in the Shepherd.

Here is a great truth to ponder: it is not what you choose for Him to bless, but what He blesses as His choice for you. Never forget, He does all He does "for His name's sake." The Good Shepherd cares for the sheep because He loves them unconditionally and wants to maintain His own good name, or reputation, as a faithful shepherd. It is out of loyalty to His own character that He upholds His own name. His reputation is at stake! He proves Himself to be what He declared Himself to be. He is loving and powerful, and He keeps His promises. He desires for us to know Him fully so we may trust Him fully and delight ourselves in Him.

 My heavenly Shepherd, it is my prayer that I will trust You in a way that results in straightforward obedience. Thank You for Your leadership and for Your character. In Christ's name, Amen.

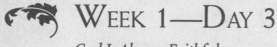# Week 1—Day 3

God Is Always Faithful

He leads me beside the still waters. He restores my soul.

Psalm 23:2, 3

As you read and reflect on Psalm 23, always remember that the writer considers himself to be a sheep in the Good Shepherd's care. It is as though he has been given the unique opportunity to brag about the benefits of being in His flock. His Shepherd takes great care of him!

A sheep's body is typically composed of about 70 percent water. Water is necessary for the vitality, strength, and vigor of the sheep; without it, the sheep becomes weak. When sheep are thirsty, they become restless and set out in search of water. To see that their needs are met, a shepherd will lead the sheep to the place of "still waters." Sheep are afraid of rushing water; if necessary, a shepherd will dam up a portion of it to create a quiet stream so they can drink in a peaceful place.

Sheep are often raised in very dry climates, and it can be difficult to find fresh water supplies. The sheep usually begin to stir early in the morning in order to find heavy dew on the grass. In my own personal devotional life, there are not many days I drink from a deep well or a running spring; on most days, my Shepherd uses the dew from a few verses of Scripture or a paragraph in my devotional book to quench my soul's thirst. When I am really thirsty for the Word, I will rise well before daylight in order to graze in His rich pastureland—to read His Word. There, the Good Shepherd refreshes my soul.

Undoubtedly, the psalmist could remember times when he wandered away from the flock and found unhealthy sources of water. In his wandering, he could testify to the Good Shepherd's faithfulness to come and find him, and then restore his distressed soul. When you wander, always remember that the Good Shepherd will come looking for you until He finds you. He rescues, refreshes, and restores.

 Heavenly Father, I praise You for Your faithfulness. You are so true to Your name, and I am Your benefactor. I am grateful for the refreshment and restoration You provide. Thank You for not giving up on me. In Jesus' name, Amen.

DR. JOHNNY HUNT, WOODSTOCK, GA

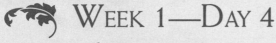# Week 1—Day 4

God Is Our Protector

Yea, though I walk through the valley of the shadow of death, I will fear no evil; for You are with me; Your rod and Your staff, they comfort me.

Psalm 23:4

David came to learn through years of being led by the Good Shepherd that his security did not lie in his environment, whether "green pastures" or "still waters" (Psalm 23:2), but in his Shepherd. His words in today's verse are, "You are with me."

Many read Psalm 23:4 and immediately think of the grave; however, the word translated as *death* can also refer to "deep darkness." It seems that if we live long enough we will become acquainted with times of darkness and depression. Sometimes the Lord leads us along these dark paths, where only a ray of light is seen, where the light casts a shadow of His presence within our view.

Sheep have poor vision—they can only see about 20 or 30 feet in front of them—so dark places can be especially difficult to navigate. At times, a shepherd will lead his sheep through narrow, frightening mountain passages. When our Shepherd does this with us, there is a comforting truth we ought to remember: while the path is new and daunting to us, He never leads His sheep to places He has not already traveled. He is very much aware of the dangers. As a result, He is no longer out front leading the flock; He is now beside them, assuring them of His protection and care. Remember, nothing concerns you that does not concern Him.

A shepherd carries a rod and a staff with him. The rod is used for protection from anything and anyone who might seek to harm one of his sheep. The staff is often used to snatch one of his sheep from harm's way. As a result of having the Lord as his Shepherd, the psalmist found comfort in His rod and staff, and said, "I will fear no evil."

Praise Him today that He Himself is our Protector who walks through our valley with us.

 Heavenly Father, thank You for Your presence. Thank You that when answers aren't enough, there is Jesus. When I don't understand the "dark times," I am grateful that You are here with me. In Jesus' name, Amen.

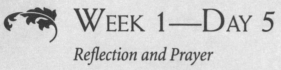

WEEK 1—DAY 5
Reflection and Prayer

When in your life have you sensed the Lord walking beside you instead of ahead of you? How can you thank Him?

_____

_____

_____

_____

_____

_____

_____

_____

_____

Reflect back on the Shepherd's leading you to green pastures and still waters. Has He ever had to make you lie down?

_____

_____

_____

_____

_____

_____

_____

_____

DR. JOHNNY HUNT, WOODSTOCK, GA

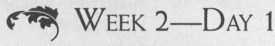

WEEK 2—DAY 1

Joy in God's Presence

God gives wisdom and knowledge and joy to a man who is good in His sight.

Ecclesiastes 2:26

*A*chieve the American dream. Get what's mine. He who has the most toys in the end wins. These are all phrases that describe what many think of as the be-all and end-all of life these days. They represent the idea that the way to true happiness is the accumulation of things, titles, and resources. Sure, we can spend our entire lives working toward these goals and looking for happiness in things that have no eternal value. In the end, however, they will ultimately disappoint.

God presents a different perspective on this topic. His Word says that to those who are good in His sight—those who please Him and have the right perspective—He will give true wisdom, knowledge, and joy. True joy is different than happiness, because happiness is based on circumstances. Happiness is when we say, "Things went my way, so I'm happy." Joy, however, is a choice. It's a *state* that results from knowing and serving Christ. It's not based on circumstances. Through Christ we can choose joy, even when the circumstances in our life aren't going our way.

Considering today's verse, true wisdom and knowledge appear to be gained through pleasing God. Perhaps one aspect of true wisdom and knowledge is the ability to understand the difference between joy and happiness. Ultimately, the pursuit of happiness based on the accumulation of things or good circumstances will just leave us lacking. May we come to realize that a relationship with Christ and the awesomeness of His presence are what will bring us true joy and fulfillment.

 Father, today, I choose joy. I commit to having my focus on You and having passion for You. May everything else short of Your goodness fall away. Lord, today, I serve You. I pray that You will be pleased with my life— may it be a life of worship! I thank You in advance for the wisdom, knowledge, and joy that come from my time with You. Thank You, Lord. In Jesus' name, Amen.

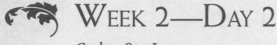

WEEK 2—DAY 2
God as Our Lover

He brought me to the banqueting house, and his banner over me was love.

Song of Solomon 2:4

The world watched a real-life fairy tale when Prince William took a commoner for a wife. Even though she fell short of royal standards, the future king of England chose her. Enough said. He showed her off to the world, brought her into his kingdom, and invited her to share in all his splendor. His act made her official royalty—Kate Middleton became Her Royal Highness the Duchess of Cambridge. We can only imagine that her response was naturally one of intense love, thankfulness, and devotion to the man that made her his very own.

The same is true in our relationship with God. His love for us, His pleasure in us, and His willingness to identify with us should naturally intensify our passion for Him and loyalty to Him. He is the One who has called us to Himself. He has chosen us and loves us. He claims us as His own and He wants the world to know. Just the thought of this kind of love should draw us to Him and cause us to feel a complete dedication to Him and desire for Him. We should simply find ourselves helpless to do anything less than truly falling in love with Him. This ought to be our response to His love and it should increasingly intensify because of what He has done for us.

Charles Wesley wrote the words for a great hymn entitled, "Lover of My Soul." The thought of God as our lover might sound a bit strange to some. Yet when you think about it carefully and see it from a fresh perspective, an overwhelming passion for Christ seems to be a reasonable result from the fact that we are His! It is the reality of being so overwhelmed by this kind of grace that we want nothing more than to live for Him, please Him, and adore Him. Verse 3 of Wesley's hymn says, "Thou, O Christ, art all I want, more than all in Thee I find; raise the fallen, cheer the faint, heal the sick, and lead the blind. Just and holy is Thy name, I am all unrighteousness; false and full of sin I am; Thou art full of truth and grace."

Father, today I rest in You and Your love for me. I bring nothing into this relationship but sin, yet You still love me. You still choose me and identify me as Your own. My prayer today is that I would be overwhelmed with You and that my response would be a deep love for You, my Savior and heavenly Father. Amen.

MATT SURBER, NASHVILLE, TN

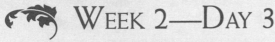

WEEK 2—DAY 3

What a Friend We Have in Jesus

His mouth is most sweet, yes, he is altogether lovely. This is my beloved,
and this is my friend, O daughters of Jerusalem!

Song of Solomon 5:16

You know those couples you see at a restaurant who are leaning in toward each other? One speaks while the other intently listens. Generally that type of focus is a result of some intense admiration. When you're quite taken with someone, you just can't seem to get enough of what they have to say. You find yourself hanging on their every word.

It is the beloved's words that are sweetest to the female speaker. His words are what she longs for and enjoys. The more she hears those words, the more she comes to say, "This is my love. This is my friend."

It's a similar situation in our relationship with Christ. To keep our love and devotion for our Lord healthy and strong, the lines of communication have to be kept open. The WWII soldier is a great example of this. Before cell phones and e-mail, the man overseas had to write letters to his sweetheart. His words were what assured her of his love and calmed her anxieties. He knew that sending his thoughts home on paper, full of his words of affection for her, would keep her going while he was away. His sentiments made her miss him. And in missing him, she wanted to be with him more and more. The words are what brought them close, even though they were miles apart.

Jesus' words to us are found in the Bible. We call it the Word of God. By spending time with His words, we get to know Him. The more we come to know Him, the more we find that we love Him. In time, we begin to realize that not only has Christ become the greatest love of our lives, He has become, and is, our Friend.

 Heavenly Father, I pray today that Your Word will come alive to me. Reveal more of Yourself to me, and in turn, may I grow to love You more and more. Jesus, thank You that You are not only my Savior but also my Friend. Amen.

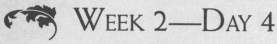# Week 2—Day 4

Knowing All of God

---

*I will betroth you to Me forever; yes, I will betroth you to Me
in righteousness and justice, in lovingkindness and mercy.*

Hosea 2:19

God asked the prophet Hosea to take a prostitute as his bride, and Hosea obeyed. God's purpose was to use his marriage to show the people of Israel that even though they'd been repeatedly unfaithful to Him and they were utterly unworthy of His love, He would continue to be faithful to them. He said, "I will betroth you to Me forever." Did you notice that He said that twice in this verse? He was saying, "I will tell you again: I am going to make a covenant with you forever."

Through the picture of Hosea marrying a prostitute, God shows us that He has done the same thing with us. Romans 3:23 says, "All have sinned and fall short of the glory of God." We've all messed up. We've all been unfaithful to Him. None of us are worthy. But in spite of our sin, our shortcomings, He takes us as His very own anyway. In both the case of Hosea and Gomer and of God and Israel, the relationship was initiated by the one who would be true.

Interestingly, it's our mess that brings out who He really is. His actions show us what kind of God we're dealing with. When someone does wrong toward you or me, we want to tell the world and see that they're punished. That's human nature. But God doesn't do that. He handles it differently. Aren't we grateful that He does? Experiencing this kind of grace, love, and forgiveness brings us to a deeper knowledge of our great God, stirring our hearts to worship and adore Him more and more.

 God, I am overwhelmed by Your grace, Your lovingkindness, and Your mercy. I admit that I am unworthy, but You love me anyway. Thank You that You reveal Yourself to us in this way and that we can truly know You, not because we deserve it, but because You allow us to. Thank You, God. Amen.

MATT SURBER, NASHVILLE, TN

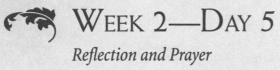 # Week 2—Day 5

Reflection and Prayer

Is your relationship with God growing? Are you closer to Him today than yesterday? Than last year?

_____

_____

_____

_____

_____

_____

_____

_____

_____

How are you investing in your relationship with God? What spiritual action steps need to be taken to improve your relationship?

_____

_____

_____

_____

_____

_____

_____

_____

_____

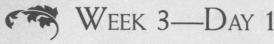# Week 3—Day 1

Develop an Attitude of Listening

He said, "Go out, and stand on the mountain before the Lᴏʀᴅ." And behold, the Lᴏʀᴅ passed by, and a great and strong wind tore into the mountains and broke the rocks in pieces before the Lᴏʀᴅ, but the Lᴏʀᴅ was not in the wind; and after the wind an earthquake, but the Lᴏʀᴅ was not in the earthquake; and after the earthquake a fire, but the Lᴏʀᴅ was not in the fire; and after the fire a still small voice.

1 Kings 19:11, 12

This is a day of much talking. Talk radio, around-the-clock television news, blogs, tweets, and social network ramblings dominate the lives of many. They are all filled with constant chatter. All too frequently these talkers have nothing to say . . . at least nothing profitable to the child of God. There are too many voices today that howl like strong winds, disrupt like earthquakes, and spread like wildfire. These are the voices of criticism, division, and destruction. They never minister grace; they are content to survive on slander, gossip, and misinformation. It should be remembered that when the Lord revealed Himself to Elijah, He was not in the wind, the earthquake, or the fire. We shouldn't expect to find Him in those places today!

Christians must learn to overlook those noisy, negative, nagging voices and to hear the voice of God—because He does indeed speak, and we need to hear Him. It is time to be silent before Him and listen for His still, small voice. James wrote in his epistle that God's children should be slow to speak and swift to hear (James 1:19). That's some good advice for the twenty-first century! Resist the urge to be talking all the time. A sign in a stationary shop advertised a cheap ink pen with these words: "Runs freely when almost empty." Therein lies the problem today. Too many people are letting their words run freely when they are almost spiritually empty.

Develop the art of listening, especially to the voice of God. He rarely shouts. In words of gentleness and kindness, He speaks to our hearts. Are you listening?

 Heavenly Father, thank You for being a God who speaks to Your children. I pray that You will speak to my heart today. Give me the ability to distinguish Your voice from others of lesser importance. May I be like Samuel who said, "Speak, for Your servant hears" (1 Samuel 3:10). Grant that I would not only hear Your voice but heed it as well. Today I promise to listen for Your still, small voice. Amen.

BOB PITMAN, MUSCLE SHOALS, AL

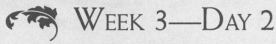

Week 3—Day 2

How Can God Use an Imperfect Person Like Me?

If we confess our sins, He is faithful and just to forgive us our sins
and to cleanse us from all unrighteousness.

1 John 1:9

Every believer desires to be used by God. We all have different talents, abilities, and spiritual gifts, but God will use anyone who is available to Him. He is not impressed with what we can do. No lack of talent or physical handicap renders the child of God useless. One thing causes us to be put on the shelf—sin. God commonly uses a broken vessel, but He rarely uses a dirty vessel.

You may say, "But all of us are sinners." That's true. The Bible declares, "All have sinned and fall short of the glory of God" (Romans 3:23). We are sinners by birth and by choice. When you received Christ as Savior and Lord, He forgave you of every sin you had ever committed. He wrote your name in His Book of Life and set you on your way to heaven. But you are not there yet. We still live in this world and we have to deal with sin. Our sin is no more acceptable to God now than it was before we were saved. Sin hinders our usefulness to God.

How do we deal with our sin? First, we must *see it as God sees it*. He sees it as unrighteousness—that means moral wrongfulness. God sees sin as wrong! Second, we must *confess our sins*. *Confess* means "to agree with another." We must not only see sin as God sees it but also agree with Him about it. We cannot hide it; we must admit it. Third, we must *ask Him to forgive us*. When we see sin as God sees it and agree with Him about it, then we can honestly ask for forgiveness. Because of His faithfulness, He forgives our sin and cleanses our hearts. Then He will use us!

 Dear Lord, You know me better than I know myself. You know my heart
with all of its deceitfulness. You know all my deeds and all my thoughts.
Today I want to be right with You. I do not want to be put on a shelf, but
to be active in Your vineyard. May the Holy Spirit reveal any wrongfulness
in my life so that I may confess it and experience Your cleansing. In Jesus'
name, Amen.

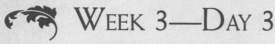 # Week 3—Day 3

What Happens When We Praise the Lord?

Praise the LORD! Praise God in His sanctuary; praise Him in His mighty firmament!
Praise Him for His mighty acts; praise Him according to His excellent greatness! . . .
Let everything that has breath praise the LORD. Praise the LORD!

Psalm 150:1, 2, 6

The Bible exhorts us to praise God, and He is worthy of our praise! We can praise Him anywhere. *Sanctuary* in verse 1 refers to the temple or to planet earth. *Mighty firmament* refers to the regions beyond, the heavens. God can be praised on earth or in heaven.

There are many reasons to praise God. First, praise Him for who He is. This passage proclaims that He is Lord and He is God. *LORD* is a translation of the Hebrew word *Yah*, an abbreviation of *Yahweh*. That is God's covenant name. It refers to His eternal love for all people and His willingness to enter into a covenant relationship with them. *God* is a translation of the Hebrew word *El*, an abbreviation of *Elohim*. That name refers to His power and glory.

Second, praise Him for what He has done—"His mighty acts." This refers to all He has done in the past, all He does in the present, and all He will do in the future.

Third, praise Him for "His excellent greatness," which literally means "the multitude of His greatness." There is no one like Him. Praise should come from everyone ("everything that has breath"). Sadly, there are billions of people on earth that never give Him praise. May that never be said of those of us who claim Jesus as Lord.

When we praise God, we are obeying Scripture. Obedience always honors the Lord and demonstrates the reality of our faith. When we praise Him, our lives spiritually shine for Him. One of the meanings of *praise* is "to shine." In Matthew 13:43, Jesus said the righteous will shine at His coming. We can shine for Him now as we consistently praise Him. When we praise God, we are also loving Him. Praise is an act of devotion, adoration, and worship. Offer praise to God out of a heart of love for Him today!

 Holy Father, thank You for Your overwhelming love. Thank You for salvation through Your Son, Jesus Christ. As I live this day, may my lips praise You and my life be an offering of praise that is acceptable in Your sight. In Your name, Amen.

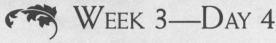# Week 3—Day 4
How Does God Define Sin?

My people have committed two evils: they have forsaken Me, the fountain of
living waters, and hewn themselves cisterns—broken cisterns that can hold no water.

Jeremiah 2:13

A certain theological professor announced to his class, "There is no definition of sin. That which is called 'sin' has been dreamed up in the minds of fundamentalist preachers who are killjoys of our fun." Sheepskins on the wall do not eliminate ignorance. Sin is real and the Bible makes no joke about it.

Sin is *something we are*. We were conceived in sin and we were born with a sin nature. Sin is *something we do*. It is doing that which God tells us not to do. Sin is also *something we don't do*. Inactivity doesn't always equate goodness. "You shall" is just as important as "You shall not."

Sometimes we think sin in the life of the believer is less serious than sin in the life of the unbeliever. Not so! In this text God spoke to those whom He called "My people." Believers are not exempt from committing sin or experiencing its consequences.

God always views sin as a double whammy—committing two evils. First, sin is a departure from that which is holy and good. To forsake the Lord is to depart from Him. As the words of an old hymn declare, "Prone to wander, Lord, I feel it; prone to leave the God I love." To depart from the Lord is to abandon the only source of real blessing. He alone is the source of living water. How deceitful sin is! The wells of this world cannot satisfy. Second, sin is embracing that which is unholy and useless. Broken cisterns represent human attempts to provide what only God can give. Sin is not only deceitful; it is totally unreasonable. Why abandon God for broken pots? Determine today to live the rest of your life for Him.

Dear Father, today I realize the wickedness of my heart. I know that I am prone to wander. At this very moment I ask You to take my heart and seal it for Your purpose and for Your glory. May I walk in Your will and way throughout this day. Do not let me yield to any temptation. If I do, please do not allow me to make excuses for my sin. May Your goodness lead me to repentance. In Jesus' name, Amen.

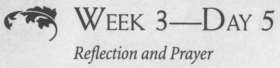 # WEEK 3—DAY 5

Reflection and Prayer

Since God speaks to His children, why do so many never seem to hear His voice? What can you do to guard against that happening in your life?

_____

_____

_____

_____

_____

_____

_____

_____

What impact does sin have in the life of a Christian? How should a Christian deal with sin?

_____

_____

_____

_____

_____

_____

_____

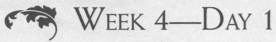

Week 4—Day 1

How Can I Really Hear God?

I desire mercy and not sacrifice, and the knowledge of God more than burnt offerings.

Hosea 6:6

Superficial religious activity is unacceptable to God. Going through the motions of being spiritual is no substitute for true dedication to God. The Almighty is not attracted to pious deeds but to pure devotion. External activity is meaningless to God if there is no internal adoration. First Samuel 16:7 tells us, "The LORD does not see as man sees; for man looks at the outward appearance, but the LORD looks at the heart." Our hearts lie continually on the heavenly X-ray machine.

God instructed Hosea to take a harlot as a wife to demonstrate how Israel had "played the harlot against their God" (Hosea 4:12). The Book of Hosea is to be understood against the backdrop of the Book of Deuteronomy, which records the covenant relationship between God and Israel. Like an unfaithful wife, the people of Israel had broken their covenant with God through their disobedience. Outwardly they looked good, but inwardly they were unfaithful and unclean.

Why do we not hear and heed the voice of God? Maybe we are not His children. Maybe we have never repented of our sin and by faith embraced the truth of Jesus' death, burial, and Resurrection. Or maybe as His children we're living in sin, and disobedience gives us bad "spiritual hearing." Our brains filter out many sounds that are not perceived as valuable because they cannot respond to every stimulus they receive. If we are unfaithful, the voice of God has been replaced by other stimuli and we do not perceive His "still small voice" as valuable (1 Kings 19:12). Sacrifices and burnt offerings were commanded, but closeness to God comes from devotion and faithfulness. Do you know God? *Really* know Him? Or are you depending on the activities of baptism and the Lord's Supper without a genuine, growing relationship with God? Learn from the Israelites' mistakes—be careful not to go through the proper motions without the proper motives.

> *Oh God of heaven, I realize You are looking into my heart today. You see all the filth and ugliness it contains. All things are open and naked before Your all-seeing eye. With the blood of Jesus, bathe me on the inside so that I may be pleasing to You. May the meditations of my heart—my motives and attitudes—in every situation I face today be acceptable to You. By Your grace, may I live in true devotion to Your glory. Amen.*

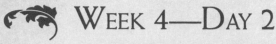

Week 4—Day 2

How Can I Find Renewal and Restoration?

He makes me to lie down in green pastures; He leads me beside the still waters.
He restores my soul; He leads me in the paths of righteousness for His name's sake.

Psalm 23:2, 3

Deism asserts that God has set everything in order, established certain laws of nature, and now sits idle while the universe runs on its own. He is the "absent landlord" who does not intervene in human affairs. Yet Scripture shows God to be a very personal God. The fact that He is personal distinguishes Him from false gods!

Notice the personal aspect of David's relationship with God as seen in Psalm 23: "The Lord is *my* shepherd . . . He makes *me* to lie down . . . He leads *me* . . . He restores *my* soul" (vv. 1–3, emphasis added). David used seventeen personal pronouns in this psalm. If God is not a personal God, then David sure had a flawed theology!

We see God active in human affairs in the verbs David used: "The Lord *is* my shepherd . . . He *makes* me to lie down . . . He *leads* me . . . He *restores* my soul . . . He *leads* me in the paths of righteousness" (vv. 1–3, emphasis added). I count nine verbs in Psalm 23 showing God's activity. God is not lying in some heavenly hammock while the world drifts by unnoticed!

Right in the middle of Psalm 23, we find this great statement: "You are *with* me" (v. 4, emphasis added). Go ahead and stop reading for a moment so you can shout, "Glory!" No wonder the angel told Joseph that "they shall call His name Immanuel," a name that means "God *with* us" (Matthew 1:23, emphasis added).

Like the traveler in the parable of the Good Samaritan (Luke 10:25–37), the devil will beat us up and religion will pass us up, but—praise God!—Jesus will pick us up. He is with us and can restore our soul. If you need some renewal and restoration today, then lie down with your Shepherd in His green pasture and beside His still waters. He has prepared a table for you. Your cup will run over!

    Lord, I take great comfort in knowing that the ear of my God hears, the eyes of my God see, and the heart of my God pities! Because You have taken personal responsibility for me and my eternity, I confess today that You are my God. In Jesus' name, Amen.

ALLAN TAYLOR, WOODSTOCK, GA

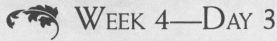

Week 4—Day 3
What Does the Bible Say When Life Leaves You Lonely?

The LORD will not forsake His people, for His great name's sake,
because it has pleased the LORD to make you His people.

1 Samuel 12:22

Perhaps no pain hurts like the pain of loneliness. Most people experience loneliness at some point in their lives, and Christians are not immune to it. Many great Bible characters incurred loneliness. Elijah felt alone in 1 Kings 19. King David felt alone when others were trying to take his life. Paul wrote that "Demas has forsaken me" (2 Timothy 4:10). Even Jesus cried out from the Cross, "My God, My God, why have You forsaken Me?" (Mark 15:34).

Although Christians walk through the trials of loneliness, we do not walk alone or without hope. Today's verse gives great encouragement when we feel lonely: "the LORD will not forsake His people." The assurance of God's personal presence is observed throughout the Bible. God spends quality and quantity time with His children. He is the Good, Great, Chief Shepherd, and "we are His people and the sheep of His pasture" (Psalm 100:3).

God walked with Adam in the cool of the day (Genesis 3:8). God promised Isaac, "I will be with you" (Genesis 26:3). God told Jacob, "I will be with you" (Genesis 31:3). God assured Moses at the burning bush, "I will certainly be with you" (Exodus 3:12). He then reassured him in the wilderness wanderings, "My Presence will go with you" (Exodus 33:14). Moses told the Israelites, "The LORD your God walks in the midst of your camp" (Deuteronomy 23:14). God reminded King David through the prophet Nathan, "I took you from the sheepfold, from following the sheep, to be ruler over My people, over Israel. And I have been with you wherever you have gone" (2 Samuel 7:8, 9).

Jesus told His disciples, "I am with you always, even to the end of the age" (Matthew 28:20). Mark it down: a believer is never alone, even if he or she feels that way.

    Lord, You taught us to address You in prayer as "our Father" (Matthew 6:9), and as my Father, I am not an orphan or left alone. The world may walk away from me and leave me lonely, but I praise Your name that You never will! I am Yours and You are mine. Therefore, I will claim, stand on and relish Your promise for me this day. I pray in Christ's name. Amen.

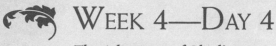

Week 4—Day 4

The Adventure of Obedience

*Your ears shall hear a word behind you, saying, "This is the way, walk in it,"
whenever you turn to the right hand or whenever you turn to the left.*

Isaiah 30:21

God is not looking for talent, charisma, personality, or skill; He is looking for obedience. Here is a great truth: obeying God is the most spiritual thing you can do. But it is not the easiest thing to do. Obedience has *adventure* in it. God often moves in a way that disrupts and interrupts our lives. We look for the convenient; God looks for the compelling.

Obedience has *anxiety* in it. We view insecurity and instability as being outside the will of God, when it may be the very center of God's will for us. God drags His disciples from a comfortable and calculable life into an adventurous one. The biblical program is that God is on mission and asks us to join Him. When we join God on His mission, He has to get us from where we are to where He is—usually that's quite a stretch!

Obedience has *adjustment* in it. Obedience requires us to make the needed adjustments in our lives to align with God's will. How long has it been since you sat down in a quiet place with an open Bible and an open heart and allowed God to speak into your situation?

Obedience has *allegiance* in it. The essential prerequisite to knowing the will of God is a willingness to do it. Regardless of our circumstances, our faith must stand tall. God needs no heroes (He is the hero), just obedient children. Solomon said the conclusion to all his wisdom was, "Fear God and keep His commandments" (Ecclesiastes 12:13).

Obedience has *abundance* in it. Our perceived adversity could be full of God-given opportunity because God only blesses obedience. Hymn writer John Sammis had it right: "Trust and obey, for there's no other way to be happy in Jesus, but to trust and obey."

 Heavenly Father, I want to be an obedient child. But like Paul, I often find that I do that which I should not do and don't do what I should. Whisper in my ear today, "This is the way, walk in it." Hedge me in so I must walk the path You have for me. Strengthen me to walk in faithful obedience to Your will. Amen.

ALLAN TAYLOR, WOODSTOCK, GA

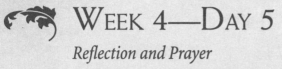# WEEK 4—DAY 5

Reflection and Prayer

Are you a for-real Christian, devoted to your relationship with Jesus? Or are you just going through the motions of superficial religious activity?

_____

_____

_____

_____

_____

_____

_____

_____

_____

How can you better adjust your life to the commandments of God so that you may be obedient to His will?

_____

_____

_____

_____

_____

_____

_____

_____

_____

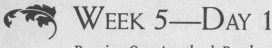# WEEK 5—DAY 1

Bearing One Another's Burdens

Bear one another's burdens, and so fulfill the law of Christ.

Galatians 6:2

When I was in college, I severely sprained my ankle in a pickup basketball game. As you might suspect, when it happened, every part of my body went into action to take the pressure off my ankle—my healthy leg bore the majority of my weight, my arms reached down to stabilize the injured ankle, and my mouth opened to yell for help. Christ used the way the human body works as a metaphor for the way those who are His own are to relate to one another. When one part of the body is under a burden, the other parts of the body respond to help support it. When the body acts this way, as it should naturally, then it is fulfilling the law of Christ.

The phrase "the law of Christ" is a curious one. In a letter where Paul explicitly reminds believers that they are no longer under the law (Galatians 5:18), he still exhorts them to fulfill the law of Christ. What is the law of Christ? We know it to be love (John 15:9–13), and the foundation of love is sacrifice. The Lord Jesus expressed sacrificial love when He gave His life for the world. This, therefore, is our model for how we treat the other parts of the body.

It is a privilege to join Jesus in bearing the burdens of others, and doing so is simply an act of receiving His invitation. He has invited us to take His yoke upon us because His strength compensates for our weakness (Matthew 11:28–30). We don't bear another's burden alone! Look for ways that you, while yoked to Jesus, can be a loving burden-bearer for your brothers and sisters.

Lord Jesus, Your strength and loving sacrifice are the source of my strength and love. Help me to be sensitive to the burdens that weigh down my brothers and sisters in Christ, and to enter lovingly into their burdens alongside You. Please give me eyes to see the needs of others, strength to walk alongside them, and grace to look like You in burden-bearing. Your strength is perfect and Your grace is sufficient not only for my need, but also for the needs of my brothers and sisters that I will undergird. Help me fulfill Your law of love. Amen.

JERRY GILLIS, GETZVILLE, NY

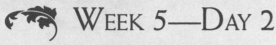 # Week 5—Day 2

How Do I Deal with Pride?

As for you, my son Solomon, know the God of your father, and serve Him with a loyal heart and with a willing mind; for the LORD searches all hearts and understands all the intent of the thoughts. If you seek Him, He will be found by you; but if you forsake Him, He will cast you off forever.

1 Chronicles 28:9

Years ago, when I was leaving Florida to move to New York to take my first position as the lead pastor of a church, my father shared some wisdom with me. He said, "Don't go up there and act like you know everything." He was warning me about pride.

Our passage today tells of another father giving his son some wise counsel. King David was speaking to Solomon around the time that Solomon was to be recognized as king of Israel. Solomon would have a great task ahead of him. He would be charged with the building of a permanent temple for Yahweh and would experience unparalleled peace and prosperity. It sounds appealing enough, doesn't it? But underneath peace, prosperity, and success lies the potential for self-destruction due to pride. Unfortunately, we know from the biblical record that Solomon gave in to the lure of pride and didn't embrace the warning of his father. His personal failures sowed the seeds of his kingdom's downfall.

While you and I may not have the riches or power of Solomon, we still have one thing in common with him—the lure of pride. We would do well to heed the advice that David gave his son, and recognize that the Lord knows our hearts, understands our thoughts, and wants us to seek Him with our whole being. Here is the only antidote for pride: bathing ourselves continually in the reality of all that God is. The gospel was not only the best news you had ever heard when you came to faith in Jesus; it is the best news you will hear today, because it will keep you from the self-destructive power of pride.

 Father, I know that the less I seek You, the more self-reliant I become. Please give me a hunger and thirst for You. Help me to swim in the ocean of Your grace so that I will gain a deeper understanding of all that You have done for me. Awaken me, Lord, to the gift of Your grace in Jesus, and help me to live in dependence upon You. You are my sufficiency and my boast. May I decrease that You may increase. In Jesus' name, Amen.

WEEK 5—DAY 3

What Role Does Obedience Play in a Mature Christian's Life?

*All the people, from the least to the greatest, came near and said to Jeremiah the prophet,
"Please, let our petition be acceptable to you, and pray for us to the LORD your God, for all
this remnant (since we are left but a few of many, as you can see), that the LORD your
God may show us the way in which we should walk and the thing we should do."*

Jeremiah 42:1–3

As a child, I hated brushing my teeth. I would do it because my mom or dad told me I had to, but I would do it reluctantly. As I got older and began to notice girls more, I could not brush my teeth enough—I wanted to have pristine-looking teeth and minty, fresh breath. I didn't have to be instructed or coaxed by anyone to brush my teeth; it was something I wanted to do. So what happened? Maturity changed my perspective.

When we speak of obedience in the life of a follower of Christ, sometimes it can be a daunting word. It reminds us of hearing our parents or teachers give us strict directives that we didn't particularly feel like obeying. In the young life of a follower of Jesus, that may be the case at times. We obey simply because Jesus told us to obey Him. But I can assure you, maturity in Jesus changes one's perspective.

As we mature in our faith, obedience to Jesus becomes joyful, not laborious. It becomes willful, not reluctant. The reason for the change is that as we continue to grow in grace, we will see new shades of the faithfulness, holiness, trustworthiness, and love of God, and seeing them inspires a new perspective on obedience. We want to obey Him because we are convinced He knows better. We are convinced that God is good. We are convinced that God, in His Sovereignty, has a trustworthy plan to unfold His glory through our lives. So, as we mature, obedience becomes more than just an act of willful submission to God *when He asks us to do something*; it is an act of willing submission to God *before He asks us to do anything*. May we be increasingly quick to trust Him and take joy in obeying Him!

Heavenly Father, I know that You can be trusted completely. I want to answer yes to You before You even ask me a question, because I know that whatever You ask of me is for Your glory and for my good. Show me the ways I should walk and the things I should do, and may I have a deep joy in bringing pleasure to Your heart. Thank You for being so faithful and trustworthy. Amen.

JERRY GILLIS, GETZVILLE, NY

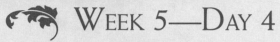 # WEEK 5—DAY 4

Why Is It So Important to Forgive Others?

Let all bitterness, wrath, anger, clamor, and evil speaking be put away from you, with all malice. And be kind to one another, tenderhearted, forgiving one another, even as God in Christ forgave you.

Ephesians 4:31, 32

Radical forgiveness is at the heart of the Christian gospel. It is virtually inexplicable that a holy God would send His one-of-a-kind, sinless Son to die for the sins of the world so that we might receive forgiveness of sin and have a way to be reconciled to Him. The forgiveness that God has extended to the world through His Son, not based on humanity's merit or works but solely on God's grace, is perhaps the most profound thing the human mind can ponder. It is also the basis for why we forgive other people. We are to forgive others as God, in Christ, has forgiven us.

What Paul writes in Ephesians is not new. It is clearly an amplification of how Jesus taught His followers to pray. Included in His model prayer in Matthew 6 is this statement: "Forgive us our debts, as we also have forgiven our debtors" (v. 12). Jesus teaches us to pray in such a way that as we ask God to forgive us, we ask Him to forgive us *in the same way* we forgive others. Simply put, Jesus reminds us that the forgiveness we extend to others needs to be motivated and informed by the forgiveness that has been extended to us.

Forgiving others can be difficult, but it is important that we do it. First, it magnifies Jesus. Second, it teaches us a lifestyle of forgiveness (since forgiveness is not typically just a single act but an ongoing posture of the heart). Third, it keeps us from locking ourselves into a self-built jail where bitterness, wrath, anger, clamor, evil speaking, and malice are our cell mates. Bathing in the gospel is our only hope for understanding forgiveness deeply and then extending it to others.

 Lord, I pray that You will give me the grace to live out the reality of forgiveness. Help me to appreciate more fully the depths of Your grace in forgiving my sin so that I will look at people I need to forgive with Your eyes. Teach me never to lose sight of the radical and immeasurable gift of forgiveness shown to the world—to me—at the Cross. Amen.

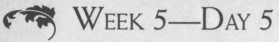 # WEEK 5—DAY 5

Reflection and Prayer

Is God calling you to forgive or to help bear the burden of someone in your life? How will you respond?

_____

_____

_____

_____

_____

_____

_____

_____

_____

Are you willing to set aside pride (self-reliance) and joyfully submit to obeying God in what He asks of you? If so, what will it mean for you to do that?

_____

_____

_____

_____

_____

_____

_____

_____

JERRY GILLIS, GETZVILLE, NY

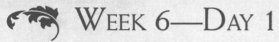

WEEK 6—DAY 1

How Do I Guard Against Temptation?

No temptation has overtaken you except such as is common to man; but God is faithful, who will not allow you to be tempted beyond what you are able, but with the temptation will also make the way of escape, that you may be able to bear it.

1 Corinthians 10:13

You may have heard the saying, "It doesn't matter what you know, but who you know." That may be true when trying to achieve something here on earth, but it falls short when fighting temptation. Being in a proper relationship with God is of the greatest importance, but when the temptation comes, it is crucial to know God's Word.

Matthew 4 gives an account of when Jesus was tempted by Satan in the wilderness. Jesus used Scripture to refute the devil's lies. Jesus did not negotiate with Satan or try to rationalize what He was tempted with; He simply went to God's truth to defeat Satan's lies.

When we are being tempted, it is important for us to do the same thing. Often, we try to justify the temptation, or we try to rely on our own power to resist the devil. We are no match for Satan in our flesh. However, when we have meditated on and memorized God's Word, we are able to use God's truth to resist the temptation. David said it this way in Psalm 119:11: "Your word I have hidden in my heart, that I might not sin against You."

We not only need to make sure we are meditating on God's Word every day—we also need to memorize Scripture so that when we are tempted, we can be quick to respond with God's truth. It worked for Jesus and it will work for us!

 Lord Jesus, I am reminded in Scripture that You were tempted just as I'm tempted. I also know that You used the power of Your Word to resist temptation. Thank You for giving me Your Word and help me use it when I'm tempted. Amen.

Week 6—Day 2

What Are the Characteristics of a Godly Person?

*While he thought about these things, behold, an angel of the Lord appeared to him in
a dream, saying, "Joseph, son of David, do not be afraid to take to you Mary
your wife, for that which is conceived in her is of the Holy Spirit."*

Matthew 1:20

The Bible warns that individuals can have the appearance of being godly, but when they are examined closely, they are far from God. The Pharisees were seen as the godliest of all the Jews. They prayed so that all could hear and they fasted so that all could see. They tithed and gave offerings, but Jesus showed that their hearts were far from God.

While the Pharisees had an outward appearance of godliness, they were disobedient to the will of God by refusing to receive Jesus as the Messiah. Compare them with the carpenter from Nazareth named Joseph. When Mary told Joseph she was pregnant with Jesus, Scripture says that he was going to leave her. However, when the angel revealed to Joseph that this was true, he was obedient to the will of the Father. Joseph took Mary as his wife and helped raise Jesus. Because he chose to be obedient to the will of God, he was able to be an integral part in the "God Incarnate" theme of the Bible.

Is it your desire to be a godly person? If so, make obedience to the will of God your highest priority. Choose obedience to God over fame, fortune, popularity, or political correctness, and then watch how God will bless this in your life. As a pastor, I've often said that if I had one word to preach to those who are saved, it would be the word *obedience*. This is what God desires from us, because when we are obedient to Him, we reveal the truest form of godliness.

 *Father, I confess that there are times when I am disobedient to You and
for this, I ask for Your forgiveness. My desire is to be obedient in everything
You ask of me. Help me to be an example of true godliness for others to see.
Help me live a life that is pleasing to You! Amen.*

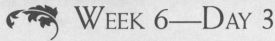

WEEK 6—DAY 3

What Does It Mean to Live in Fear of the Lord?

*You shall not oppress one another, but you shall
fear your God; for I am the LORD your God.*

Leviticus 25:17

Back in the early 1990s, someone coined the phrase "No Fear." You could find these words on T-shirts, automobile windows, and various other places. It speaks of living life without the boundaries of fear that often hold us back.

This "No Fear" philosophy may work well when it comes to skydiving or rock climbing, but it is not compatible with our walk with Jesus Christ. Numerous places in Scripture deal with a healthy fear of the Lord. God is our Creator and we are to show Him the proper reverence He deserves.

There are two extremes that can be demonstrated when it comes to fearing God. One extreme is to have a "No Fear" mentality that one can live any way they want to live because they are under God's grace. It is the belief that it does not matter what you do on earth because you are saved. The other extreme is walking around paralyzed by fear. It is the belief that if you sin, God is going to take away your salvation or strike you dead.

Neither extreme demonstrates the healthy fear that the Lord asks for in Scripture. It should be our ultimate desire to please Him in all areas of life because of our reverence for Him. If we have this proper fear of God, it will motivate us to pray that He would keep His hand on our lives and ministry, so that we might live in a manner worthy of our Father in heaven.

 Father, help me to fear You as You would have me fear You. I desire to live a life that is honoring and pleasing to You. I know I can't do this without a proper, biblical fear of You, my Creator and sovereign God. I love You, Father, and pray that my life pleases You. Amen.

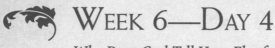

WEEK 6—DAY 4

Why Does God Tell Us to Flee from Evil?

*You shall do to him as he thought to have done to his brother; so you shall put
away the evil from among you. And those who remain shall hear and fear,
and hereafter they shall not again commit such evil among you.*

Deuteronomy 19:19, 20

Living on the East Coast, we hear about the paths of coming hurricanes every year. The National Weather Service is continually trying to improve the warning time they can give people when a storm is heading their way, believing that the longer warning time a person has to evacuate an area, the better chance they have to flee the impending storm.

Through God's Word and Spirit, we are warned of an impending storm. This is not a weather-related storm of wind and rain, but a storm of evil that Satan desires to send against every believer. God's Word is clear on how we are to respond to a warning of impending evil: we are to flee from it. We are not able to stand and fight the wiles of the devil. He is called the deceiver for a good reason. Because of this, God tells us to flee evil.

In our humanity, we often feel as though we can flirt with evil and remain pure. But why should we think so highly of ourselves? God's desire for us is to do just what Joseph did when he was pressured by Potiphar's wife to commit a sin. Scripture tells us, "She caught him by his garment, saying, 'Lie with me.' But he left his garment in her hand, and fled and ran outside" (Genesis 39:12). We are to flee temptation as quickly as we can. If we're hesitating and struggling, we need to pray about the sin we are desiring to commit and depend on God's help to make the right choice.

The Lord desires His followers to strive for holiness in their lives because He is holy. We should desire to model Christ to all those around us, and we will never do this as long as we allow evil to be part of our lives. Do you desire to be more like Christ? Do you desire to show Him to the world? If so, you must learn to flee evil when the deceiver seeks to tempt you to sin.

 *Father, I confess that in my humanity, I am tempted by evil each day. I
also confess that I cannot withstand the devil on my own. Help me flee any
evil that comes into my life. Lord, I desire to be more like You each day. Help
me to be close to You and clean in Your sight every day of my life. Amen.*

MARTY JACUMIN, RALEIGH, NC

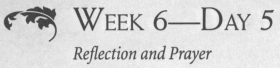

Week 6—Day 5

Reflection and Prayer

In what areas of your life are you most tempted to sin? What are you doing to resist the temptations?

_____

_____

_____

_____

_____

_____

_____

_____

_____

In what areas of your life are you being fully obedient to the Lord?

_____

_____

_____

_____

_____

_____

_____

_____

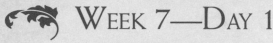

Week 7—Day 1

Does the Devil Have Control of My Life?

*The light of a lamp shall not shine in you anymore, and the voice of bridegroom
and bride shall not be heard in you anymore. For your merchants were the great
men of the earth, for by your sorcery all the nations were deceived.*

Revelation 18:23

In the scripture passage today, God did for His people what they could not do for themselves. He vanquished an enemy from their lives. Babylon was a destructive, influential controller over the Israelites for a very long time. God pronounced an irrevocable judgment that freed His children from that sinful stronghold.

Jesus warns us in Luke 11:24–26 that if we remain void of His presence and power as we attempt to rid ourselves of sinful habits, we will revert to those same habits, which will become accompanied by even worse controlling factors. It is one thing to replace old habits; it is another for God to do a cleansing work in our lives. It is one thing to resolve to do better; it is another for Christ to make us new creations. Who is controlling your life? You? Has the flesh returned with even more sinister influences? Or has Christ vanquished the enemy of sin and taken up residence in your life where He presides?

Whatever controlling demons you need to be rid of—whether it is drugs, illicit sex, alcohol, greed, lust, or desire for power—remember that only the power of the Holy Spirit can pull those strongholds down. When He replaces them with Himself, they will never be able to control your life again, just as Babylon would never be allowed to reign over Israel again.

The question now becomes, has the Holy Spirit regenerated your life? Did old things pass away? Did all things become new? Can you sin now, and not receive discipline from God? If not, then ask Christ to forgive you and cleanse you today.

Father, You are so good and holy, and You do for me what I cannot do for myself. I thank You that You love me and have given Your love to me even while I was unlovely. Reveal to me anything about me that is not submitted to You. Please fill me with Your presence and power so that I may live victoriously over the desires of the flesh. Empower me to know who I am in Christ that I may stand against the attacks of the Enemy. In Jesus' name, Amen.

Week 7—Day 2

What Can I Do When Life Feels Hopeless?

Though the fig tree may not blossom, nor fruit be on the vines; though the labor of the olive may fail, and the fields yield no food; though the flock may be cut off from the fold, and there be no herd in the stalls—yet I will rejoice in the Lord, I will joy in the God of my salvation.

Habakkuk 3:17, 18

Over a hundred years ago, a missionary to China stood up in a meeting and read the above scripture. After pausing a moment he declared, "What could the devil do to a man like that?" then sat down.

Isn't it true that when problems come our way, our first reaction is to try to get out from under them, run from them, and get rid of them as fast as we can? Normally we will focus on the problems and make them the object of our attention and energy.

Often when the problems seem insurmountable and we have no solutions, we pray and come away from the prayer time thinking that God hasn't heard and, frankly, doesn't appear to care. What do you do when you can't find the answers, and heaven seems like brass? Let me offer a little formula that I have suggested to many through the years.

First, recognize that hopelessness does not come from God. Admit that there are some problems that you simply cannot handle.

Second, reject any notion that you are defenseless against those problems. Spend time talking to the Lord and let Him be your defense.

Third, replace those thoughts of hopelessness with the Word of God and the promises that He has guaranteed in regard to your problems. A missionary named Edith Edman once said, "Never doubt in the dark what God has promised you in the light."

All of us will experience trials and frustrations; no one is exempt. What we do with those trials is our choice. We can grow despondent, fear, and doubt, or we can choose to trust our God.

 Father, Your Word declares that there is nothing in this life we will experience that You Yourself did not face. You have the resources to meet every need. You are aware of my need right now. Please grant me strength to stay focused on You. You have promised that I can do all things through You as You strengthen me. I give You thanks, Father. Amen.

Week 7—Day 3

What Does It Mean to Be Conformed to the Truth?

*Whom He foreknew, He also predestined to be conformed to the image of
His Son, that He might be the firstborn among many brethren.*

Romans 8:29

Although this verse is controversial regarding the issue of predestination, the primary message of the verse is meant to encourage us in our walk with Christ. We can expect a lot of difficult days in our pilgrimage serving the Lord: loss of job, family crises, health problems, financial stress, betrayal, misunderstandings, and a host of other challenges. One of the main points of Romans 8:28, 29 is that we can rest assured that our Lord will use all of our life experiences, including the negative ones, to make us look more like Jesus—His ultimate goal and plan for believers. So when the exigencies of this life land right on top of us, instead of running away from them, questioning "Why?" or praying for them to depart (although that is not a bad thing to do), why not let each be filtered through the fact that God intends to use them to help us look more like Jesus?

Recently I looked at my sister and found her beauty quite staggering. When she was a little girl, there was not the slightest hint that she looked like my mother. Even in her young adult life, no one ever saw the resemblance. But now she is almost the exact image of my mom. The day you received Christ as your Savior, you had very little resemblance to Him. Even after baptism, the likeness could scarcely be seen. But as you respond to the difficulties of life with the mind of Christ, you become more and more like Him. One day, because of His predestination, you will look just like Jesus.

 Heavenly Father, You have desired that all should come to repentance, that none should perish. Thank You for allowing me to be a part of Your wonderful heavenly family. I am so thankful that I am not as I once was. I am not everything that I ought to be now, but by Your grace and mercy, I will one day be everything that You have intended me to be. May the circumstances of this life conform me to look more like Jesus, who is the truth. Amen.

WEEK 7—DAY 4

The Importance of Scripture

All Scripture is given by inspiration of God, and is profitable for doctrine,
for reproof, for correction, for instruction in righteousness, that the man of
God may be complete, thoroughly equipped for every good work.

2 Timothy 3:16, 17

Jeremiah 29:11 speaks of the fact that God has a plan for each of our lives. Yesterday's devotion makes it plain His plan for us includes conforming us to the image of Christ. But the fact of the matter is we often think we know what is best for our lives and have a plan that contradicts His plan.

We have the notion that if we search Scripture and discover His plan for us, it will not be a plan that is beneficial for us and we will miss out on a "fun" life. So we set out to do it our way and eventually find ourselves disheartened, disillusioned, and discouraged with life. But God says that if we dig into the Word and discover His ways, it will be profitable for us—we will know the truth, be corrected in our wrongs, and discover the right way to live. Only then can we become mature believers, equipped to live a life that is pleasing to God.

It is true that on His path you will miss out on some things. Things like fear of the future, because God's Word says that you will spend eternity with Him. Things like depression and anxiousness, because God says that He gives a peace that is different from what the world can give. Things like loneliness, for He says He will never leave you. Things like purposelessness, for His plans are to give us a future and a hope. You will miss out on the guilt of sin, for He says He will always be faithful to forgive those who repent.

Begin a quest to make Bible study a part of your daily lifestyle. The benefits are out of this world!

   Father, Your ways are not my ways and Your thoughts are not my thoughts. Help me to discover more of You through the Bible. My desire is to live a life that is pleasing to You, so correct me and guide me through Your Word. When You come back to earth or when I go to be with You, may You find me complete and mature as a result of Your Holy Spirit teaching me through the pages of Your Word. Help me hide Your Word in my heart so that I won't sin against You. In Jesus' name I pray. Amen.

Week 7—Day 5

Reflection and Prayer

Consider where you are in life right now; what evidence makes you believe that you are becoming more like the person God wants you to be?

_____

_____

_____

_____

_____

_____

_____

_____

_____

What life adjustments do you need to make to allow God's Word to enable you to weather the storms of life and to become more like Jesus?

_____

_____

_____

_____

_____

_____

_____

_____

_____

WEEK 8—DAY 1

The Pathway to Binding Satan

And I will give you the keys of the kingdom of heaven, and whatever you bind on earth
will be bound in heaven, and whatever you loose on earth will be loosed in heaven.

Matthew 16:19

What a tremendous opportunity the church has been given to unlock the doors of understanding for lost men, women, boys, and girls to the glorious gospel of Christ. Jesus' mention of "the keys to the kingdom" was a figure of speech familiar to the disciples. On another occasion, referring to the religious experts of His day, Jesus said, "Woe to you lawyers! For you have taken away the key of knowledge. You did not enter in yourselves, and those who were entering in you hindered" (Luke 11:52). It was the role of the rabbis to unlock the doors of understanding and knowledge. They were instead locking the doors and keeping people from understanding.

Jesus tells today's church that we have the keys of the kingdom. We have been given the gospel, the keys to the kingdom of heaven. Along with those keys comes every believer's responsibility to use them. Nothing that the Enemy throws at us should deter us, slow us down, or cause us to give up, because we possess the keys of authority. The power of heaven binds what we bind, and the power of heaven looses what we loose.

The only thing that can come between the power of heaven and these keys of authority is sin. Isaiah 59:2 says, "Your iniquities have separated you from your God." But we know from 1 John 1:9 that if we confess our sins, God will forgive and cleanse us. So we must do all we can to stay close to Jesus, remembering that He told His disciples, "Abide in Me, and I in you. As the branch cannot bear fruit of itself, unless it abides in the vine, neither can you, unless you abide in Me" (John 15:4). Apart from Jesus we are nothing and can do nothing! May we abide constantly in Him, and help others come closer to Him as well.

 Lord Jesus, help me to be faithful every day to use the keys of the kingdom of heaven to point people to You. Thank You for making possible the way of salvation! Amen.

WEEK 8—DAY 2

The Immense Value of Meditation

Let it please You to bless the house of Your servant, that it may continue before You forever; for You, O Lord GOD, have spoken it, and with Your blessing let the house of Your servant be blessed forever.

2 Samuel 7:29

As David meditated on the Lord, a desire was born in his heart to build God a permanent dwelling place for His glory. But God's answer was no. David's response is a wonderful example of what we should do when God looks at our dreams and aspirations and says no. He humbly gave thanks, praised God for His character and works, and expressed his dependence on Him (2 Samuel 7:18–29).

David had hoped to build the Lord a house, but God turned it around and built David a house. His house is known in Scripture as the Davidic covenant, a promise made by God to establish David's throne forever. What a promise! In David's prayer recorded in today's verse, he sought the blessing of God on his family and his descendents. He knew that God is a God of covenant, and He would keep His covenant to bless His people for generations.

David's desire to build God a house was a good one, and even though God didn't will for it to be fulfilled, He did praise David for having the desire in his heart (2 Chronicles 6:8). When we find ourselves having specific desires to serve God, we should thank Him, and then find out for sure that our dreams are in line with His plan for our lives. Sometimes we experience the death of our dreams. We see things not turn out as we had hoped, but we must always remember the Lord's promise in Romans 8:28: "All things work together for good to those who love God, to those who are the called according to His purpose."

 Lord, thank You for this new and wonderful day You have created. I pray that You would guide me through this day and that I would be sensitive to follow in all the ways that You choose to lead. Amen.

WEEK 8—DAY 3

How God Speaks to Us

---

*When He had made an end of speaking with him on Mount Sinai, He gave Moses
two tablets of the Testimony, tablets of stone, written with the finger of God.*

Exodus 31:18

I will never forget the first time God spoke to me. I had only been a Christian a couple weeks, and I was at a revival prayer meeting at my brother's home. That moment was the most intense communication with God I had experienced since the night I was saved. I knew the presence of God in prayer, but that night I learned a valuable lesson about how clearly God speaks. God is not vague in His leading!

Hebrews 1:1 says that in the past God spoke "at various times and in various ways . . . to the fathers by the prophets." There have been times when God spoke to people in a literal voice. When God spoke to Moses on Mount Sinai, it was amidst the sounds of thunder and trumpets (Exodus 19). When God spoke to Elijah, it was in a still, small voice (1 Kings 19:12). There were also times when God spoke through dreams, for instance, when He gave dreams to Joseph (Genesis 37). In New Testament times, God primarily spoke to people through the Old Testament scriptures, but that wasn't His final word either.

The writer of Hebrews says that God "has in these last days spoken to us by His Son" (Hebrews 1:2). Only at the coming of Jesus do we begin to understand His full significance. As we draw near to Jesus, we come to understand that He is the full, complete, and final word of God to us—even if we have yet to hear all of it!

 Lord, I am grateful that You not only love us but also lead us in this new life! I know that there have been times I didn't see or feel Your presence, but Lord, by faith I know You were there! Thank You for Your ever-present Spirit. Amen.

WEEK 8—DAY 4

How Can I Gain Wisdom from God?

My son, if you receive my words, and treasure my commands within you, so that you
incline your ear to wisdom, and apply your heart to understanding . . .
If you seek her as silver, and search for her as for hidden treasures;
then you will understand the fear of the LORD, and find the knowledge of God.

Proverbs 2:1, 2, 4, 5

The separation between God and humanity began when sin entered the Garden of Eden. Humanity was cut off from the wisdom of God as a result of sin. Ever since then, we have found it difficult to understand and interpret our circumstances and conflicts. We need the wisdom of God to understand these things and to know God.

James makes it crystal clear that there are two kinds of wisdom in the world. In James 3:15–17, earthly, human wisdom is compared with heaven's wisdom. Earthly wisdom is sensual, demonic, envious, and self-seeking, causing confusion and every kind of evil. God declares that this kind of human wisdom will never achieve knowledge of Him! In contrast, "the wisdom that is from above is first pure, then peaceable, gentle, willing to yield, full of mercy and good fruits, without partiality and without hypocrisy" (v. 17).

How can we gain this heavenly wisdom? James assures us, "If any of you lack wisdom, let him ask of God, who gives to all liberally and without reproach, and it will be given to him" (James 1:5). Clearly, heaven's wisdom is a gift from above. When we acknowledge our spiritual destitution and our own inability to deal with the conflicts of life, and turn in faith to God, He will give His gift of wisdom. With this kind of wisdom, we learn to see things from heaven's viewpoint as God begins replacing our spiritual destitution with spiritual insight!

 Lord Jesus, how we desperately need Your wisdom and understanding as we navigate through life. Help me every day to depend totally on You for the wisdom that comes as a gift from heaven. Amen.

NORMAN HUNT, CANTON, GA

WEEK 8—DAY 5

Reflection and Prayer

What are your thoughts and feelings concerning your responsibility as a believer to "use" the keys of heaven you've been given?

_____

_____

_____

_____

_____

_____

_____

_____

_____

How has God spoken to you and guided your path since you came to know Him?

_____

_____

_____

_____

_____

_____

_____

_____

Week 9—Day 1

How Does the Wisdom of God's Word Help Us in Our Christian Walk?

The Lord gives wisdom; from His mouth come knowledge and understanding; He stores up sound wisdom for the upright; He is a shield to those who walk uprightly.

Proverbs 2:6, 7

Christianity is not some ethereal, feel-good, emotion-driven religion. Rather, Christianity is eminently practical in our daily lives. Once a person accepts the Lord Jesus Christ, there is no separation between secular and sacred. Our lives are to be lived for Him.

How can we know how to live for Him and please Him? How can we learn to walk as we should as Christians and conduct ourselves wisely in our daily lives? By reading His instruction manual! Today's passage says knowledge and understanding come from His mouth. What comes from His mouth has been written down in Scripture. When Paul told Timothy, "All Scripture is given by inspiration of God" (2 Timothy 3:16), he used a Greek word that literally means "God-breathed."

Proverbs 2:6, 7 shows us that God wants us to be wise. He wants us to walk in His protection. Therefore, it is imperative that we spend time reading the Bible each day. As the Israelites were about to enter the Promised Land, Moses told the people, "Man shall not live by bread alone; but man lives by every word that proceeds from the mouth of the Lord" (Deuteronomy 8:3). Jesus reiterated the same message to Satan when Satan tempted Him in the wilderness (Matthew 4:4). Health experts tell us good nutrition is vital to good physical health. The Spiritual Expert, Jesus, tells us that taking in the Word of God is vital to good spiritual health. Commit to living wisely by taking in God's wisdom daily.

    Heavenly Father, I acknowledge that I am not wise enough to know how to live to please You or to enjoy being Your child. Thank You for having Your wisdom written down so I can learn to walk wisely and securely. Help me make taking in Your wisdom a daily priority in my life. In Jesus' name, Amen.

Week 9—Day 2

What Does God Really Think of Me?

Being justified freely by His grace through the redemption that is in Christ Jesus.

Romans 3:24

Paul began his letter to believers in Rome by pointing out that whether a person is immoral, moral, or religious, "There is none righteous, no, not one" (Romans 3:10) and that "all have sinned and fall short of the glory of God" (Romans 3:23). Then in Romans 3:24, Paul made a glorious statement that counteracts, outweighs, and cancels out our sinfulness—we are "justified freely."

We do not use forms of the word *justification* very much in our daily conversations. It is a legal term that means "to be acquitted, found not guilty." Just as a judge might declare a person charged with a crime to be not guilty, God, the Righteous Judge, has declared those who believe in the Lord Jesus to be not guilty of their sins!

An earthly judge would declare a person not guilty on the basis that the person did not commit the crime. God declares a person who accepts Jesus as not guilty not because he or she didn't commit the sins, but because Jesus paid the penalty for his or her sins. When a person confesses Jesus as Lord, that person is justified, seen by God as righteous—as the phrase goes, "just as if I'd never sinned"!

Another wonderful aspect of being justified is that it is a present condition. In the Greek language of the New Testament, *justified* is a present participle, which means it is current—it is happening right now—and it is an ongoing condition. Followers of Jesus Christ are right now being justified through the work of Jesus Christ on the Cross.

What does God really think of me? If I am more than a church member, if I have truly turned from myself and my sin and received Jesus as my Lord, then God really thinks of me as justified, innocent, and accepted . . . because of Jesus.

 Dear heavenly Father, thank You for loving me and sending Jesus to pay my sin debt, to take the punishment I deserved. Thank You for opening my eyes to see that in Jesus, You really do see me as Your justified child. In Jesus' name, Amen.

Week 9—Day 3

How Do I Rightly Know God's Truth?

As it is written: "Eye has not seen, nor ear heard, nor have entered into the heart of man the things which God has prepared for those who love Him."

1 Corinthians 2:9

Every religion has its "holy book." For Christians, it is the Bible. There are many differences between the Bible and other "holy books" that validate that the Bible is true. The most important proof is the hundreds of prophecies of the Old Testament that were fulfilled in the Person of Jesus Christ. So we know the Bible is true. In addition, Jesus said to His Father, "Your word is truth" (John 17:17).

But how do we understand the truths of the Bible? The verse above clearly states that it doesn't come by merely looking at it with our eyes or hearing it with our ears, and it's not the power of positive thinking. The next verse, 1 Corinthians 2:10, gives us the answer: "But God has revealed them to us through His Spirit." The Holy Spirit is the One who allows us to understand the truth of God's Word. Jesus told His disciples that after He left the earth, He would send the Holy Spirit, saying, "When He, the Spirit of truth, has come, He will guide you into all truth" (John 16:13).

This means it is imperative that you and I be clean and pure, having confessed our sins, when we read the Word. We must be filled, controlled, and led by the Holy Spirit to understand God's truth. We need to take time *before* we read the Bible to examine our lives. Will you ask God to show you right now any unconfessed sin in your life that would hinder the Holy Spirit from teaching you? Do this, and you will be in a position to know God's truth rightly.

    Heavenly Father, thank You for proving that Jesus is the only way to You by raising Him from the dead and fulfilling Old Testament prophecies. Thank You for giving us Your Holy Spirit to teach us. Please show me anything in my life that is displeasing to You and keeping me from rightly knowing Your truth. In Jesus' name, Amen.

DENNIS NUNN, DALLAS, GA

WEEK 9—DAY 4

How Can I Develop a Better Self-Image?

We are His workmanship, created in Christ Jesus for good works,
which God prepared beforehand that we should walk in them.

Ephesians 2:10

Hundreds of books have been written about how to build self-confidence and self-esteem. Magazines and newspaper articles give self-help advice. Seminars, videos, and television shows are intended to help people improve their self-image. There is no shortage of ideas, suggestions, and plans to help people feel good about themselves.

Paul, in writing to the Ephesian believers, gives us God's way of developing a better self-image. In the two verses before Ephesians 2:10, Paul says that it is not by our good works, but through our faith in the crucified and risen Lord Jesus Christ that we are delivered from the penalty of our sins. Salvation is a free gift, not earned by or deserved because of the good things we do. The fact that God would punish His Son for your sins immediately grants you VIP status with God! As a child of God, you have been given tremendous worth.

But coming to faith in Christ Jesus is just the beginning. Ephesians 2:10 gives us a key to developing a better self-image—doing the good works God prepared for us to do. You may experience great frustration and lack of fulfillment if you find yourself in a boring and unchallenging job. You may have trouble seeing yourself as valuable and important. However, walking in godliness and obedience and doing the good things that God has uniquely called and gifted you to do will cause you to develop a better self-image . . . and more importantly, you will be bringing Him glory! Look for opportunities to use your abilities for God's purposes, and depend on Him to lead you and work through you.

 Oh God, thank You for loving me so much that You had Jesus die for me!
Thank You for raising Him from the dead so I could have a new life. Help
me today, and every day, to see myself as valuable and important. Help me
do the good things You have prepared for me to do. In Jesus' name, Amen.

Week 9—Day 5

Reflection and Prayer

How highly have you been valuing daily Bible reading? Be honest—this is just for you. Do you need to make changes? If so, what are they?

_____

_____

_____

_____

_____

_____

_____

_____

How have you been viewing your self-worth? Do you need to make changes? If so, what are they?

_____

_____

_____

_____

_____

_____

_____

DENNIS NUNN, DALLAS, GA

WEEK 10—DAY 1

How Can I Claim God's Promises?

Let us hold fast the confession of our hope without wavering, for He who promised is faithful.

Hebrews 10:23

Promises are never any better than the character of the one who makes them. It doesn't matter how much faith someone has if the one in whom that faith is placed cannot be trusted. As children of God, the issue must never be the sincerity of our trust, but the steadfastness of the One we trust. That's why the writer of Hebrews confidently exhorted believers not to be "wavering" in their confession. The phrase "without wavering" is literally translated "standing without leaning." It is a clear portrait of an erect believer positioned with his feet securely planted on a firm foundation—a position lovingly prepared for him and faithfully promised to him.

How comforting it is to know that God has chosen to accomplish His will within the framework of clearly stated parameters. These self-limiting restrictions are known in the Bible simply as promises. He has interwoven those pledges with His attributes and has demonstrated what He is like through the promises of what He will do. Those promises are gracious windows through which the inquisitive believer may view His likeness. Do you want to know what God is like? Then look at what He has promised!

What God was like yesterday and what He will be like tomorrow is nothing more or less than what He has promised to do today. For He has said, "I am the LORD, I do not change" (Malachi 3:6). What a wonderful truth that is! It is the very foundation upon which all of our faith is built. Everything we are or ever hope to be in Christ is securely resting upon that unshakable pillar. May we keep our faith in this firm foundation, without wavering!

 Dear Lord Jesus, I praise You because You are as good as Your word and You never lie. I am grateful that my hope of salvation is as secure as the integrity of Your character. Please grant me confidence based on Your grace, and humility in Your presence. Help me remember that You have begun a good work in me and will complete it until the day of Jesus Christ. I pray in Your holy name. Amen.

Week 10—Day 2
What Do I Do When I Really Need to Hear from God?

Incline your ear, and come to Me. Hear, and your soul shall live; and I will make
an everlasting covenant with you—the sure mercies of David.

Isaiah 55:3

Listening has never been one of the greatest virtues of fallen humans. Failing to listen well is usually an expression of one's utter disinterest in what others have to say. A person's appreciation for someone else's words is always in direct proportion to their appreciation of the speaker. In the plainest of terms, not listening is simply a matter of people not hearing what they hear.

We can see accounts of people not listening in hundreds of verses in the Bible. Jesus said of His listeners, "I speak to them in parables, because seeing they do not see, and hearing they do not hear … For the hearts of this people have grown dull. Their ears are hard of hearing" (Matthew 13:13, 15). That scathing rebuke was directed not to those who could not hear, but to those who *would not* hear.

That's why God said to His people through His prophet Isaiah, "Incline your ear, and come to Me. Hear, and your soul shall live." The phrase "incline your ear" means far more than merely receiving vocal sounds. It literally calls for one "to hearken, to offer up, to cause to yield." It clearly infers a willingness to heed even before one hears. And interestingly, it is the first step toward discerning what God has to say to us. That's why the phrase "incline your ear" appears before the phrase "come to Me." It is as if He is saying, "If you are not willing to listen to what I intend to say and to obey it, then there is no need for you to come."

Before you ask God to speak to your heart, be absolutely sure that you are willing to obey what He says.

Precious Master, before I ask You to speak to me today, I pray that You will touch my ears and make them submissive to Your voice. Help me remember that what You ask me to do is not a suggestion that I may consider, but a command I must obey. It is my sincere desire to be like Samuel, who earnestly prayed, "Speak, for Your servant hears" (1 Samuel 3:10). In Jesus' name, Amen.

WEEK 10—DAY 3

How Can I Enrich My Time Alone with God?

Draw near to God and He will draw near to you. Cleanse your hands,
you sinners; and purify your hearts, you double-minded.

James 4:8

How close we are to God always depends on how close we are to sin. While the Lord loves us and will never leave nor forsake us, He has no desire to be second place to anyone or anything. As the rather timeworn saying goes, "He must be Lord of all, or He will not be Lord at all."

As no right-minded husband or wife would ever consent to share their marriage partner with someone else, the Lord will not share His fellowship with those who belong to Him with anything other than Himself. The Greek word translated as *purify* in this verse also means "to make chaste." It correlates with spiritual adultery, just as when James called believers to have pure, humble hearts and said, "Adulterers and adulteresses! Do you not know that friendship with the world is enmity with God? Whoever therefore wants to be a friend of the world makes himself an enemy of God" (James 4:4). Imagine being seen as an enemy of God! As frightening as that is, it is precisely what James said. While most Christians would be highly insulted if they were accused of committing adultery with someone else's spouse, they take lightly their infatuation and flirtations with the world.

But not God!

When it comes to sin, the word *trivial* never appears in His dictionary! A gospel that so plainly speaks of dying to self leaves no room for the half-hearted commitment of an indifferent and unrepentant person. Those who have any serious interest in having fellowship with the Lord must come before Him with clean hands, pure hearts, and an undivided mind. Anything less than that is a waste of time. For the Lord has said, "Can two walk together, unless they be agreed?" (Amos 3:3).

     Gracious Lord, it is my sincere desire to have fellowship with You today. I honestly want to draw near to You so that You will draw near to me. According to Your Word, I cannot do that unless my hands are clean, my heart is pure, and my mind is undivided. Reveal to me anything that displeases You and causes separation between us. Make me willing to confess it and forsake it. I ask this in Your dear name. Amen.

WEEK 10—DAY 4

Where Can I Look for Good Advice?

By pride comes nothing but strife, but with the well-advised is wisdom.

Proverbs 13:10

It is never good for people to think they know more than they actually do. The most obnoxious characteristic of people like this is their appalling insistence on telling everyone about it. That's why the Greek word for *pride* literally means "to inflate with self-conceit, to be lifted up." The difference between the vain and the humble is often no more than the tense they choose to attach to their verbs. Fools tell us what they have learned; the wise tell us what they are learning. The proud are ever on their thrones, constantly boasting of how much they have seen, while the wise are content to tell how much they wish they could see.

History has a way of taking men and women who thought they were nothing and making them heroes, and dethroning others who thought they were something and making them nothing. It is no mere coincidence, therefore, that the Book of Proverbs links pride with strife and wisdom with being well-advised. Rarely does one appear apart from the other. The proud will always be afflicted with problems; the wise will always be blessed with perception. Pride may give you the knowledge of what you need, but only God's wisdom can tell you where to get it. Someone has humorously quipped, "Pride may make you smart enough to believe only half of what you hear, but wisdom will make you smart enough to know which half to believe."

The best part is that God's wisdom is free to all! James 1:5, 6 says, "If any of you lacks wisdom, let him ask of God, who gives to all liberally and without reproach, and it will be given him. But let him ask in faith, with no doubting."

 Dear Father, give me wisdom I do not have. Today, in simple faith, I choose to believe Your promise to provide me with wisdom as I ask for it. I admit that apart from You, I can know nothing of eternal value. With You, I can know all I need to know and all You want me to know. In Jesus' name I pray. Amen.

JUNIOR HILL, HARTSELLE, AL

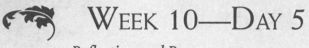

WEEK 10—DAY 5
Reflection and Prayer

How has my trust that God will keep His promises affected the sincerity of my prayers?

_____

_____

_____

_____

_____

_____

_____

_____

_____

What areas of my life are displeasing to God and causing me to be distant from Him?

_____

_____

_____

_____

_____

_____

_____

_____

Week 11—Day 1

The Value and Meaning of Hard Work

The LORD was with Joseph, and he was a successful man; and he was in the house
of his master the Egyptian. And his master saw that the LORD was with him
and that the LORD made all he did to prosper in his hand.

Genesis 39:2, 3

Success. Everyone seems to pursue it, but few are able to define it. At first glance, it appears that Joseph was successful because God rewarded his hard work. Closer examination, however, reveals that Joseph was successful before *and* after being promoted in Potiphar's house. Through years of heartache and suffering, Joseph remained faithful to the Lord, and God was faithful to him. The key phrase is "the LORD was with Joseph." This statement appears in today's passage, while he was in slavery, and in Genesis 39:21–23, after he was demoted to prison. In other words, Joseph's success was marked by the presence of God rather than his position in life. Knowing the Lord personally was more important than serving the Lord powerfully.

This is precisely where we miss it. Ours is a world that measures success solely on impact rather than intimacy. Being known by others seems to drive us more than being known by God. We long to be the main character of our story, when what makes us successful is having the Lord with us. Don't forget that Joseph's pain was instrumental in preserving the nation that would produce the Messiah. The young patriarch's trials were indications of God's presence, not His absence.

Are you willing to serve God when your world falls apart? Will you be faithful to a God that you cannot understand? Will you choose to value the presence of God more than His grandest blessings? If you judge success in terms of achievement alone, you will be tempted to rebel against God when dark days come. This is the lesson of Joseph. Certainly there are moments of reward and victory along the way, but life affords many difficulties, too. True success requires us to forsake our expectations of God in order to live with adoration for God in all things.

Lord, I know that my life exists for Your glory. Forgive me, God, for my tendency to be self-absorbed when life seems difficult. Help me to value Your presence more than the blessings or recognition You give. Thank You for working through my suffering in ways that I do not understand. Help me to serve You faithfully during the dark days of life. In Jesus' name, Amen.

DR. ADAM DOOLEY, MOBILE, AL

Week 11—Day 2

God's Empowering Presence

Then said I: "Ah, Lord God! Behold, I cannot speak, for I am a youth." But the Lord said to me:
"Do not say, 'I am a youth,' for you shall go to all to whom I send you, and whatever I command you,
you shall speak. Do not be afraid of their faces, for I am with you to deliver you," says the Lord.

Jeremiah 1:6–8

Qualifications. Some have more than others, and life seems to reward an extensive résumé. Yet in the economy of God this principle seems inverted. Jesus challenges the notion by saying the first will be last (Matthew 20:16), the greatest must become like the least (Luke 22:26, 27), and the meek are blessed (Matthew 5:5). No amount of preparation, no matter how strenuous, qualifies a person to serve God. In fact, asserting such appears to be a form of self-idolatry that accomplishes just the opposite. Thus, when the prophet Jeremiah protested his calling from God because of his inability to speak and lack of experience, he unknowingly demonstrated exactly why he was the perfect candidate for the task at hand. From this incident, the following perspective emerges: our inabilities provide the right platform for God to put His abilities on display.

God's response to Jeremiah encourages us to serve without hesitation when the Lord leads. In verse 8 God promised Jeremiah, "I am with you." He did not promise him a loving congregation, numerous conversions, or notoriety among the Jewish people. Actually, Jeremiah enjoyed none of these contemporary measurements of God's affirmation. But the young preacher possessed the one ingredient we still need more than any other to serve God effectively—the presence of the One who sent us. This does not mean we should ignore our gifts when we serve God. We should remember, however, that personal skill is a poor substitute for the Almighty's presence.

Do you find yourself making excuses rather than serving God faithfully? Have you considered that doing so is a form of false humility? Any lack of qualification used as justification for refusing God's calling is a cowardly way of propping up our inadequacies while diminishing the empowering nature of God's presence. Is it possible that what we see as limitation is actually God's way of making Himself known to us and to others?

 God, thank You for the privilege of serving You in ways that I never dreamed possible. Forgive me when I resist Your leading and opportunities. Protect me from false humility that supposes my abilities are more important than Your will. Show Yourself to be strong through me. Amen.

WEEK 11—DAY 3

The Value of Being a Diligent Follower of God

In the morning sow your seed, and in the evening do not withhold your hand; for you do not know which will prosper, either this or that, or whether both alike will be good.

Ecclesiastes 11:6

Unpredictability. Of all the things we desire to change about life, mysteriousness might top the list. Why do things happen the way they do? Why do we face the difficulty of forgetting the past and the impossibility of knowing the future? How can we navigate a world where everything can change in a moment?

Ecclesiastes gives us counsel from the wisest man who ever lived. His admonition? Work hard, trust God, and leave the rest to Him. To illustrate, Solomon wrote in chapter 11 that only farmers who sow will have the chance to reap a harvest. Though we cannot predict what misfortune will occur on the earth (v. 2), we can be certain that those paralyzed by fear will have nothing to show for it (v. 4). The diligent farmer plants his crops and is ready if the rain comes. Likewise, God calls every Christian to live without fear of calamity, focusing instead on what we know to do. Refusing to walk with God because we cannot predict what lies ahead is not an option. Seasons of joy and heartache are the consequences of a fallen world, but God calls us to rest in Him rather than retreat from Him.

Though life is often a mystery, trusting in God is not. Don't allow the burdens of the past to prevent you from trusting the Lord today. Refuse to let the uncertainty of tomorrow tempt you to doubt the goodness and purposes of God. Plant the seeds of faithfulness, righteousness, hope, and love while waiting for the rain of heaven. Position yourself for the blessings of God, and if they don't come, trust Him anyway. Choose to believe Scripture when your circumstances entice you to doubt. God knows what He is doing so you don't have to.

 Father, help me to trust You when I don't understand what You're doing in my life. Free me from demanding answers rather than trusting in You. Give me the strength and wisdom to be faithful in my Christian walk despite the anxieties I sometimes feel. Forgive me for doubting Your goodness in my life. Thank You for working all things together for my good according to Your good pleasure. In Jesus' name, Amen.

DR. ADAM DOOLEY, MOBILE, AL

WEEK 11—DAY 4

How Can I Find Courage in Times of Adversity?

Be strong and of good courage, for to this people you shall divide as an inheritance the land which I swore to their fathers to give them.

Joshua 1:6

Have you ever faced an overwhelming challenge? Maybe it was something that seemed insurmountable, or a goal that felt just out of reach. Perhaps it was a task that left you troubled and anxious. If so, consider the example of Joshua. Though following Moses may not be history's greatest obstacle, it certainly wasn't an assignment for the faint of heart. Yet the Lord told Joshua to be strong and of good courage. God even instructed him not to fear or be dismayed (Joshua 1:9), leaving us to wonder about the basis for this unusual courage. How can we face life's burdens without wilting under the pressure?

Apparently, this admonition stemmed from both the promise and presence of God. In verse 6 the Lord assured Joshua that He would use him to divide the Promised Land among the people of Israel. Translation: God always keeps His promises. In verses 7 and 8 God implored the young leader to know His precepts so that he would not deviate from them. Filling our minds with the Word of God allows us to live in light of His promises. Often our anxiety grows because we are ignorant or not mindful of the reassurances found in Scripture. Though the people in God's story continually change, the principles and promises of His Word do not.

God guaranteed that He would be with Joshua wherever he went (Joshua 1:9). Peace that passes understanding is not attributed to the absence of adversity, but to the presence of God in the midst of it. Appreciating the nearness of God would be impossible apart from times of desperately needing Him. In this sense, life's challenges are a necessary means of creating intimacy with your Savior. Rather than running from difficulty as if God is not there, you might be surprised to discover that this is where He is most present.

Lord, the possibilities of this day overwhelm me. I pray that You will continually bring Scripture to my mind as I face various challenges. Protect me from anxiety as I yield to Your Word and rest in Your presence. Assure me with certainty of Your goodness toward me and Your purposes for me. I choose to acknowledge You rather than leaning on my own understanding. Thank You for the hope I have in You, Lord Jesus. Amen.

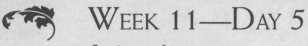

Week 11—Day 5

Reflection and Prayer

How do you measure success? What do the circumstances of Joseph teach you about your life?

_____

_____

_____

_____

_____

_____

_____

_____

_____

What promises from Scripture mean the most to you? When have you needed them most?

_____

_____

_____

_____

_____

_____

_____

_____

_____

DR. ADAM DOOLEY, MOBILE, AL

WEEK 12—DAY 1

How Can I Find Fulfillment in My Work?

Whatever your hand finds to do, do it with your might; for there is no work
or device or knowledge or wisdom in the grave where you are going.

Ecclesiastes 9:10

When I was a kid, my mom used to hang pictures on the wall using the heel of her shoe to hammer in the little nails. How strange! Why did she use a shoe? Because a real hammer wasn't handy, and the shoe could do the small job just fine. Can you imagine going to a construction site to build a house and, instead of bringing a hammer, you brought a high-heeled shoe? It may work in a pinch to hang a picture or two, but it wouldn't work for a hammering job of any size or significance.

You know what I have found to be one of the biggest problems people have with their jobs? They are like a shoe doing the work of a hammer. They are doing a job that doesn't really fit their passion or skill set. As a result, they are frustrated and unfulfilled. Could that be true of you?

Regardless of how much money a particular job pays, if it is not what you were made to do, you are wasting your life continuing in that work. God has made you for a job that you can do well and really enjoy. Seek the Lord and see what that job might be for you. Don't be afraid to take a step backward so you can take two steps forward. Life is too short to miss out on God's best. If all jobs paid the same, what would you do for a living? Follow that answer and you'll never "work" a day in your life.

Lord, I believe You made me with specific gifts, talents, and abilities. I want to use those things to glorify You. Show me what You created me to do and want me to do. Help me work hard in the job You have provided, knowing that I really serve You, not my human boss. If I am not in the right spot, Lord, open a different door for me. I don't want to be a shoe doing the job of a hammer. In Jesus' name, Amen.

WEEK 12—DAY 2

How Do I Deal with Burnout?

*Those who wait on the LORD shall renew their strength; they shall mount up
with wings like eagles, they shall run and not be weary, they shall walk and not faint.*

Isaiah 40:31

I know the feeling of burnout all too well. When you are burned-out, your mind wanders easily, your energy level drags frequently, and your temper gets harder and harder to control. The simplest tasks seem to take a long time to complete. Burned-out people just want to run away from all the responsibilities and pressures of life. What are you and I to do when we face burnout?

God tells us to come to Him, and wait and linger in His presence. Sounds easy . . . but it is not. When burnout comes, we really start to feel the pressure of our to-do list. Our production efficiency continues to falter, so we throw more and more time at our responsibilities in order to get things accomplished. As a result, we feel we can't afford the time to wait and linger in God's presence—but that is *exactly* what we need to do. A woodsman is not wasting time when he stops to sharpen his axe.

What does it mean to "wait on the LORD"? It is not sitting on your hands doing nothing, but rather putting your burdens in His hands and leaving them there. It is seeking the face of God in an unhurried manner. It is resting in the lovingkindness of the Lord and looking to Him for strength and renewal.

One of the best things you can do when you feel burned-out is to take a much-needed break. Go on a vacation, even if only for a couple of days. Turn off the TV and get alone with God. Let Him recharge your batteries and revive your heart. He specializes in giving us times of refreshment when we simply come to Him, curl up in His lap, and stay awhile.

  Lord, I confess that I have not been seeking You like I should. I have gotten so busy that I have failed to take the time just to rest and linger in Your presence. I choose today to wait on You and leave my problems in Your hands. Renew me, Lord, just as You have promised. Sharpen my axe, refresh my soul, and help me soar. Thank You, Jesus, for being my Friend, my Savior, and the One who renews my strength. Amen.

JEFF SCHREVE, TEXARKANA, TX

WEEK 12—DAY 3

How Can I Feel Secure in the Lord?

"Yet now be strong, Zerubbabel," says the Lord; "and be strong,
Joshua, son of Jehozadak, the high priest; and be strong, all you people
of the land," says the Lord, "and work; for I am with you," says the Lord of hosts.

Haggai 2:4

The Lord said these words when the people of Israel were back in their own land after their captivity in Babylon. During the Babylonian attack in 586 BC, the temple of God had been completely destroyed, so it was time to rebuild. But the job seemed too great, too overwhelming, too impossible . . . and the people were discouraged and left the job unfinished. Ever been there? Discouraged about the mess your life has become? Unsure and insecure in your relationship with the Lord due to some bad decisions you have made, and the adverse circumstances you face as a result of those bad decisions? What is the answer?

God says, "Be strong, work, and *know that I am with you.*" The Lord's presence is the key to overcoming discouragement, insecurity, and fear. If you have received Christ as Savior and Lord, you can be assured that He is with you. He promises He "will never leave you nor forsake you" (Hebrews 13:5). Even if you have to walk through the dark valley of the shadow of death, you can be secure and fearless because He is with you every step of the way (Psalm 23:4).

Are you facing tremendous difficulties today? Do you have to start over in business, in restoring your marriage or family relationships, in rebuilding your name in the community? Does the task seem too great? Don't quit! The Lord will be with you as you trust Him! He will give you strength as you roll up your sleeves and get to work on the rebuilding project He has put before you. Be encouraged. There is no need to fear when Jesus is near.

      Lord, I thank You for Your presence in my life. I thank You that You are
with me and will see me through every trial and difficulty, even those that
are self-inflicted. Give me strength and a will to work on the things in my
life that desperately need rebuilding. I praise You that I don't work and walk
alone. The God who spoke the world into existence is with me. Wow! Thank
You, Lord. In Jesus' name, Amen.

WEEK 12—DAY 4

When and How Am I Filled with the Holy Spirit?

*They were all filled with the Holy Spirit and began to speak with
other tongues, as the Spirit gave them utterance.*

Acts 2:4

What does it mean to be Spirit-filled? Does it mean you speak "with other tongues" as they did in Acts 2? Does it mean you perform miracles as the apostles did? What exactly does it mean, and how can you and I get in on it?

To be filled with the Holy Spirit simply means the Holy Spirit has control of you. It means your life is completely and willingly yielded to the leadership of the Holy Spirit. It means you are living with the attitude of Christ when He prayed, "Not My will, but Yours, be done" (Luke 22:42). You don't have to beg God to fill you with His Spirit, for that is what He wants to do. But you do have to ask God in faith to fill you and keep yourself yielded to His Spirit moment by moment.

When you are filled with the Spirit, it shows in your actions and reactions. You begin to act and react like Jesus. There is a power about your life that wasn't there before—a power to do right and overcome wrong. You are supernaturally able to bless those who curse you and love those who hate you. You experience the fruit of the Spirit: "love, joy, peace, longsuffering, kindness, goodness, faithfulness, gentleness, self-control" (Galatians 5:22, 23).

Do you want to be filled with God's Spirit? It will require you to vacate the throne of your life and let the Lord take His rightful place as your King. Someone has well said, "When self is on the throne, Christ is on the cross; when Christ is on the throne, self is on the cross." Are you ready to lay down your scepter and crown, and let the Spirit of the holy King take full control?

King Jesus, I yield to You this day. Take total control of me. Fill me with Your Spirit. Change my life by Your power. I want You to act and react through me. I resign from being captain of my own ship. By faith, I turn the reins of my life completely over to You, and I look forward to the wonderful results of living life Spirit-filled. In Jesus' name, Amen.

WEEK 12—DAY 5

Reflection and Prayer

If all jobs paid the same, what would you do for a living? What are you really passionate and excited about that God may enable you to do for a living?

_____

_____

_____

_____

_____

_____

_____

_____

_____

How much differently would you live if you knew beyond a shadow of a doubt that Jesus Christ was walking with you every step of the way? How would that change the way you view problems? The way you deal with temptations? The way you hope and dream?

_____

_____

_____

_____

_____

_____

_____

_____

_____

WEEK 13—DAY 1
The Awareness of God's Presence Stimulates Us for Our Work

Whatever you do, do it heartily, as to the Lord and not to men.

Colossians 3:23

Whatever you do is everything you do. What kind of work do you do? Do it for the Lord and not for humans. Having this perspective turns every secular job into a spiritual job. Class work, homework, office work—all work is for Him!

In life, we all have to do things we don't particularly like. As Christians, we must learn to do our work without complaining. Some people seem to think of their negative attitude as their purpose in life—they think, *How many things can I grumble about today?* or, *How much satisfaction can I derive from making others miserable?* When you are around complainers, pray that God will change their heart, and show them the goodness of a joyful, grateful, productive attitude.

In whatever situation you are in, be dependable. Dependability can be the greatest ability. Christians should be the best employees or employers in the workplace. Many people stop looking for work when they get a job! Be self-motivated. Look for work that needs to be done. Don't wait until someone has to tell you what needs to be done.

Be responsible. Strive to be the best student, athlete, musician, artist, secretary, stay-at-home mom, worker, or boss you can be. If you are miserable at your job, God either wants to change your job or change you.

Be accountable. There will be a payday someday. God will reward us if we faithfully serve Him. While we all answer to human authority, we ultimately answer to God. When people criticize or disapprove of you, don't get upset. You are not doing it for them; you're doing it for Him! Seek the approval of your heavenly Father. One day you will hear Him say, "Well done, good and faithful servant" (Luke 25:23).

Father, every day is a gift from You and holy unto You. May every place I go today be holy ground because You are there. May my heart be pure and my work be passionate as I seek to please You in all that I do. Amen.

DR. GRANT ETHRIDGE, HAMPTON, VA

Week 13—Day 2

Why Give Thanks to God?

We, Your people and sheep of Your pasture, will give You thanks forever;
we will show forth Your praise to all generations.

Psalm 79:13

Of all people, Christians have the most to be thankful about. We are children of God! God is the Creator of everyone, but only Father to His children. God has always had a people. Starting with Adam, Abel, Seth, Noah, Abraham, Isaac, Jacob, Israel, and then the church. Have you identified with the people of God? Are you part of the family of God?

If so, you are one of His sheep and He is your Shepherd. The Good Shepherd provides for us and protects us. As sheep, we tend to stray and go our own way. Jesus was willing to leave the ninety-nine to go after that one little lost lamb (Matthew 18:10–14). Those who have been found can't help but thank Him and praise Him forever!

How can you hand down your faith to your children so that it becomes personal to them? How can you teach them to be thankful? At home and on trips, talk with them about your relationship with the Lord. Count your blessings. It should be a natural part of daily conversations. We must pass the torch to the next generation.

As I write this, my wife and I are expecting our first grandchild. We are also blessed to be "grandparents" to several foster children. We enjoy and want to spend time with the next generations, and we pray for them daily. Our greatest gift and work in the kingdom may not be through us, but through the generations who will follow us.

 Heavenly Father, I thank You for the work You started in my life. Lord,
I must decrease and You must increase. Let others see Jesus in me. Don't let
me become lazy. May those who come behind us find us faithful. Help me
run the race You have set before me. Today, I recommit my life to You. I will
not quit. I will not turn back. Help me finish strong. Amen.

Week 13—Day 3

Spiritual Kinship to Christ Begins with Obedience

Whoever does the will of God is My brother and My sister and mother.

Mark 3:35

Do you ever have any problems with family members? If you have problems with people in school, chances are you'll never have to see them again after graduation. But when it comes to family, you have to see them at holidays, weddings, and funerals. It may comfort you to know that Jesus had problems with His family members, too.

Jesus' own family thought He had lost His mind. After all, He claimed to be God in the flesh. Too religious! Too radical! They were concerned He had gone off the deep end and came to rescue Him. They did not know until after His Resurrection that He had come from heaven to rescue *them*.

He left a good-paying job at the carpenter's shop . . . for what? He had no place to lay His head. He had a band of questionable disciples following Him. Tax collectors? Ignorant fishermen? His family did not understand or approve.

Have you ever noticed that when people are consumed with nutrition and health, it does not seem to bother their family? If they are running every day, no one gets worried. But if they are reading their Bible every day, the family becomes alarmed. When a person is excited about sports, people call them a fan. But if you are excited about spiritual things, people call you a fanatic. Someone once called an old-fashioned preacher a nut. The preacher replied, "At least I am screwed on the right bolt!"

Jesus issues an invitation: "Let Me be the Lord of your life." Having your family's approval is desirable, but having the approval of heaven is more desirable. Obey God today and you will hear your heavenly Father say, "This is My beloved child, in whom I am well pleased."

 Heavenly Father, I bring my situation and request before You. I do not know what to do, nor will I try to tell You how to work things out. Help me simply trust and obey. I stand on Your Word. Help me do Your will. Thank You for the privilege of being adopted into Your family. Amen.

DR. GRANT ETHRIDGE, HAMPTON, VA

Week 13—Day 4
What Does It Mean to Be Set Free in Christ?

Jesus said to those Jews who believed Him, "If you abide in My word, you are My disciples indeed. And you shall know the truth, and the truth shall make you free."

John 8:31, 32

If you abide in My word, you are My disciples. There is power in the Word. When you get in the Word, the Word gets in you! Church rolls are filled with people who have made a decision for Christ but have never continued in the Word. Have you cut back on your commitment to God, or are you continuing in your commitment? The true test of salvation is not a past experience but a present walk with God. The Word of God tells us how to live and how to think. It gives us guidance for everyday life.

"You shall know the truth." Jesus did not say you "might" know. The Holy Spirit will make sure you know. What do you believe? How you believe will determine how you behave. What you believe as a Christian should be based on the Bible alone.

"The truth shall make you free." Are you still in bondage? Are you addicted? Are you a slave to sin? Jesus can deliver you from whatever binds you. Whether it's poverty, debt, sickness, fear, worry, panic, anger, insecurity, jealousy, lust, addiction, demons, sin, guilt, destructive habits, depression, misery, or just life without meaning—*Jesus will set you free!* All around the world, people are crying out for freedom. What humanity longs for most desperately can only be found in Jesus.

When God gives us a command, He knows what is best for us. He is not restricting us. He is freeing us. Call on Him and run to Him today with open arms. He will set you free!

 Father, I stand on Your promise that "whoever calls on the name of the Lord shall be saved" (Joel 2:32). Deliver me from self and sin, and tear down the strongholds of the Enemy in Jesus' name. Cleanse me with the blood of Jesus and fill me with the Holy Spirit. Help me take every thought captive to the obedience of Christ. My desire is to hide Your Word in my heart that I might not sin against You. Thank You for victory in Jesus' name. Amen.

WEEK 13—DAY 5

Reflection and Prayer

If you stood before God today and were judged for your attitude toward and obedience to Christ, how would God evaluate you? In what ways, if any, would you like to change your influence on the next generation?

_____
_____
_____
_____
_____
_____
_____
_____
_____
_____

In what areas of your life do you still long for freedom in Christ from the things that hold you in bondage? How is your time or lack of time in God's Word influencing your deliverance from these areas of bondage?

_____
_____
_____
_____
_____
_____
_____
_____
_____
_____

DR. GRANT ETHRIDGE, HAMPTON, VA

WEEK 14—DAY 1

How to Control Your Temper

Do not be furious, O LORD, nor remember iniquity forever;
indeed, please look—we all are Your people!

Isaiah 64:9

When we're not careful about controlling our anger, it will control us. It may start with a minor frustration, but when left unchecked, it grows into something nasty and harmful. This is the natural course our sinful flesh takes. When we harbor resentment, constantly remembering injustices and living in a state of discontentment (if not barely contained rage), it's as if our hearts are being stewed in a big cauldron of anger. The heat keeping it going is our conceit, and the boiling water is like our bubbling emotions that splash up haphazardly and scald anyone nearby. Our hearts are certainly changed as a result of harbored anger. They become darkened by our narcissism and bitterness, and the words and actions overflowing from them hurt those around us. This kind of situation is rooted in the sin of self-interest; we are, in fact, bowing before the idol of self.

Experiencing anger is a natural part of life. It would be a mistake to equate anger with sin, for God Himself expresses anger. Yet in our anger we must not be guilty of sin. We must not allow the anger we feel produce the sin we must avoid.

The key to controlling our temper is communion with God. When we dwell in God's gracious presence, the heat of bitterness is turned down and we find peace. Tuning our hearts to His grace cools animosity's selfish blaze. Obsessions of self fade as we delight in God's presence and purpose. No longer bowing at the altar of our ego, we rest in the embrace of Christ and we become a living sacrifice for His glory. In worshiping Him, we smother the fire of ire.

Lord God, help me become a patient person who is slow to anger. Rather than exploding with tirades of wrath, I want to quiet the conflicts around and within me. I want to have inner peace that comes from a settled faith in You. Grant me faith to understand that You are completely in control over every situation and that You are working to lead me to the very best in life. By Your Spirit, grant me grace to engage my world with the faith-filled assurance that You are moving in and through every situation. Amen.

WEEK 14—DAY 2
Obeying God's Will in All Situations

You shall command the priests who bear the ark of the covenant, saying, "When you have come to the edge of the water of the Jordan, you shall stand in the Jordan."

Joshua 3:8

Sometimes obedience just doesn't make sense. Sometimes God asks us to do something that seems incompatible with what we feel or understand. I imagine that this was the Israelites' experience when God told the priests to stand in the Jordan River. They may have found it hard to believe that God would again heap up waters like He did at the Red Sea. Still, He called them to trust and obey Him.

In every relationship and in every circumstance, we are to live to celebrate our God and bless Him through obedience. Through the day and into the night, both when people watch us and when no one is near, we must be resolved to make God smile. Our hearts must beat for His honor and our souls must sing for His pleasure. We are to live each moment in a manner that is worthy of His love and empowered by His grace. The Spirit awakens our hearts to think first of God's joy before we speak, write, or take action. As God's Word unveils His heart and opens our eyes to what gives Him delight, we determine to weave every fiber in the fabric of our lives into a garment of praise.

There is no higher calling and no greater joy than to give all that we are to glorify God. To pursue His pleasure is the aim of our obedience. To know His pleasure is our supreme treasure.

 Glorious God, when I stand on the brink of difficulty or on the summit of success, may my heart embrace Your will and seek Your pleasure. May the resounding song of Christ's love rooted deep in my soul propel me to step forward in concert with Your purposes for me. I pray that I might adjust every thought, word, and action of my life according to Your desire, as unveiled by Your Spirit and through Your Word. Amen.

ERIC THOMAS, NORFOLK, VA

Week 14—Day 3

Develop a Discerning Spirit

These words which I command you today shall be in your heart.

Deuteronomy 6:6

When the sign on a backcountry trail forbids me to go forward, I can be prideful, certain of my own invulnerability. I tell myself that warning signs are for those who have less knowledge or sub-par skill. But such pride will end in disaster. Warning signs apply to all people, regardless of their skill level or experience on the trail, for all who make the journey beyond the warning will face the same danger.

The signposts set up by God warn us and help us keep our soul from sin's pathway. But we can be prideful, certain of our own strength to navigate dangerous trails safely. Discernment, planted in our hearts through God's Word and pressed on our minds by His Spirit, dispels our pride and directs our steps away from disaster and dishonor.

Living for God's glory demands a careful and diligent walk. We have to take time to look around us and within us so we don't rush headlong into danger. To live wisely and with discernment, we need to rescue every moment for God's glory. Looking inside and out, we must ask, *Am I honoring God with my life and service?*

When we allow God's Word to sink deep into our hearts, we will be able to understand His plan for situations we face. His Word is the filter through which we gain discernment. Our relationship with God through faith in Christ is more than words on a page. It is who we are, if indeed the Spirit of God dwells within us. God promises that when we are saturated with His loving wisdom through His Word, our hearts will be transformed and we will be given discernment to navigate through every terrain of life for His glory.

 Lord Jesus, I humble myself before You today and embrace Your Word that gives me life. I pray that this day might be marked by the discerning spirit You offer to me through intimate fellowship with You. I pray that the glorious grace of Your rescuing love might enlighten my heart with insight and direct my steps toward Your glory. Amen.

WEEK 14—DAY 4
Seek God's Guidance

Wait on the LORD; be of good courage, and He shall strengthen your heart; wait, I say, on the LORD!

Psalm 27:14

Up the hill and down the slope, through the woods and over the streams, my brother and I played the game with great skill. Of course, he was the leader because he was the elder, but I was the expert at following in his steps. The game was simple, even through tough terrain. I was going to follow the leader. Upward to the summit and down to the valley, we made the journey with focus. Making our way through the woods and the waters, we found courage to follow the path before us.

The key to making a journey for God's glory is following the Leader. We must become experts at following in Christ's steps. The journey is simple, even through the toughest terrain. Life is most satisfying when we walk in His steps.

It seems like an easy enough task. It's sensible, too. If we want to bake a cake that is edible, then we will follow the directions in the recipe. If we want to arrive at an appointment on time, then we will follow the directions on the map. But the creeping, slinking serpent of pride lures us away from the directions. We convince ourselves that we don't need them anymore. So, ignoring the directions, we get lost and confused.

God gives us directions to follow, and He has given us His Son to show us the way. When we follow Jesus Christ in the details of our days and through every maze, we will taste the pleasure of life. Anything else will be tarnished by pride and filled with sorrow. When we keep God as our Boss and stay close to Jesus, we will follow His directions and stay on track.

> *Lord, show me the path You would have me walk. I will wait upon Your direction and find Your strength as I give myself to God-sized faithfulness and not me-sized solutions. Right now, I confess that my vision and wisdom are so very limited; Your vision and wisdom are eternal and unlimited. Would You show me how to move today? Would You make my paths straight, showing me every day what steps to take? Lead me in every decision. Amen.*

Week 14—Day 5

Reflection and Prayer

What is the filter you are using to make daily decisions? Is it your experience, desires, emotions, or something else?

_____

_____

_____

_____

_____

_____

_____

_____

Spend some time thinking about how your life might be different if you adjusted your decisions, emotions, actions, and relationships to fit God's Word. Do you need to make any changes?

_____

_____

_____

_____

_____

_____

_____

_____

_____

WEEK 15—DAY 1

How the Holy Spirit Will Guide You

When He, the Spirit of truth, has come, He will guide you into all truth; for He will not speak on His own authority, but whatever He hears He will speak; and He will tell you things to come.

John 16:13

The Lord God Almighty does a marvelous service for us! He does what no other religion or religious leader can do. What is it that He does? He, by the mighty work of the third Person of the Godhead, indwells and fills every child of His. Everyone who has given his or her life to Jesus receives God the Father's and Jesus' presence through the Holy Spirit.

This is why Jesus told His disciples, "It is to your advantage that I go away; for if I do not go away, the Helper will not come to you; but if I depart, I will send Him to you" (John 16:7). This is amazing! The Holy Spirit encourages and leads us. Rather than simply accompanying us physically, He indwells us and guides us. The Lord keeps His promise to direct our paths. The Spirit helps us understand, know, and execute God's will.

It is just as if Jesus were by our side. Because the Spirit dwells in us, however, it is better still. The Spirit who does all things in counsel with God the Father and Jesus the Son guides us on a daily basis.

Today we rejoice in the fabulous, wonderful ministry of the Holy Spirit. May we be so attuned to His will and purpose that we do not miss His plan and remain fit vessels for His service and use.

 Heavenly Father, thank You for the wonderful ministry of the Holy Spirit. Thank You for being a gracious God who knew my needs and met them before I was even aware of them. Through the Holy Spirit, You guide my life. May He have full control over all that I say and do. Thank You for this most remarkable gift! May I know His fullness and His leadership as I step into today's activities and challenges. I honor You in Jesus' name. Amen.

DR. R. PHILIP ROBERTS, KANSAS CITY, MO

Week 15—Day 2

Why Do I Sometimes Fail to Hear God When He Speaks?

I spoke to you in your prosperity, but you said, "I will not hear." This has been your manner from your youth, that you did not obey My voice.

Jeremiah 22:21

Since the Garden of Eden, humans' inclination is to be totally self-reliant. Prosperity often brings this upon us. We think that the blessings we enjoy are a result of our own abilities and resources. The Word of the Lord, however, asks, "What do you have that you did not receive?" (1 Corinthians 4:7). Self-sufficiency can be a destructive and deadly spiritual state.

There are many other concerns that may hinder us from hearing the Lord's voice. Even good and proper duties—the responsibilities of life—may press us to neglect fellowship with and dependence on our Lord Jesus. Luke 10:38–42 gives an account of Jesus' visit to Mary and Martha's house. Martha was diligent in preparing dinner for Jesus while Mary sat at Jesus' feet, listening to Him. Jesus told Martha that Mary had chosen the better part—spending time with Him! While the meal Martha prepared would soon be forgotten, Mary would forever be changed by her fellowship with Christ. Dependence upon Him and union with Him are to be the cornerstone of our life.

May we be very aware today of our dependence upon the Lord, whatever the conditions we face. We need Him for everything, even as we need the air we breathe to survive. May God graciously grant you today the blessing of dependence, and prompt you to hear and obey His voice.

 Heavenly Father, thank You for Your great and wonderful care for me. It is so easy for me, especially when I prosper, to think that I have been the cause of all of the good things that have come my way. Remind me that every good and perfect gift is from Your hand, and keep me steadfast in my faith, allegiance, and dependence upon You. I pray in Jesus' name. Amen.

Week 15—Day 3
God Will Always Show You His Will

*Blessed be the L*ORD *God of Israel, who made heaven and earth, for He has given*
King David a wise son, endowed with prudence and understanding,
*who will build a temple for the L*ORD *and a royal house for himself!*

2 Chronicles 2:12

Dear follower of Jesus Christ, do you desire to know the will of God? Then He is prepared to show it to you. He may not always show it exactly when or in the manner we would wish it to come. But He will not leave us without His guidance and care. In due time, sometimes after trouble or in tribulation, He will make His will known. The psalmist said, "Wait on the LORD" (Psalm 27:14). God told His people through His prophet Isaiah, "In quietness and confidence shall be your strength" (Isaiah 30:15). That quietness and dependence come when we wait upon the Lord, even as Hiram, who is speaking in today's verse, was taught to do in his life of faithfulness.

If we are impatient and hear nothing, it is God's choice to answer us with, "Not yet." More is to come. As events unfurl, circumstances change, and our prayers remain persistent, the will of the Lord will be made known.

Isaiah said, "Those who wait on the LORD shall renew their strength; they shall mount up with wings like eagles, they shall run and not be weary, they shall walk and not faint" (Isaiah 40:31). Sooner or later, either with a yes or a no, the will of God will be clarified. When it is, we will proceed with the power of the eagle and the persistence of the runner. May God grant you such a life and such a willing obedience to do His will. May we be found faithful!

      Heavenly Father, thank You that You have a will and a plan for my life.
Help me rely on You. Help me trust Your Word and lean not on my own
understanding, but in all my ways acknowledge You. I believe You will lead
my way and guide my path. Thank You for being faithful in the past. I claim
Your promises for the future. May Your hand of blessing guide me as I seek
to follow Your will. I pray in Jesus' name. Amen.

DR. R. PHILIP ROBERTS, KANSAS CITY, MO

WEEK 15—DAY 4

The Will of God Begins in Your Heart

Bondservants, be obedient to those who are your masters according to the flesh, with
fear and trembling, in sincerity of heart, as to Christ; not with eyeservice,
as men-pleasers, but as bondservants of Christ, doing the will of God from the heart.

Ephesians 6:5, 6

What an amazing statement this is from Scripture. Bondservants were admonished to follow the direction of their masters in order to set an example of faithfulness to Christ. Many of these servants were abused, punished, and ridiculed, but because their first desire was to please God, they aimed to reflect the life of Christ through their love for and obedience to their masters.

How was this obedience possible in the face of such injustice and cruelty? They kept their eyes on the reality that they were serving God! They knew they belonged to Christ, and they wanted to serve and honor Him. Servants who lived according to this truth knew they could rely on the Lord of the universe to sustain and encourage them in all their undertakings.

While their obligations in this life might have restricted them, they did experience freedom of the heart, will, and spirit. The forgiveness that comes through the Cross of Jesus truly set them free to serve and honor Him!

May all of us who breathe the air of freedom be found faithful, doing the will of God. May our example shine like lights in the darkness, even as servants of old under much more rigorous circumstances were found faithful. May our hearts be attuned to the Lord's will so that we may one day hear those words: "Well done, good and faithful servant" (Matthew 25:21).

     Heavenly Father, I desire to know Your will. I know that before You reveal
it to me, however, I should be willing to accept it. May my life reflect a love
for Christ that honors You. Guide me in all that I do today. Thank You for
loving me, and I ask for Your help to serve and follow You perfectly. I pray
in Jesus' name. Amen.

Week 15—Day 5

Reflection and Prayer

How dependent are you, on a daily basis, on the Holy Spirit? Are you allowing Him to direct and control your life as you should?

_____

_____

_____

_____

_____

_____

_____

_____

Are you quiet, thoughtful, and still enough to realize on a daily basis that you are utterly dependent on the grace of the Lord? Is that dependence reflected in your walk with God?

_____

_____

_____

_____

_____

_____

_____

_____

DR. R. PHILIP ROBERTS, KANSAS CITY, MO

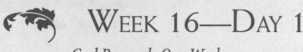

WEEK 16—DAY 1

God Rewards Our Work

Behold, I am coming quickly, and My reward is with Me, to give to every one according to his work.

Revelation 22:12

Your daily attitudes and actions have the potential of impacting eternity. In the final words of Revelation, God proclaims that He is going to reward His followers according to what they do. Your works do not secure your place in heaven, but they do make a difference. If there were neither heaven nor reward, it would still be worth it to follow Christ, but we get Jesus *and* all this, too!

God gives His reward according to our works. God offers His reward, which means it will be perfect. God could offer nothing less. It will also be personal; it will come from Him to you. This reminds us of God's promise in Matthew 16:27, "He will reward each according to his works." If you are a follower of Jesus Christ, He is coming to reward you. *Come* is one of God's favorite words. Usually Scripture commands us to come, but in the case of Revelation 22:12, God Himself is coming quickly to reward His followers perfectly and personally.

You may be asking, "What have I done to deserve God's reward?" Ultimately, your only hope is the grace of God. However, Scripture presents several reasons why you would receive heavenly rewards. You are rewarded for how you share (Mark 9:41), serve (Colossians 3:23, 24), sacrifice (Luke 6:35), and suffer (2 Corinthians 4:17).

Why does God reward you? The answer is simple. God rewards you so that He might receive glory. Your rewards bring honor to Him. While heavenly rewards are nice, they are not yours to keep. Rewards give you an opportunity to give God the glory He desires and deserves.

Do you fervently want more than this world has to offer? Live today for the rewards of another world. Make this day have eternal significance.

 Heavenly Father, thank You for rewarding me with eternal life. I realize it is only by Your grace that I have the hope of heaven. I am so grateful that this world is not my home. I long for a better place. Help me live this day in light of Your promised rewards. May my attitudes and actions impact eternity, and may You receive the glory, honor, and praise. In Jesus' name, Amen.

Week 16—Day 2
Will God Meet All Your Needs?

My God shall supply all your need according to His riches in glory by Christ Jesus.

Philippians 4:19

Do you really believe God will meet *all* of your needs? If so, worry will be absent from your life. This is not the case for most people. In spite of God's promised provision, much of their time is spent worrying. Right after challenging us not to worry, the apostle Paul reminds us of God's promise to provide.

What are you worrying about today? Your family, finances, future? Worry appears when hopes pull you in one direction, fears pull you in another, and you feel pulled apart. It demonstrates that you place more confidence in the possibility of problems than you do in the promises of God. It causes you to feel strangled.

How do you win the war over worry? Paul provides the answer in Philippians 4. First, you present your worries to God (vv. 6, 7). Nothing you face catches God off guard. Has it ever occurred to you that nothing ever occurs to God? Persistent prayer will result in powerful peace, which ultimately defeats worry in your life. Next, protect your thoughts (v. 8). Think about the things that matter most. Most of the things you worry about never happen. Think instead about things that are true. Finally, practice godly living (v. 9). Do the things you know to do. If you focus less on what you don't know and more on what you do know, life will be more enjoyable. Focus on what you can actually do something about. When you live according to this pattern, it becomes easier to trust God's provision.

In a world of uncertainty, worry may be natural, but the Christ-follower is called to live supernaturally. Look at your life differently. Place more confidence in God's promises than your problems. An improper evaluation of your situation will always result in an inability to embrace God's supply.

 *Jesus, please forgive me for not trusting Your provision. I confess the sin of worry in my life. I believe that You will supply **all** my needs. Thank You for this powerful promise. Protect my thoughts today as I depend on You for worry-free living. In Your name I pray. Amen.*

PAUL PURVIS, TEMPLE TERRACE, FL

Week 16—Day 3

How Important Is It to Set Goals?

Brethren, I do not count myself to have apprehended; but one thing I do, forgetting those things which are behind and reaching forward to those things which are ahead, I press toward the goal for the prize of the upward call of God in Christ Jesus.

Philippians 3:13, 14

*A*re we there yet? As a father of four, I've been asked that question many times. As a son, I've asked it a few times myself. The question is based on an assumption that a destination will be reached. God has a desired destination for your life. Are you there yet?

The Christian life must always be lived with a destination in mind. While your ultimate destination is heaven, your earthly goal must be holiness. The spiritual life is a never-ending journey in constant pursuit of God's best for your life. God's best always involves transformation into His holy image.

Are you headed in the right direction? The apostle Paul modeled several attributes that enabled him to press on. Use his words as a checklist for yourself today. First, he was honest and self-aware. He knew that he was not there yet. Do you live like you have already arrived? In order to go where God wants to take you, you must first understand you are not there yet! This means you must be both vulnerable and secure.

Secondly, Paul was committed to God's purpose in his life. He understood that God's plan was worthy of active pursuit. God has a divine purpose for your life, but it will not be achieved by default. You must constantly pursue His best. You are here to become all He wants you to be, not what others want you to be, or even what you think you should be. Focus on why you are *here* instead of fretting because you are not *there* yet.

Finally, forget the past and forge ahead! What do you need to forget? Don't let anything in your past keep you from God's purpose for your present—there is a high and holy purpose for your life today!

    Holy God, sometimes it's hard to believe that You have a plan for my life. Thank You for loving me and creating me for a divine purpose. I know I'm not there yet! Please expose the blind spots in my life that may keep me from Your best. Help me passionately pursue Your plans today. In Jesus' name, Amen.

Week 16—Day 4

The Chastisement of God Is for a Holy and Helpful Purpose

The king spoke, saying, "Is not this great Babylon, that I have built for a royal dwelling by my mighty power and for the honor of my majesty?" While the word was still in the king's mouth, a voice fell from heaven: "King Nebuchadnezzar, to you it is spoken: the kingdom has departed from you!"

Daniel 4:30, 31

*T*his is going to hurt me more than it hurts you. I can remember hearing that as a child and thinking, *You've got to be kidding me.* I've said it as a parent, and I'm sure it evoked the same response. Can discipline be both painful for the parent and profitable for the child? Yes.

It should come as no surprise that your heavenly Father may willingly discipline you for the purpose of your betterment. This does not mean He enjoys seeing you punished. God has a plan for your life that involves your good and His glory. Consequently, He reserves the right to do whatever it takes to pull you toward Himself, further along the path of holiness.

Nebuchadnezzar made two mistakes. First, he boasted that he had built Babylon. Anytime you take credit that God alone deserves, you create the need for His discipline. Our God is a jealous God. He will not share His glory. The king's second mistake was having the wrong motivation—"the honor of my majesty." Desiring praise that God alone deserves is idolatry. Your goal as a Christ-follower is holy living, not higher praise.

God responded accordingly; He disciplined the king. Make no mistake; God still resists the proud (James 4:6). Scripture clearly states that after pride, a fall will come (Proverbs 16:18; 29:23). Are you in danger of receiving God's discipline? God never disciplines His children to hurt them, but He will allow them to be chastised for His holy and helpful purpose. Nebuchadnezzar learned his lesson. Daniel 4 ends with the king giving God praise and receiving God's restoration. When you pursue holiness, God will liberally pour out grace in your life. If you don't want to be disciplined, then discipline yourself today. Pursue holiness!

Gracious Father, thank You for disciplining me. Help me see Your hand at work in my life. Thank You for loving me enough to pull me toward holiness. Rid me of the desire to take credit and receive glory for what You are doing. Give me an intense drive to pursue holiness. I give You all the praise and glory today in Jesus' name. Amen.

Week 16—Day 5

Reflection and Prayer

Are you relying on God's promise to meet the needs of His followers today, or are you focusing on the problems of this world? Do you need to confess or repent of any worries in your life?

_____

_____

_____

_____

_____

_____

_____

_____

_____

Has pride become a problem in your life? Is there any area of your life that deserves God's discipline today? What specific things can you do to demonstrate your pursuit of holiness?

_____

_____

_____

_____

_____

_____

_____

_____

_____

WEEK 17—DAY 1

What Part Does Humility Play in a Christian's Life?

Likewise you younger people, submit yourselves to your elders. Yes, all of you be submissive to one another, and be clothed with humility, for "God resists the proud, but gives grace to the humble."

1 Peter 5:5

What part does humility play in a Christian's life? A *very large* part. A few people define humility as the center of Christian morality, and pride as "the great sin."

Here's some good news: if you're like most people, you're way above average—at almost everything. Psychologists call this the state of "illusory superiority." It simply means that we tend to inflate our positive qualities and abilities, especially in comparison to other people. We are proud. We think better of ourselves than we really are, we see our faults in faint black and white rather than in vivid color, and we assume the worst in others while assuming the best in ourselves.

When we say we are Christians, we are saying far more than the fact that Christ has saved us from the consequences of our sins. It is also a declaration that we intend to live a Christlike life. Submitting to elders and to one another means we have the kind of spirit that Christ calls on us to have. Grace and humility prove an authentic faith, while pride and resistance send a different message.

What does a spirit of humility look like? Keeping a check on your motives, regarding others as better than yourself, and not limiting yourself to personal interest only. Humility does not mean thinking less of yourself, but allowing God to direct every aspect of your life.

 Lord, today I am asking that You help me submit to others. This does not come easily for me; I will need Your power to do it. Help me not to make excuses about my pride. I know it is something You don't want in my life. Help me not to make little of my sins while making much of others' sins. I need Your grace, and I know the pathway to more grace is through humility. Help me follow You completely today. Amen.

RICK WHITE, FRANKLIN, TN

WEEK 17—DAY 2

The Deadliness of Anger

The women sang as they danced, and said: "Saul has slain his thousands, and David his ten thousands." Then Saul was very angry, and the saying displeased him; and he said, "They have ascribed to David ten thousands, and to me they have ascribed only thousands. Now what more can he have but the kingdom?"

1 Samuel 18:7, 8

Recently I was traveling to the West Coast to officiate a wedding. As I was exiting the airplane and walking into the waiting area, an announcement came across the loudspeaker concerning a flight that was being delayed for a second or third time. A man grabbed his carry-on bag and threw it against the wall, shouting a venomous tirade of complaints at the airline staff members. Wow, was he angry! His behavior was deplorable and embarrassing to everyone around him.

Sometimes we experience what I call circumstantial anger, like the guy in the airport. Hopefully afterward, once we have had time to cool down and think about it, we adjust our attitude, repent of wrongdoing, and move on. But sometimes we get angry because of a foul spirit within us. Many times relational anger like that of King Saul is brewing beneath the surface, and it is deadly. Anger is one of those emotions that we have to guard against; it is hard to handle and it is capable of bringing devastation to our lives and the lives of others.

The psalmist declares, "Cease from anger, and forsake wrath; do not fret—it only causes harm" (Psalm 37:8). James says, "My beloved brethren, let every man be swift to hear, slow to speak, slow to wrath; for the wrath of man does not produce the righteousness of God" (James 1:19, 20). The scripture is clear—we can never accomplish the purposes of God through our anger.

Saul's heart was filled with jealousy. The most popular song of the day was all about David, and Saul could not listen to it any longer. Anger on the outside simply points out that there is something terribly wrong on the inside. Don't allow anger to poison the relationships in your life. Get rid of it. Confess it to God, ask Him to forgive you, and try to repair any damage your anger has caused.

     Lord, today I confess my anger to You. I realize that Your purposes will never be achieved through my anger. I acknowledge that this sin could be destroying me as well as others around me. I bring my anger to You, and I ask You to wash me clean and fill me with the joy of Your salvation. Amen.

Week 17—Day 3

Ask God for Specific Things

At Gibeon the Lord appeared to Solomon in a dream by night;
and God said, "Ask! What shall I give you?"

1 Kings 3:5

Every Monday the Senior Management Team of our church staff has lunch together following our morning meeting. The scenario is always the same: I ask, "Where would you guys like to have lunch today?" Nobody claims to care where we eat, just so long as we eat. But then when we are at restaurant, looking at the menu, someone will say how tired they are of eating there and they wish we could go somewhere else. I always say, "Speak up next time! I want to take you someplace you like, so tell me specifically where you want to go."

It isn't that big of a deal when it's just a restaurant menu, but what about the things we need in life that only God can give? At Gibeon, the Lord very clearly said to Solomon, "Ask! What shall I give you?" It is apparent that Solomon was ready with an answer: "Give to Your servant an understanding heart to judge Your people, that I may discern between good and evil" (1 Kings 3:9). The opportunity could have been squandered on self, but Solomon knew what he really needed was wisdom for leadership. God gave Solomon exactly what he asked for, plus so much more.

Over and over in the New Testament we are told by God to ask and we will receive. We are also told, "You do not have because you do not ask," and sometimes when we do ask, we ask with wrong motives and our desires are totally self-centered (James 4:2, 3). God is not like a genie in a bottle, a great slot machine in the sky, or even a kindly, old grandfather figure that passes out gifts to his children. But He is the God of this universe and He does stand ready to meet the needs of His children who trust Him and will ask Him specifically for the real desires of their heart. Just ask Him.

 Father, help me think deeply about this passage today. Had I been in Solomon's position, it would have been tempting to ask for all the "stuff" that brings temporary pleasure. Help the desires of my heart be the desires You have for me. Help me ask for, believe, and receive the things that will first bring You glory and then bring me good. Just like Solomon, I ask for the wisdom to lead and care for Your people. In Jesus' name, Amen.

RICK WHITE, FRANKLIN, TN

WEEK 17—DAY 4

The Many Faces of Prayer

*We ... do not cease to pray for you, and to ask that you may be filled with the
knowledge of His will in all wisdom and spiritual understanding ... giving thanks
to the Father who has qualified us to be partakers of the inheritance of the saints in the light.*

Colossians 1:9, 12

How would you classify most of your praying? Do you pray more about physical matters or spiritual matters? The prison prayers of Paul are somewhat unique. He prayed more for others than he did for himself, and most of his prayers for others regard spiritual rather than physical matters. This is the kind of prayer partner we should all desire to have.

Paul prayed specifically for three things. First, he prayed for spiritual intelligence for the church in Colossae. He wanted believers to know, understand, and experience the will of God for their lives. That only takes place as we get to know His Word and His Spirit, and as we live in community with one another. All three—Word, Spirit, and church—are absolutely essential to Christian growth.

Second, he prayed for their practical obedience in living out God's will. Someone has rightly said, "The devil finds his arsenal in the stockpile of our disobedience." In the New Testament, learning and living go hand in hand. Our confession and our conduct should be one and the same. If we know to do the right thing but don't do it, then for us it is sin. We cannot compartmentalize what we believe from how we live. In Paul's words, we are to "walk worthy of the Lord" (Colossians 1:10), which means we must live out a consistent, authentic faith.

Third, Paul prayed for their moral character. Knowledge, conduct, and service should always lead to character development. Have you ever met people who seemed to know a lot about the Bible, yet the way they treated others did not resemble Jesus' words about loving and caring for people? One of the greatest detriments to the Christian witness in today's world is not our message, but our lack of character.

 Father, thank You for recording Paul's prayer so that I could ponder it today. I confess that sometimes my prayer life can be reduced to a list of personal physical needs. Help me know, understand, and experience Your will for my life. Help me live out what I say I believe. Help me continue in the process of transformation on a daily basis. In Jesus' name, Amen.

WEEK 17—DAY 5

Reflection and Prayer

Take a moment and think about the last time you were really angry with someone. What were the results of your anger? If you could relive that experience, how would you handle it differently knowing what God says about anger?

_____

_____

_____

_____

_____

_____

_____

_____

If God were to ask you to tell Him specifically what you wanted, what would you say? How much would it resemble Solomon's request? How would it differ?

_____

_____

_____

_____

_____

_____

_____

_____

_____

RICK WHITE, FRANKLIN, TN

WEEK 18—DAY 1

How to Tackle a Prayer Burden

I pray, LORD God of heaven, O great and awesome God, You who keep Your covenant and mercy with those who love You and observe Your commandments, please let Your ear be attentive and Your eyes open, that You may hear the prayer of Your servant which I pray before You now, day and night.

Nehemiah 1:5, 6

A burden is something you go to bed with, wake up with, and live with each day of your life. A burden grips your heart and does not let you go easily. As you mature in the Lord, you learn that a burden is actually a wake-up call from God. It's a way He speaks to you, alerting you to something that requires your attention.

For Nehemiah, God was speaking to him about his home city of Jerusalem. The gates were down, the city was plundered, and God was calling him back to Jerusalem to do something about it. This was a time when prayer was not enough. God wanted more. He wanted action! He wanted to prove Himself strong not only to Nehemiah but also to all of Jerusalem. Nehemiah tackled his prayer burden with the actions of going, doing, fasting, and obeying God in all areas.

What is your prayer burden? What is gripping your heart? Call out to the Lord about this burden! For Nehemiah, it was a wall; what is it for you? Fast over this burden. Be willing to go and do. Be willing to transform your prayer burden into action! This is no time to push the snooze button in your life. God is waking you up and speaking to you. He wants to do a new thing in you, through you, and around you. This is what burdens do.

    Lord Jesus, this prayer burden is Your wake-up call to me. Speak to me loudly and clearly. I release myself to You; do whatever You want to do in and through me. Amen.

WEEK 18—DAY 2

The Principle of Intercession

The prayer of faith will save the sick, and the Lord will raise him up. And if he has committed sins, he will be forgiven. Confess your trespasses to one another, and pray for one another, that you may be healed. The effective, fervent prayer of a righteous man avails much.

James 5:15, 16

My mother is dealing with acute leukemia. Many people in our church have said to me, "We are praying for your mom." Others have said it another way, "We are interceding for your mom." When one intercedes for another, one is intervening on behalf of the other. They are standing in the gap, representing another person before God in prayer.

When we pray, God can do more in a moment than someone could ever do in a lifetime. When we are sick or burdened to the point that we appeal to our spiritual leaders to pray over us, we are positioning ourselves to be a part of a miracle. God alone heals and forgives, but He also challenges us to humble ourselves before our spiritual leaders, confess our sins to one another, and have others intercede for us in prayer. As you demonstrate humility and practice obedience, God will raise up someone to pray for you.

When you have a need, ask others to pray for you. When others have a need, pray over them. Intercession is one of the most beautiful principles in all of Scripture. Why? It is just a matter of time before I need you to pray for me. It is just a matter of time before you need me to pray for you. Standing in the gap for another person in prayer is a huge privilege, responsibility, and opportunity. God honors the energetic, passionate, and pure prayers of His children. Through intercession, He works miracles.

 Lord, show me the people You want me to pray over today, and raise up people to pray for me when I have a need. In the name of Jesus, Amen.

DR. RONNIE FLOYD, NORTHWEST ARKANSAS

Week 18—Day 3
How Can I Learn to Pray Effectively?

I set my face toward the Lord God to make request by prayer and supplications, with fasting, sackcloth, and ashes. And I prayed to the Lord my God, and made confession, and said, "O Lord, great and awesome God, who keeps His covenant and mercy with those who love Him, and with those who keep His commandments."

Daniel 9:3, 4

In our walk with God, there are seasons when He calls us to a different level of sacrifice. Usually, He creates desperation in us, which causes us to set our face toward Him, refocus our spiritual lives, and cry out to Him. This new season is calling us to new sacrifice. This can involve humbling ourselves by adding fasting to our prayers. Fasting is abstinence from food with a spiritual goal in mind. Fasting denies the most natural thing your body desires, which is food, in order to pursue intently the God of heaven, asking Him to do something new and fresh in your life.

This is exactly where Daniel was in his life. He was desperate for God to move. He was desperate for God to establish again some of the spiritual practices among His people. He humbled himself before the Lord in prayer and fasting. Is this a formula? Is this a hoop you jump through to get God's favor? Absolutely not! At the same time, we know God works in specific ways. Most of all, He gets us ready.

Desperation begins. Prayer occurs. Humility happens. Fasting follows. God shows up. When God shows up, He can do more than we can imagine. Effective prayer occurs when you talk to God and when God talks back to you through His Word. Effective prayer occurs through a relationship between you and God. Prayer that is joined by fasting creates an incomparable intimacy with God. It takes your relationship with God to a different level. Prayer becomes more effective than ever before.

 Oh Lord, give me a passion to go to heights I have never been with You before. I pray for this for Your glory. Amen.

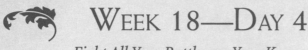

Week 18—Day 4

Fight All Your Battles on Your Knees

Pray without ceasing.

1 Thessalonians 5:17

Battles are real in the Christian life. As long as our flesh is our home, we will be in battles. None are easy. Some are draining. Most are discouraging. All are exhausting. When I think of battles, I am reminded of a small figurine I have of a soldier returning to his home from the Civil War. Still in the saddle, but hanging over the horse in complete exhaustion, the figurine is entitled *Nothing Left*. I have been in battles like that in my Christian life; I have come to God with nothing left.

It is in these types of battles that we move from sitting before the Lord in prayer to fighting the battle on our knees or on our face. We come to Him like the soldier who came home with nothing left. We not only pray, but we pray without ceasing. This does not mean we never break from prayer, but it means we come to God regularly about the battle before us. It means that we do not give up until God comes through. In other words, we are persistent. We ask Him and keep on asking Him. We seek Him and keep on seeking Him. We knock on His door and keep on knocking until He opens the door. We don't give up until God wins the battle through us and for us! This is praying without ceasing.

Are you in a battle today? You are probably in at least one. Perhaps there is something difficult happening in your family, in your job, or in your heart, something you're struggling with personally. Perhaps you have battles in all of these areas simultaneously. What do you do? Get out of your chair and get on your knees. Pray about that battle and do not give up. Continue to do this daily, perhaps even more than just once a day. In time, God will prevail. And in the meantime, remember that the battle is not yours, but God's.

 Father, I need You more today than ever before. Help! Amen.

WEEK 18—DAY 5

Reflection and Prayer

Are you trying to face desperate battles in your life without ceaseless prayer? Do you need to incorporate fasting into your prayer life?

_____

_____

_____

_____

_____

_____

_____

_____

_____

Are you praying for friends and colleagues by name each day, interceding for them? If not, what can you do to develop this habit of prayer?

_____

_____

_____

_____

_____

_____

_____

_____

_____

WEEK 19—DAY 1

How Can I Make My Prayer Life Fresh and New?

Call to Me, and I will answer you, and show you great and mighty things, which you do not know.

Jeremiah 33:3

The prophet Jeremiah gives us one of the most promise-filled prayers of the Bible. This verse has been called "God's telephone number"—JER-333. How can you as a disciple maintain freshness in your daily prayer time with God? Freshness in prayer comes from understanding the position of desperation from which you are praying. Jeremiah was in prison and the Babylonian army was destroying the city of Jerusalem. Then God gave him the promise we read in today's passage. There is nothing we can do, humanly speaking, to make an eternal difference. Yet what humans cannot do, God can!

Freshness in prayer comes as you consider whom you are approaching in prayer. The Lord says, "Call to Me." This is the invitation of the eternal, covenant-keeping God who is also the Creator and Sustainer of all things. He is all-powerful, all-knowing, and always present.

Freshness in prayer is experienced by the promise and power of God's response. The Lord says, "I will answer you." The only prayer that God does not answer is the prayer not prayed. God always gives the right answers to prayer, but they vary. He always answers our prayers with messages of yes, no, or wait. As you claim by faith God's promise to answer your prayer, you will experience the power of prayer—just as He promised to show Jeremiah "great and mighty things." Though His power is invisible and beyond human comprehension, when we pray, God releases His power in visible ways!

 Heavenly Father, I realize that I am desperate and that my needs go far beyond my abilities. I call to You in this prayer, thankful that You expect me and desire me to be in Your presence. I pray in faith, knowing that You will answer me and that You will display Your might and power. Thank You that Your grace and power are such that I can never ask too much! In Jesus' name I offer this prayer. Amen.

DR. MICHAEL LEWIS, PLANT CITY, FL

WEEK 19—DAY 2

How Do I Handle Nagging Doubt?

He said to them, "Why are you troubled? And why do doubts arise in your hearts?"

Luke 24:38

This is a probing question the risen Lord asked His disciples in the Upper Room, and He could very well ask us the same question today. We face difficulties, and doubts arise in our hearts. We find ourselves feeling uncertain, confronted by troubling questions.

Earlier in this chapter, the two disciples walking on the road to Emmaus were questioning the reality of Jesus' reported Resurrection and whether He had accomplished the work of redemption as promised. It was at that point in their journey of doubt that Jesus revealed Himself to them and explained all the things concerning Himself in the Old Testament.

So how do we handle daunting doubts that come our way? Allow the living Christ to open your heart to the living Word and fill you with the truth of who He is and what He has done. Doubts arise when our minds are focused on half-truths and uncertainties. Faith is built when we receive the whole counsel of God from Scripture.

Doubts can also be driven away when you realize that the living Christ who walks with you is the One who lives in you. When the disciples' eyes were opened and they realized they had been speaking with Jesus, they said to one another, "Did not our heart burn within us while He talked with us on the road, and while He opened the Scriptures to us?" (v. 32). Doubts fade when you experience the reality of "Christ in you, the hope of glory" (Colossians 1:27).

Heavenly Father, in the busyness and pressures of our world, my mind can become clouded with doubt. Please drive back these dark clouds of doubt. Open my eyes that I may see You and open my ears that I may hear You speaking through Your Word. May I experience "holy heart-burn" as I daily walk with You. I pray in the name of our living Lord Jesus. Amen.

WEEK 19—DAY 3

How Can I Combat My Fears?

God has not given us a spirit of fear, but of power and of love and of a sound mind.

2 Timothy 1:7

We all have to face fears in life. The young pastor Timothy was no exception, battling fears as he led the church in Ephesus. There were many things that may have contributed to his fears. Maybe it was his feeling of inadequacy to be the spiritual leader of a local church. Maybe it was the size of the task, for Ephesus was largely an unreached population and the work would have required great spiritual stamina. Maybe it was the presence of false teachers who were subverting the gospel into a message of good works.

The aged apostle Paul encouraged young Timothy with the promise that the Holy Spirit's presence would be in him and work through him. The Spirit would give him spiritual strength for the battle, a capacity to love those who are difficult, and sound judgment to make critical decisions. It is interesting to notice that Paul included himself in this statement of truth by using the word *us*. There are seasons of life when even great spiritual giants are tempted to fear and doubt. In every case, the Holy Spirit who lives in us gives us power to overcome doubts and fears.

How can you combat fears in your life? Simply live by faith and acknowledge the Spirit's presence in your life. Recognize that feelings of fear, insecurity, and apprehension do not come from God, but from the Enemy who seeks to keep you from reaching your spiritual potential in Christ. Grow in your relationship with the Holy Spirit and depend wholly on His power, loving presence, and wisdom for daily living.

 Father in heaven, I pray that Your Spirit would fall fresh on me. Fill me with spiritual strength so I can face challenges. Fill me with love so I will treat everyone I encounter with kindness. Fill me with soundness of mind so I will make godly decisions when I am pressed by circumstances. I humbly pray these things in full dependence on You in the name of Jesus. Amen.

DR. MICHAEL LEWIS, PLANT CITY, FL

Week 19—Day 4

How Can I Deal with Someone Who Is Angry or Bitter?

The heart knows its own bitterness, and a stranger does not share its joy.

Proverbs 14:10

Each day we encounter people who are full of anger and bitterness. A bitter person is someone who has been hurt, has let that hurt fester within, and consequently hurts others. Maybe the bitter person you will encounter will be a friend, a stranger, a coworker, a fellow church member, a family member, or perhaps even your spouse.

How can you deal with someone who is angry and bitter? God's counsel in Ephesians 4:32 applies here: "Be kind to one another, tenderhearted, forgiving one another, even as God in Christ forgave you." Kindness toward someone who is angry is a Christlike attitude—He responded to cursing with blessing. Being tenderhearted means being moved with the compassion of Christ toward the bitter person. Tenderheartedness is praying Christ's prayer from the Cross, "Father, forgive them, for they do not know what they do" (Luke 23:34). Forgiving an angry person means that you do not hold their sin against them. The only basis for these supernatural attitudes and actions is the supernatural grace of God found in Christ alone. You can only forgive bitter and angry people on the basis of God's forgiveness of you in Christ.

When someone who is angry and bitter offends you, you have two options: you can either respond the way you naturally would, with revenge, or respond the way Christ in you would, with forgiveness.

 Father God, many times I ask, "How many times shall I forgive one who sins against me?" And I can hear Your Son say, "Up to seventy times seven" (Matthew 18:22). I realize that this is not a matter of mere multiplication; it is a matter of the attitude of my heart. I pray that You would supernaturally enable me by Your Spirit to be kind to those who are rude to me, tenderhearted to those who are angry at me, and forgiving toward those who have wronged me. I pray in Jesus' name. Amen.

WEEK 19—DAY 5

Reflection and Prayer

Reflect on God's promise about prayer in Jeremiah 33:3. Identify doubts or fears that you are facing and call on the Lord to bring down any strongholds of faithlessness.

_____

_____

_____

_____

_____

_____

_____

_____

Reflect on God's power in response to prayer to show you "great and mighty things, which you do not know." Pray for any bitter people in your life. Pray for God to change their bitterness to gladness.

_____

_____

_____

_____

_____

_____

_____

_____

_____

DR. MICHAEL LEWIS, PLANT CITY, FL

WEEK 20—DAY 1

How Can I Become a Godly Influence on Others?

I sought for a man among them who would make a wall, and stand in the gap
before Me on behalf of the land, that I should not destroy it; but I found no one.

Ezekiel 22:30

It is tempting to believe that problems today are so enormous that a single individual cannot make much difference. The truth, however, is the opposite. The most momentous advances in history have occurred when one person stood up to the indifference of the times.

In Ezekiel 22, God identifies at least four levels of Judah's culture that should have been faithful and were not. Prophets, priests, princes, and the people themselves were corrupt and dishonest (vv. 25–29). Finally, God said, "I sought for a man." One life could have been a "wall" of protection for a doomed city. The Bible is full of examples of individuals who changed the world, and individuals still provide a godly influence today.

In the 1980s, the late David Wilkerson was walking through Times Square in New York City where prostitution, drugs, and crime were rampant. The famous author and preacher was praying that God would raise up a witness in that city when he sensed the Lord saying, "You do it." So David Wilkerson started Times Square Church. Now, a little over twenty years later, the church reaches several thousand people each week in worship and ministry. In the beginning, it must have looked like a nearly impossible dream, yet today it is a strong witness in a part of New York City not known for vibrant churches. What's more, when David Wilkerson started Times Square Church, he was fifty-five years old—not the average age of a church planter! Yet, with God, one man is a majority against the tidal wave of sin and compromise that can destroy an entire culture. It is not too late to "stand in the gap," interceding on behalf of your family, your workplace, or your nation. You can be the one.

 Lord, use me today to bless someone else's life. I am only one—but I am *one who believes that today, in Christ, I can make a difference. I am avail-* *able, and I am ready for every opportunity You bring. In Jesus' name, Amen.*

WEEK 20—DAY 2

How Can I Walk with the Holy Spirit?

As you therefore have received Christ Jesus the Lord, so walk in Him, rooted and built up in Him and established in the faith, as you have been taught, abounding in it with thanksgiving.

Colossians 2:6, 7

Do you have any habits that your family and friends recognize? I find myself singing the chorus to one particular song almost every day, and it has nearly driven my kids crazy! If they never hear "Over the Rainbow" again, they will be happy.

Habits are those repeated actions that help define our lives. In the New Testament, the word *walk* describes the things we do habitually. In Colossians 2:6, 7 believers are instructed to "walk in Him" as a way of life. The word *walk* in verse 6 is a combination of two words in the Greek New Testament meaning literally "to walk around." It doesn't mean we are walking in circles, instead it is a word that describes our "walk of life" or our lifestyle, the things we do again and again.

Our spiritual lives grow through the discipline of habits and repeated actions, but they need not be dull. The verb *walk* is present tense, which suggests that the Spirit-filled believer walks with Him every day. As a result, the scenery changes along the way.

I am glad we are instructed to "walk" and not "run." I can walk a lot farther and a lot longer than I can run! Walking is also the most fundamental and universal mode of human motion and progress. Not everyone can run or drive or fly, but almost everyone can walk. Walking in Him is a habit, but it can never be dull because of the company we keep—we are walking in Him!

So our spiritual life has a pace; we walk. Our spiritual life is about progress because we are walking. Our spiritual life is a partnership because we walk with Him. Today, take a walk with Jesus.

 Father, today I will claim every promise for living the spiritual life, promises You have given for my good and for my growth. By Your Spirit, I surrender to Your authority as Lord of my life. Amen.

KIE BOWMAN, AUSTIN, TX

WEEK 20—DAY 3

How Can I Be the Kind of Faithful Person God Honors?

We desire that each one of you show the same diligence to the full assurance of hope until the end.

Hebrews 6:11

The Book of Hebrews was written to a persecuted church with several members thinking of rejecting the gospel and returning to Judaism. The writer urged his readers to keep going in faith and not to quit. Have you ever been tempted to give up in the Christian life? A friend of mine grew so frustrated with his circumstances that he quit his pastorate, divorced his wife, turned his back on God, and eventually developed a serious drug addiction. He finally came back to Christ, but he lost eleven years of his life in that whirlwind of rebellion. He was living his life in reverse at full speed!

The best rewards in the Christian life are at the finish line, not at the starting gate. The writer of Hebrews urged "diligence" in the Christian life. That word in the New Testament means "to have an earnest desire to accomplish a thing"—not just to start it, but to finish it as well. We are to set our sights on "the end." The Greek word for *end* is related to the cry of Jesus from the Cross, when He said, "It is finished!" (John 19:30). The word means "the limit of activity" or "the final result."

When my daughter was young, she was a fast sprinter, and like all young runners, she had to learn not to watch the other runners. To finish first she had to focus on the finish line, not on anything else. The same is true in our faithfulness to Christ. In order to keep going, we have to learn to take the long view and keep our eyes on the prize.

    Oh God, You have blessed me with every spiritual blessing in Christ, and I won't look back or turn back from serving You. Lead me today, Lord, and I will follow. Amen.

WEEK 20—DAY 4

Can I Really Trust that God Will Provide What I Need?

Do not be like them. For your Father knows the things you have need of before you ask Him.

Matthew 6:8

If you have driven to the gas station or been to the grocery store lately, you may have felt a little uneasy. The twenty-first century has unfolded as a time of war, bad weather, and gloomy economic conditions. When the stock market lost seven trillion dollars in one week a few years ago, Christian author Phillip Yancey was asked how to pray during a bad economy. Yancey gave a multilayered response, but it started with the advice to cry, "Help!" There is nothing wrong with that advice. God loves simple desperation in prayer. But we can also have some confidence when we pray.

Jesus reminds us in Matthew 6:8 that even in tough times, including periods of unemployment or a national recession, God never forgets what we need. The first teaching in the New Testament on the subject of prayer includes this assurance that while God expects us to pray, we never need to worry about Him understanding our requests. He knows "before you ask Him."

Recently my wife needed her driver's license renewed so I went with her to the Department of Public Safety and we waited our turn. The officer working behind the desk seemed to hate his job. He frequently answered people's questions before they could finish asking them. He must have heard it all a thousand times and his answers never changed. None of us wanted to be there, but his obvious impatience with everyone didn't help.

It is true that God, like the DPS officer, knows what we need before we ask, and he has heard every request before. But unlike the impatient officer, God is "your Father." That loving relationship makes all the difference. So go ahead and ask. God loves to answer!

 Father, You know every need I have today, and You already know how the needs will be met. I am trusting You as You minister to me and build my faith in Your constant care for me. Amen.

WEEK 20—DAY 5

Reflection and Prayer

Is there one habit, unconfessed sin, or insecurity that keeps you from believing you can make a difference, or influence someone else's life today?

_____

_____

_____

_____

_____

_____

_____

_____

What are the factors in your life that undermine your faith and consistent Christian walk? How would daily prayer, Bible study, and confession of sin strengthen your steadfastness in Christ?

_____

_____

_____

_____

_____

_____

_____

_____

WEEK 21—DAY 1

How Do I Keep My Focus on God?

If the LORD delights in us, then He will bring us into this land and give it to us, "a land which flows with milk and honey." Only do not rebel against the LORD, nor fear the people of the land, for they are our bread; their protection has departed from them, and the LORD is with us. Do not fear them.

Numbers 14:8, 9

We live in a world of distractions. New headlines, e-mails, voicemails, texts, tweets, and podcasts clamor for our attention every hour. Our smartphones and computers are constantly beeping with new information, drawing our focus to one new subject after another. We are sometimes overwhelmed by the things that surround us. In this passage the people of Israel had just received a bad report and they were in a state of panic. Joshua told them they must stay focused on the Lord. They could trust that He would do exactly as He had promised.

It is so easy for us to get caught up in our circumstances and lose sight of what God has for us. We must make sure our focus stays on Him. Doing that involves four important actions.

First, we must regularly spend time with God in His Word. So often we listen to the voices around us rather than communicating with Him. Our time in the Word will always give us a better perspective.

Second, we have to remember He has a plan for us. No matter what the circumstances, He is still God and He is still in control. He is not frustrated by our circumstances.

Third, we must keep our eyes on Him. We must constantly look to Him rather than the people or events around us. That means He is our priority. We must be seeking to put Him first and give Him the glory in everything that we do.

Fourth, we have to remember that He is the God who makes and keeps promises. The people of Israel continually forgot that God had made them a promise. Just as He was faithful to them, so He will be faithful to us. He has promised to sustain, protect, guide, and support those who have put their trust in Christ. You can trust Him to do what He has promised!

Lord, I live in a world that is so distracting. It is easy to focus on things that do not deserve my attention. In times of great stress and pressure, help me stay focused on what You want to do in my life. I pray I can trust You in every circumstance. We ask this in the precious name of Jesus. Amen.

MIKE HAMLET, SPARTANBURG, SC

WEEK 21—DAY 2

How Can I Praise God When Life Doesn't Go Well?

Let us search out and examine our ways, and turn back to the LORD.

Lamentations 3:40

The Lord does not promise us that everything in life is going to go our way. In fact, in James 1 we are told to "Count it all joy when you fall into various trials" (v. 2). The scripture teaches us that these trials can come at us from all directions. But the testing of our faith produces "patience" (v. 3). When things do not go so well, we are given the opportunity to learn to be patient and steadfast in our faith. James says that as a result, we can "be perfect and complete, lacking in nothing" (v. 4). This is a phrase that describes the believer who has a mature faith. When we face trials in life, it gives us the ability to "grow up" in our faith. God allows us to experience difficulties because God's purpose is not that we would just be happy, but that we might be conformed to the image of His Son. Receiving that honor is certainly a reason for praise!

Another reason is that the Lord gives us the opportunity to be involved in the great works He is doing. As a part of the body of Christ, we have a chance to touch the world as we share the light of the gospel and to help carry out God's will on earth. This gives us a real sense of purpose. We must constantly be seeking to bring our lives in line with His will, considering what might need to change every day. When we live in such a way, the fact that things don't always go so well pales in comparison to what God is doing in and through us!

Lord, I praise You today not because of what has happened or what will happen, but because You are God and You loved me so much You sent Your Son to die on the Cross for my sin. When I get caught up in what is going on around me, I pray that I will be reminded of what You have done for me. Help me evaluate everything in my life on the basis of what will bring glory to You. May I always be in the process of turning to You. Amen.

Week 21—Day 3

Why Do I Still Have the Impulse to Sin?

I have been crucified with Christ; it is no longer I who live, but Christ lives in me; and the life which I now live in the flesh I live by faith in the Son of God, who loved me and gave Himself for me.

Galatians 2:20

We are sinners by nature and by choice. Romans 3:23 says all of us "have sinned and fall short of the glory of God." Romans 3:10 says, "There is none righteous, no, not one." When we are saved by putting our trust in the living Lord Jesus who died for us on the Cross, we do not become perfect.

We live in a world that is works- or performance-oriented. Our success is determined by what we do and how well we do it. That is why we see so many people who are trying so desperately to work their way to heaven. No matter how hard we try, however, we cannot do it in our own strength. Galatians 2:20 is very clear. The only chance we have to deal with our sin is through the sacrifice of Jesus Christ. We'll never make progress on our sin problem as long as we try to handle it ourselves.

Today's scripture makes it clear that we cannot live in our own strength; we must live by faith in the Son of God. The world tries to tell us to make it on our own, but that is simply not possible. This is why it is so important that we confess our sin daily. It is a reminder that Jesus has paid the price for our sin and we have victory through our relationship with the One who gave Himself for us.

Temptation will always be there, but we can live with confidence because Christ is living in the life of the believer. Romans 12:2 says, "Do not be conformed to this world, but be transformed by the renewing of your mind." Transformation is a lifelong process that takes place when Christ is living in us.

Lord, I am continually amazed at Your love and Your grace. Why You would send Your Son to save a sinner like me is far beyond my understanding. I am so grateful that I do not have to do this alone, but can know joy and contentment because Christ lives in me. I know it is not because of anything I have done. May my life today reflect my dependence on You. Amen.

MIKE HAMLET, SPARTANBURG, SC

Week 21—Day 4

How Can I Overcome Anxiety?

I say to you, do not worry about your life, what you will eat or what you will drink;
nor about your body, what you will put on. Is not life more than food and the body more
than clothing? Look at the birds of the air, for they neither sow nor reap nor gather into
barns; yet your heavenly Father feeds them. Are you not of more value than they?

Matthew 6:25, 26

It seems that we are constantly seeing another report or study documenting the fact that we are worrying ourselves to death. The use of drugs to deal with worry and depression keeps growing dramatically. Everyone seems to be on "something" to deal with the anxieties of life. The world continues to turn up the pressure. It may be work, finances, marriage, kids, parents, health, emotional problems, or any of a host of other issues. Everyone has something happening in his or her life that no one else seems to understand.

Do you have something in your life about which you would say, "Not even God can do something about this." Maybe you wouldn't actually say that, but you are living that way. We have let the world inflate the power of our circumstances and shrink the power of God. That is not the way God meant it to be. We have let the world convince us there is a ceiling on what God can do. It is as if we think He has a power limit He cannot go beyond. Today's scripture says God gave special attention to the birds of the air and the flowers of the field. Certainly He can deal with the situations faced by the ones He has created in His own image, the ones for whom He made this world!

Worry is all about where you put your attention. Are you putting it on the things of this world, or the plan God has for your life? When you put Him first, your anxiety will begin to lessen dramatically. There is nothing you will face today that the Lord cannot handle. You are only a manager of what He has given to you. He will always make the right decision.

Lord Jesus, today I give You control of every part of my life. When I try
to take control and do it my way, I pray that You will remind me that Your
plan is always better than mine. I know that I need to spend my time seek-
ing Your guidance rather than trying to do things according to my desires.
Help me to see that success is not getting my way, but making sure that I live
according to Your will. Amen.

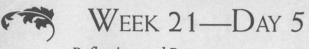

WEEK 21—DAY 5

Reflection and Prayer

What are some things you need to do to be more available to the Lord in your walk with Him?

_____

_____

_____

_____

_____

_____

_____

_____

What are the areas in your life where you are trying to keep control? How can you be more submissive to the Lord in these areas?

_____

_____

_____

_____

_____

_____

_____

_____

_____

MIKE HAMLET, SPARTANBURG, SC

WEEK 22—DAY 1

What Are Your Priorities in Life?

Seek first the kingdom of God and His righteousness, and all these things shall be added to you. Therefore do not worry about tomorrow, for tomorrow will worry about its own things. Sufficient for the day is its own trouble.

Matthew 6:33, 34

In Matthew 6, we see Jesus teach His disciples how to pray. In His prayer are the words, "Your kingdom come. Your will be done" (v. 10). He follows up this prayer with our text, "Seek first the kingdom of God"—a command, not a suggestion, about how to live our lives. We are told to have proper priorities. It goes without saying that if we are going to seek His kingdom, we are going to have to submit to the King.

Submission is the key to obeying this command. Who is Jesus to you? If He is your King, you will willingly follow His plan for your life rather than your own. Jesus does not invite us to be casual acquaintances of His; He calls us to be fully devoted followers of God!

Having proper priorities has its rewards. In Matthew 25:23 Jesus said those who follow Him faithfully will hear the words, "Well done, good and faithful servant; you have been faithful over a few things, I will make you ruler over many things. Enter into the joy of your lord." Because of our commitment to God, we will receive affirmation ("Well done"), promotion ("I will make you ruler over many things"), and His eternal presence ("Enter into the joy of your lord")!

What are your priorities in life? Stop for a moment and ask yourself, "Who is Jesus to me?" If He is your Lord, you will allow Him to have control of your life.

Heavenly Father, it is so easy to get busy and forget who we are and what You have called us to be! Help me today to refocus my priorities and to make You the center of all that I do. Amen.

Week 22—Day 2
Why Doesn't God Answer My Prayers?

You ask and do not receive, because you ask amiss, that you may spend it on your pleasures.

James 4:3

If you've been a Christian for any amount of time, you've probably asked at some point, "Why doesn't God answer my prayers?" If you've ever felt that way, you are not alone. In fact, the Bible is filled with accounts of people who questioned God's silence.

The thought of God not answering your prayers may bother you, but I believe there are often specific reasons why God is silent. Sometimes it's because of our own sinful choices. The most obvious obstacle that could prevent my prayers from being heard is my own disobedience. The psalmist made this very clear when he wrote, "If I regard iniquity in my heart, the Lord will not hear" (Psalm 66:18).

There are also times when God is silent because our prayers are selfish or trivial. He may not answer simply because our prayers aren't very good ones. James warned against these kinds of prayers when he wrote, "You ask and do not receive, because you ask amiss, that you may spend it on your pleasures" (James 4:3).

Of course, sometimes God is silent for reasons we'll never know. It's in those instances that we must wait, trust, and believe.

However, with all that said, I think that God's question for us might be, "Why don't you pray more?" After all, God is far more justified in complaining about our absence than we are in complaining about His!

 Heavenly Father, please help me learn how to pray. May I be more concerned about Your will than my own. I know You truly know best. Help me to trust You as I pray! Amen.

JERRY WALLS, WARNER ROBINS, GA

WEEK 22—DAY 3

What Does God Promise When We Are Faithful?

I am God, the God of your father; do not fear to go down to Egypt, for I will make of you a great nation there. I will go down with you to Egypt, and I will also surely bring you up again.

Genesis 46:3, 4

God is with us. I imagine that most of you reading these words already know that. Although most of us believe it at some level, I'm not sure how many of us actually embrace it. So, just for a minute, I want you to take a moment to feel the impact of that phrase. I want you to ponder what it means for God to be with you.

Now, maybe you believe this when life is good—when you're relaxing on the beach or eating at your favorite restaurant. It's easy to believe that God is with you in such moments. This principle remains true, however, no matter when we say it, regardless of whether we feel it. Frustrated at work, encouraged by kind words, or devastated by tragedy, God is with us.

This doesn't mean that God always creates a smooth path for us or gives us an easy life. It means that whatever we experience, our amazing, heavenly Father will be with us every step of the way. I find it so encouraging that God is not simply way off in the distance somewhere doing something else . . . He is actually with us!

Maybe you are hurting deeply today. God is with you. Maybe you are battling discouragement. God is with you. Maybe you are lonely. God is with you. Perhaps you are fighting a terrible disease. God is with you. Perhaps you have recently lost a loved one. God is with you. The reward of our faithfulness to God is the realization that He is—always has been and always will be—faithful to us. His faithful presence carries us through.

 Heavenly Father, thank You for being with us. We are so grateful that You aren't simply watching us or noticing us or keeping track of us, but that You are actually with us. Help us be sure that we are with You. Thank You for Your amazing promise to be with us! In Jesus' name, Amen.

WEEK 22—DAY 4

Finding Confidence in God

Through the LORD's mercies we are not consumed, because His compassions fail not.
They are new every morning; great is Your faithfulness.

Lamentations 3:22, 23

God will not let you go. Though you may find yourself in the middle of a storm of your own making, He will not turn His back on you. Though you may find yourself experiencing the consequences of your sin, you will still be loved. Because of His "mercies" and "compassions," you can be confident that He loves you and will continue to provide for you and take care of you.

You may run. He will run after you. You may hide. He will find you. You may turn on Him. He will not turn on you. Your heavenly Father is relentless in His love for you. Although He will discipline you, you will not be "consumed." He will not let you go.

Paul said it this way in 2 Timothy 2:13: "If we are faithless, He remains faithful; He cannot deny Himself." Because our God is so faithful—and also because we can be so faithless—today you and I have a chance to respond to the amazing love of God. Every morning is a chance to give back. I can't help but think that since His mercies are new every morning, our praise should be as well.

Think about it. Every morning, without fail, a fresh supply of God's mercy is made available to us. It's an all-you-can-eat buffet. Many have tried to exhaust it (including me!), only to discover that it is inexhaustible. It seems to me that we partake and partake, but rarely give thanks. Why don't we thank God right now for His steadfast love and mercy?

    Great Father, thank You for being so faithful to someone so faithless. May my gratitude be as fresh as Your mercy. I don't want to pray the same old stale prayers I've always prayed. Instead, I want to learn to speak to You each day with a renewed appreciation for who You are. Great is Your faithfulness! Amen.

JERRY WALLS, WARNER ROBINS, GA

WEEK 22—DAY 5
Reflection and Prayer

Ask yourself honestly, "What are my priorities?" Are your priorities what they ought to be? If not, how ought they to change?

_____

_____

_____

_____

_____

_____

_____

_____

_____

Do you ever wonder why your prayers go unanswered? What do you need to change or accept when it comes to your prayer life?

_____

_____

_____

_____

_____

_____

_____

_____

_____

Week 23—Day 1

What Place Does God Have in My Life?

Do not worry, saying, "What shall we eat?" or "What shall we drink?" or "What shall we wear?"...
But seek first the kingdom of God and His righteousness, and all these things shall be added to you.

Matthew 6:31, 33

A young man, anxious to serve the Lord with all his heart, asked an older Christian gentleman how he could know if God was first in his life. The elderly man noticed that the young man looked at his schedule on his phone. He also noticed his checkbook in his pocket. The man asked to hold both in his hands. The young man, puzzled by his request, gave both to him.

Holding the checkbook and the schedule in his hands, the man said, "Son, examine these two items carefully. Our real priorities always will be reflected in the ways we spend our time and our money." As the young man looked over his checkbook and calendar of events, he realized that his business and his hobbies had a greater priority in his life than the Lord.

Many people quickly say that God is first in their lives. Their actions speak differently. They believe that God blesses those who give, but they rarely give to the Lord's work. They believe the Lord honors those who obey His Word, but they constantly ignore His teachings when they are making decisions.

Too often we devote our resources, our time, and our energy to things other than our walk with our heavenly Father. It is important to remember that when we are seeking "first the kingdom of God and His righteousness," our activities and our actions will show it!

    Heavenly Father, will You show me my heart as You see it? Will You allow me to see clearly what the priorities of my heart are? Lord, help me to place You first in my life, in my actions and my activities. Help me seek Your kingdom and Your righteousness above everything else. Amen.

PHIL WALDREP, TRINITY, AL

Week 23—Day 2

How Should I Respond to Failure?

Joshua said, "Alas, Lord God, why have You brought this people over the Jordan at all—to deliver us into the hand of the Amorites, to destroy us? Oh, that we had been content, and dwelt on the other side of the Jordan!"

Joshua 7:7

Have you ever considered that some of the greatest lessons in life come through difficult times, when you've failed? Reality did not meet your expectations in some arena of life—a business venture, a church activity, a relationship. Perhaps learning to deal with that failure, and gaining wisdom and strength in the process, was a success in itself. In our modern, success-oriented society, failure is not accepted or allowed in the minds of most people. Yet some of the greatest success stories in history grew out of failure.

Take Thomas Edison, who invented the light bulb. Historians estimate that Edison tried thousands of wires until he found one that would glow for a long time. Each time Edison failed with using one kind of wire, he learned what would not work. Each failure left him with a better understanding of what might work. Finally, after numerous failures, Edison found success.

Throughout Scripture, we see that our heavenly Father uses failure to teach spiritual lessons. Sometimes, as He did with the Israelites, He uses failure to reveal sin in our lives. Other times, the Lord uses failure to teach us that we cannot do anything without Him, or that He has a better plan for our lives. Through all of these experiences, the Lord teaches us to trust Him completely.

It is encouraging to know that God never allows an experience—success or failure—to come into our lives without using it to change us into the image of His Son.

 Heavenly Father, failure is so hard to accept and even more difficult to experience. Forgive me, Lord, for having resentment and bitterness when things do not go as I plan. Help me see Your hand at work in my life in all situations. Use these times, Lord, to mold me into the character of Your Son, Jesus Christ. Amen.

Week 23—Day 3

How Can I Learn to Be Content?

We brought nothing into this world, and it is certain we can carry nothing out.

1 Timothy 6:7

A wealthy landowner was trying to buy some additional land near his estate. A neighbor observed that his only motive seemed to be to prevent someone else from buying it. So the neighbor asked, "Sire, do you want to own all the land in the world?" "No," the wealthy man replied, "just the land that joins mine."

Many people believe that contentment comes through having enough money to do whatever they wish. Others think that it comes from having a good family or having a life without any problems. That is why they constantly think that having a little more money or changing their circumstances or relationships will bring contentment.

Contentment, however, comes from a personal relationship with Jesus Christ and a belief that He will supply all our needs. Contentment is not found in things, situations, or other people. It is found in knowing that our heavenly Father loves and cares for us.

The writer of Hebrews understood this source of contentment when he wrote, "Let your conduct be without covetousness; be content with such things as you have. For He Himself has said, 'I will never leave you nor forsake you'" (Hebrews 13:5). To express it another way, discontentment comes when we think that having money or the latest gadget or fashion will make us happy. But Scripture affirms that true contentment is obtainable only through Christ. Knowing that He provides what we need when we need it produces stress-free living at its best!

Heavenly Father, teach me to be content. Help me to see my joy and purpose in You rather than material possessions. Help me avoid trying to manipulate my circumstances or other people to get what I want. Lord, help me trust You and only You to meet my every need! Amen.

PHIL WALDREP, TRINITY, AL

WEEK 23—DAY 4
How Do I Handle Financial Debt?

A certain woman of the wives of the sons of the prophets cried out to Elisha, saying, "Your servant my husband is dead, and you know that your servant feared the LORD. And the creditor is coming to take my two sons to be his slaves." So Elisha said to her, "What shall I do for you? Tell me, what do you have in the house?" And she said, "Your maidservant has nothing in the house but a jar of oil."

2 Kings 4:1, 2

Slavery was outlawed in the United States in 1865 with the passage of the Thirteenth Amendment to the Constitution. That is, physical slavery became illegal. Unfortunately, thousands of people today are enslaved by something different—something called debt. Debt can be discouraging. The lack of financial freedom causes many to wonder if they will ever be happy again.

Freedom from debt begins when we realize that our heavenly Father will supply our needs but not our wants. Selfish desires often cause us to buy things, even though we do not have the money to purchase them. With easy credit and credit cards, we quickly buy things we want but do not need. As time passes, the bondage to debt increases. Over time we lose our joy and financial freedom.

To be free again, we must immediately stop adding to our debt, regardless of the emotional pain we may experience from not having what we want. Then, with the discipline we receive under the leadership of the Holy Spirit, we must begin repaying the debts we owe. Every day that the debt decreases, even by a small amount, we can start seeing financial freedom in our future.

The mountain of financial debt did not arise in a few days. Neither will it disappear in a few months. The joy and victory, however, that we will find one day when we are financially free is worth the effort!

    Heavenly Father, give me the strength today to avoid the temptation of buying things with credit. Help me to see You as the source that will meet my needs. Lord, give me the strength and discipline to start lowering my financial obligations. Please, Lord, remind me each day of the joy and freedom that I will have when I am free from all financial debt! Amen.

WEEK 23—DAY 5

Reflection and Prayer

Take a moment to examine the way you spend your time (especially your free time), your money, and your energy. Does it reflect that God is first in your life? If not, how can you change your priorities so that He is first?

_____

_____

_____

_____

_____

_____

_____

_____

Contentment comes through knowing that God is in control and trusting Him in every situation. What is a recent experience that shows how you trusted God? What is an experience that demonstrates your failure to trust Him? From these two experiences, what did you learn?

_____

_____

_____

_____

_____

_____

_____

_____

PHIL WALDREP, TRINITY, AL

WEEK 24—DAY 1
The Lord Knows What Is Right

The LORD said to Eliphaz the Temanite, "My wrath is aroused against you and your two friends, for you have not spoken of Me what is right, as My servant Job has"... So Eliphaz the Temanite and Bildad the Shuhite and Zophar the Naamathite went and did as the LORD commanded them; for the LORD had accepted Job. And the LORD restored Job's losses when he prayed for his friends. Indeed the LORD gave Job twice as much as he had before.

Job 42:7, 9, 10

There are two key thoughts in these verses. First, the Lord rebuked Job's three comforters. God's wrath was kindled against them. Why? Because they spoke wrongly of both God and Job. They did more damage to Job's spirit than even the devil himself. When Satan had done his worst, it could still be written, "In all this Job did not sin with his lips" (Job 2:10). But as the three friends pounded their pious misrepresentations of both God and Job, the poor sufferer was driven to discouragement in his spirit (16:2; 17:1, 2; 19:2, 3). Mark this in your heart: Satan has no more dangerous tools than those who, under the guise of piety and in the name of religious orthodoxy, offer false comfort or give untrue impressions of God. It's far better being silent in the presence of suffering than saying what is wrong or doctrinally incorrect.

Second, the Lord restored the fortunes of Job when Job prayed for his friends. Job's release did not come by defending himself; it was prayer that brought the miracle. Prayer is the vital axis in the spiritual life of any Christian individual or church. There can be no genuine spiritual revival where there is no prayer. Is that not what Jesus said in Matthew 5:44–46? We are to love our enemies, bless those who curse us, do good to those who hate us, and *pray* for those who persecute us. Job prayed for his friends, and that brought about the real turning point. His liberation came not when he prayed for himself, but when he prayed for others! When I earnestly pray for others, my intercession not only brings blessing to them, it boomerangs back in blessing upon me. It's not about me. It's about others and glorifying God. Trust God and see what a difference it will make.

 Dear Lord, help me think like You. Help me remember Your love, show Your compassion, and be sensitive not only to those who are kind but also to those who are unkind. Give me the grace to forgive others and to be an ambassador for Christ. Help me pray for others knowing You will take care of me. In Jesus' name, Amen.

WEEK 24—DAY 2

Does the Fear of the Lord Lead to an Abundant and Long Life?

The LORD blessed the latter days of Job more than his beginning; for he had fourteen thousand sheep, six thousand camels, one thousand yoke of oxen, and one thousand female donkeys. He also had seven sons and three daughters.

Job 42:12, 13

As you read the last chapter of the Book of Job, you are captivated by three main thoughts. First, you see transformation in Job's character, from one who tries to justify himself to one who sees the glory of God and repents in dust and ashes (Job 42:6). He comes forth with genuine faith that is like gold "tested by fire" (1 Peter 1:7). Second, there is vindication of Job before his friends, as God calls him "My servant" (Job 42:7, 8) and calls on Job to pray for them. Finally, there is restoration to Job of all his former prosperity and indeed far more. The Lord gave Job twice as much as he had beforehand (v. 10); Job is vindicated and rewarded. Because this is a real account of God's dealings with a man, its meaning is profound. Remember, the story of Job is a divinely intended object lesson through which we are meant to apprehend certain great truths pertaining to the trials of the godly.

Whatever we go through is for our good and God's glory. Our spiritual growth does not come when everything is going well, but in times of testing when we must turn our eyes on God and trust Him for the results. Sometimes what we go through is for our own growth; sometimes we shed tears to water someone else's garden. Always know that there is a reason, and the Lord will bring us through. We will be better and stronger because of it. This world is not our home, but in Christ we are rich, and one day we will be with Him forever! Remember, after Job's trial, God gave him twice as much materially as he had beforehand. He gave him the same amount of children, and there were already seven sons and three daughters waiting for him in heaven. God is good and He knows what you need—keep the faith!

    Dear Lord, You have given me far more than I deserve to have. You have blessed me with Your love, grace, presence, and salvation. Help me realize how very rich I am in Christ, and help me be thankful for all I have. Lord, help me focus on the truths that one day I will be with You and that today I am called to be Your servant who brings glory to Your name. In Jesus' name I pray. Amen.

DR. ROB ZINN, HIGHLAND, CA

WEEK 24—DAY 3

The Reward of Sharing

May He who supplies seed to the sower, and bread for food, supply and multiply the seed you have sown and increase the fruits of your righteousness, while you are enriched in everything for all liberality, which causes thanksgiving through us to God.

2 Corinthians 9:10, 11

Giving is the very essence of God. It is His nature. As John 3:16 tells us, "God so loved the world that He gave His only begotten Son, that whoever believes in Him should not perish but have eternal life." As we grow in Christ, His nature should become our nature. We move from impulse giving to obedient giving, then to supernatural giving. We are not to give based on what we think we can afford, but as God leads us to give. Remember this: we will never be the kind of givers we should be until we understand that we are simply stewards of God's possessions. We don't own it; we simply oversee it.

Paul notes five attitudes of supernatural givers in 2 Corinthians 9. They give *generously* (v. 6). It's not about how much you can keep, but how much you can give. They give *prayerfully* ("let each one give as he purposes in his heart," v. 7), *cheerfully* ("God loves a cheerful giver," v. 7), and *faithfully* (vv. 8–12). As God leads us to give, we know by faith that He will take care of us. Nowhere in the Bible is there a command for us to give without a promise of return. If we are giving to glorify God, we can expect a return, one that is greater than the gift. Again and again we find evidence of this in Scripture: Proverbs 3:9, 10; Proverbs 11:24, 25; Luke 6:38; Philippians 4:15–19. Therefore, we should always give to receive, so that we will have the ability to give even more. Finally, a godly giver gives *sacrificially* (vv. 12–15). To give God's way, we must be willing to give up things. But whatever we give up for the cause of Christ will come back in so many different ways. Always remember, He can and He will. You will never out-give God.

 Dear Lord, give me the heart to be a good steward. Help me remember that You are my supply. All that I could ever need, You can provide! Help me be faithful and trustworthy. May the way I live and share with others be a true testimony to the love of Jesus. It's in His name I pray. Amen.

Week 24—Day 4

Finding God's Peace

*There are many who say, "Who will show us any good?" L*ORD*, lift up the light of Your countenance upon us. You have put gladness in my heart, more than in the season that their grain and wine increased. I will both lie down in peace, and sleep; for You alone, O L*ORD*, make me dwell in safety.*

Psalm 4:6–8

Be honest—where does your joy and security come from? Yes, I know the spiritual answer is "from the Lord," but I'm asking you for a truly honest answer! I have been a pastor for over thirty-four years, and I'm telling you, there are many, many Christians who have no joy, peace, or contentment. They know the right answer to the question, but they still spend their time worrying and fretting and losing sleep because what they know in their head has not taken root in their heart.

In today's passage, David says that many ask, "Who will show us any good?" These were people in God's family, not from the pagan world. They should have known the answer, but they were not living by faith. David says that God put gladness in his heart (literally more joy and rejoicing)—more gladness than the things of his earthly life could bring. As a result, David was able to experience true peace and safety in the Lord. David knew the secret! Your security cannot be found in things, but in the Lord. Your security cannot be found in your bank account, the stock market, or your property. It can only be found in your faith in the Lord—when you come to understand that God is sovereign, that He is in control, and that He loves you!

Jesus said in John 14:27, "Peace I leave with you, My peace I give to you; not as the world gives do I give to you. Let not your heart be troubled, neither let it be afraid." He also promised, "I will never leave you nor forsake you" (Hebrews 13:5). Remember, the opposite of fear is faith. Strengthen your faith, and you'll starve worry to death! If your faith is in God, you will have peace, and His peace will guard your heart and mind in Christ Jesus (Philippians 4:7).

Dear Lord, You know my heart, my thoughts, and my life. Teach me to walk according to Your wishes and in obedience to Your Word. Lord, when I doubt, remind me of Your presence and Your promises. Help me to be one who encourages others. Thank You for being my peace. I praise You, Lord Jesus. Amen.

DR. ROB ZINN, HIGHLAND, CA

WEEK 24—DAY 5

Reflection and Prayer

In what areas of your life can you observe that God has been conforming you into the image of Christ? How have you responded?

_____

_____

_____

_____

_____

_____

_____

_____

_____

_____

In the midst of trouble, how did the psalmist pray to God? What did he want God to do for him? How can you incorporate the psalmist's example into your own prayer life?

_____

_____

_____

_____

_____

_____

_____

_____

_____

_____

WEEK 25—DAY 1

God Is Our Comforter

Blessed be the God and Father of our Lord Jesus Christ, the Father of mercies and God of all comfort, who comforts us in all our tribulation, that we may be able to comfort those who are in any trouble, with the comfort with which we ourselves are comforted by God.

2 Corinthians 1:3, 4

Times of transition and tragedy are not reserved for a few unfortunates. All of us have experienced unsettled or broken times in our lives. Even the path to discipleship has pain along the way. But our pain is not purposeless. God, who is rich in compassion and steadfast in sovereignty, uses all of our experiences, including the difficult ones, for growth, healing, and ministry.

In hard times, we have a Comforter. God comforts us in our trials with His presence, reminding us that we are not alone. He strengthens us with His peace, giving us hope toward a greater purpose. Whether we suffer the loss of a loved one, financial collapse, injustice, persecution, or some other difficulty, we can look to God as our Comforter. Our personal experiences of pain, when massaged in the comfort of God's grace, often become our greatest platform for ministry. God brings us through our pain so we can encourage others who experience similar trials. The comfort He gives us in our own times of need becomes a powerful testimony for someone else. Allowing the Spirit of God to work in you during seasons of difficulty produces a greater work through you, ministering to others in their pain.

God comforts us because of His love toward us. Hard times help us see who He is—the most faithful Friend who comforts us in the midst of trials. In turn, we can show others that kind of comfort and testify to God's faithfulness to see them through. Know that you are not alone! Experience God's grace in the difficult times so you can share His grace with others. Even in pain, discipleship involves learning and growing, so you can help others to do the same!

God, I thank You for Your peace, comfort, and extravagant love. You have brought me through incredible trials. I would have never made it apart from You. Help me see You in the midst of present pain and past scars. Use me to bring Your love and peace to others who face their own hurts. I exist for Your pleasure, to bring You glory. May the experiences of Your faithfulness in my life be used to help others find You in their pain. Open my eyes to see opportunities to comfort others in their troubles. In Jesus' name, Amen.

DR. RICHARD MARK LEE, MCKINNEY, TX

Week 25—Day 2

Your Identity in Christ

---

*Holy brethren, partakers of the heavenly calling, consider the Apostle
and High Priest of our confession, Christ Jesus.*

Hebrews 3:1

Two of the aching questions of the human soul are, "Who am I?" and "Why am I here?" In different seasons of life we attempt to find the answers, desiring to know ourselves and to be known. As believers, we have an identity. We have a purpose. We belong first and foremost to the Lord Jesus Christ. We draw our purpose, direction, example, and identity from Him. We are children of God and co-heirs with Christ.

The living sacrifice of Jesus Christ bought us forgiveness of sin, victory in this life, and an eternity secure with God in heaven. He made us holy and He made us family—family with Him and family together as believers. Our purpose and focus in life is Christ and His kingdom.

Finding our identity in Jesus changes everything. The pathway to discipleship involves living a life that reflects this new identity. We no longer identify with the flesh, but with Christ. When we live according to our fleshly nature, it is a false identity. Our lives are to reflect all that His identity evokes. We are to live in community with other believers, reaching toward the goal of bringing others the Good News of the gospel.

In what ways do you need to embrace your identity in Christ and live more like Him? In what ways do other people see your true "Christ" identity in your words and actions?

 Father God, in the quietest parts of my life, I long for You. I long to know who I am and what I'm to do. I find the answers all within You. Through Jesus I unashamedly choose to follow You. As Your child, I rest in the fact that I belong to You. As Your servant, I seek to serve. As a part of the family, I accept the responsibilities that come with the family privileges. Thank You for calling me to You. Thank You for Your love that changed my everything. In Jesus' name, Amen.

Week 25—Day 3

What Does God's Love Look Like?

Now we see in a mirror, dimly, but then face to face. Now I know in part, but then I shall know just as I also am known. And now abide faith, hope, love, these three; but the greatest of these is love.

1 Corinthians 13:12, 13

What is love? People everywhere are searching for it. Our culture has redefined and cheapened it to the degree that many do not know what true love is. As a result, people struggle to receive and give love. Only after experiencing deep hurt and emptiness are some even willing to discuss God's love as an alternative.

What does God's love look like? It looks like Jesus. God's love is demonstrated by the life, sacrifice, and gift of Jesus Christ. In 1 Corinthians 13, Paul lists the attributes of love. It is patient and kind, and not easily angered, proud, rude, or self-seeking. Love keeps no record of wrongs. Wow! That's a high standard! The unconditional love of Jesus is all that and more.

As recipients of God's love, we rejoice and are thankful. As followers of Christ, we are to extend His love to those in need, especially to those closest to us. We are to be Jesus with skin on—loving others according to that same high standard! We are to express God's love at home with our family and in our everyday life relationships at school, work, or play.

Discipleship is not just knowing what to do; it's living what you know day to day. Discipleship is love in action! The greatest expression of love is the life of Jesus. He gave of Himself for the benefit of others, loving selflessly and completely. That's what love looks like. Jesus loved with actions and not just knowledge or words. He is our example and model for how we are to love others. We are able to love because He first loved us!

God, because You loved us, You sent Jesus as the ultimate gift of Your love. You've shown me how to love and to be loved. Give me the wisdom and discernment to be able to pass it on. I pray that You would use me to love others by Your grace, that they would see Your love expressed through me. May my love for You shine in such a way that it leads others to see Your love for them. Lead me to go specifically and intentionally to share Your love this day. In Jesus' name, Amen.

DR. RICHARD MARK LEE, MCKINNEY, TX

Week 25—Day 4

Is There a Limit to God's Forgiveness?

Do you not know that the unrighteous will not inherit the kingdom of God? Do not be deceived . . .
And such were some of you. But you were washed, but you were sanctified,
but you were justified in the name of the Lord Jesus and by the Spirit of our God.

1 Corinthians 6:9, 11

Many people have at some time or another wondered, *How could God ever forgive me?* The feeling of unworthiness or the inability to accept forgiveness is crippling. The truth is, we are all sinners. While the consequences of sin may vary, the reality of everyone's vulnerability to sin levels the ground at the foot of the Cross. We are all in need of forgiveness.

The Good News is that God's love knows no boundaries. The blood of Jesus paid the price for all our sin. To those who come to Him in repentance, there is no place that God's grace and forgiveness can't reach. Forgiveness is not only the beginning of the journey, when we first accept the forgiveness of sin Christ offers—it is also a steady marker on the pathway to discipleship. As Christ-followers, we continually receive and distribute forgiveness. God's love is demonstrated in us through His forgiveness of our sin—past, present, and future. As we walk the pathway of discipleship, we will stumble and falter along the way, but we will never be out of the grip of God's grace, nor beyond the limits of His forgiveness.

Gratitude for that kind of forgiveness, and the overflow of Christ's love poured out in our hearts, gives us the courage to express that same kind of forgiveness toward others. God forgave us when we didn't deserve it. There will be times when we must also forgive those who don't deserve it. Disciples reflect their leaders, so followers of Christ should lead lives steadily marked by forgiveness. God's forgiveness has no limits for those who believe in the saving power of the Cross. Forgiven people are free! Forgiven people are found. And found people find other people to tell about the Good News of forgiveness.

> *God, I have received from You forgiveness I did not deserve. Thank You. I pray that You would help me forgive as I've been forgiven. There is no limit to Your forgiveness, but sometimes there is a limit to my ability to forgive. Create in me a new heart. Help me love others as You love them. Give me the strength to extend grace and forgiveness because You first gave it to me. Help me continue to forgive when I'm reminded of the hurt. Make me more like You. In the name of Jesus, my Forgiver, Amen.*

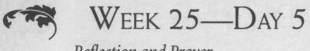

WEEK 25—DAY 5

Reflection and Prayer

The pathway to discipleship is marked by forgiveness. In what areas do you need to receive forgiveness? To whom do you need to extend forgiveness, even if it is undeserved? Are there things you've initially forgiven, but still wrestle with when the pain resurfaces? Ask God to search your heart and give you courage to continue to forgive.

_____

_____

_____

_____

_____

_____

_____

John 3:30 says, "He must increase, but I must decrease." A disciple is a reflection of the teacher. In what ways does your identity reflect Christ? In what areas can you grow to reflect more of Jesus? What changes need to be made for that to happen?

_____

_____

_____

_____

_____

_____

_____

_____

DR. RICHARD MARK LEE, MCKINNEY, TX

WEEK 26—DAY 1
How Do I Find God's Way?

Show me Your ways, O LORD; teach me Your paths. Lead me in Your truth and teach me,
for You are the God of my salvation; on You I wait all the day.

Psalm 25:4, 5

When our circumstances are urgent, extreme, and bleak, we need to know God's way ... but how? David wrote this psalm under dire circumstances; his own son Absalom had rebelled against him and desired his throne, even his life. Abraham Lincoln once said, "I have been driven many times upon my knees by the overwhelming conviction that I had nowhere else to go." David didn't know what to do, so he turned to God.

David teaches us that when God leads us in His way, it typically involves three things. First, there is the issue of what we *want*. David said, "Show me Your ways, O LORD; teach me Your paths." David wanted to be led by the Lord. Many times we don't really want God to show us His ways; what we really want is for God to approve of and affirm our ways. When God, who knows our hearts, sees that we really want Him to lead us, then He will lead us. What caused David to want God's way? He understood how destitute he was.

A second thing involved is our *will*. David not only wanted God's ways and God's paths, he was willing to follow God's leadership. Without the involvement of the will, the first pebble in the path trips us up. God has never promised us health and wealth if we follow Him. He wants us to follow Him no matter what. Why would God show you His way when you are unwilling to follow His way? David said, "Lead me in Your truth and teach me," showing us that guidance in God's way begins with a willingness to submit to the Word of God.

Third, experiencing God's leading may require us to *wait*. David demonstrated his desire and his willingness by his patience. David said, "On You I wait all the day." This is where many of us fail. We become impatient and act without God's guidance, and then complain when things go wrong. Let us remember that God is never in a hurry and that waiting on God is never a waste of time. Show God your desire to learn His ways, your will to follow Him, and your resolve to wait on Him, and He will bless you with His wisdom, truth, and guidance!

 Oh Lord, I am so lacking and destitute. Guard me, guide me, and grace me, oh God of my salvation. In Jesus' name, Amen.

How Can I Have God's Peace?

You will keep him in perfect peace, whose mind is stayed on You, because he trusts in You.

Isaiah 26:3

This verse is a part of Israel's song of salvation, which has a theme of righteousness and peace. There can be no true peace apart from righteousness, and there can be no righteousness apart from salvation in Jesus Christ! Psalm 85:10 speaks of the salvation Jesus made possible for us, describing what took place at the Cross: "Mercy and truth have met together; righteousness and peace have kissed."

Verse 1 of Isaiah 26 refers to a day when Jesus will defeat His enemies and reign over all. Blessings will follow. Israel will be strong and will sing the salvation song of Isaiah 26. There is not much peace in Jerusalem today, but on that day, Jerusalem will be a city of "perfect peace."

Jesus is the source of true peace. Angels announced Jesus' birth to the shepherds by saying, "Glory to God in the highest, and on earth peace, goodwill toward men!" (Luke 2:14). Jesus gives us peace in three ways. First, He gives us *peace with God*. We cannot have peace with God apart from the salvation that Jesus makes available.

Second, He gives us the *peace of God*. When Jesus is our Lord, "the peace of God, which surpasses all understanding, will guard [our] hearts and minds through Christ Jesus" (Philippians 4:7). When our world seems to be falling apart, Jesus can give us a peace that surpasses all understanding.

Third, Jesus gives us *peace that comes from God*. Isaiah says that when Jesus rules over this earth, "they shall beat their swords into plowshares, and their spears into pruning hooks; nation shall not lift up sword against nation, neither shall they learn war anymore" (Isaiah 2:4).

It is Jesus, the Prince of Peace (Isaiah 9:6), not the United Nations, that we need today for world peace. Today the world despises Jesus and gives Him no seat at the negotiating table. Yet our world will never know peace until Jesus rules over the world. *Prince* means "head person." When Jesus is the head person, whether in a life, a nation, or a world, He will produce peace!

 Lord, I remove myself from the throne of my life and call You my King. Occupy this throne and rule my life for Your glory. In Jesus' name, Amen.

ARDEN TAYLOR, GRAY, TN

WEEK 26—DAY 3

What Should I Do When I Feel Distant from God?

Israel was greatly impoverished because of the Midianites,
and the children of Israel cried out to the LORD.

Judges 6:6

When you feel distant from God, the first thing you must consider is why you feel distant from God. Could it be your own disobedience? This was the situation with the people of Israel in Judges 6; they had not obeyed the voice of God (v. 10). The Israelites suffered for years at the hands of neighboring nations, but they continued to tolerate or worship pagan idols.

Disobedience will always put distance between God and us. God can never be the problem, so when we are distant from Him, the problem must lie within ourselves. If disobedience pushes us away from God, what will bring us back to Him? Repentance! Repentance is the desire to turn from sin, not just escape the pain of sin.

The good news of God's discipline or chastisement is that it assures us that we are His children. His desire for us is that we would be conformed to the image of His Son (Romans 8:29). Solomon wrote, "Do not despise the chastening of the LORD, nor detest His correction; for whom the LORD loves He corrects" (Proverbs 3:11, 12).

A child of God needs to understand that God is not a passive or permissive heavenly Father, allowing us to do whatever pleases our depraved nature. Just as the Father said of His Son Jesus, "This is My beloved Son, in whom I am well pleased" (Matthew 3:17), He desires to say of us, "This is My beloved child, in whom I am well pleased." Our holy Father wants His very best for His children, and the best He can give to us is the character of Jesus. Obedience develops our character; disobedience destroys our character, and God will not sit idly by and watch us destroy ourselves.

     Thank You, Lord, for not giving up on me, even when I have given up on
myself. Forgive my sin, Lord. I repent of my sin and turn to You. While Your
chastisement is not a gratifying experience, it is a guaranteeing experience
of Your love for me, and I give You thanks for that. In Jesus' name, Amen.

Week 26—Day 4
How Can I Be Confident in Times of Distress?

God is our refuge and strength, a very present help in trouble. Therefore we will not fear, even though the earth be removed, and though the mountains be carried into the midst of the sea; though its waters roar and be troubled, though the mountains shake with its swelling.

Psalm 46:1–3

What are we to do when an enemy is about to overpower us and everything looks stacked against us? This is the problem that Hezekiah had as the Assyrian army marched toward Jerusalem. As the Assyrians marched southward through Syria and Israel, fields ripe with fruit, green with vegetation, and gold with grain lay before them; behind them they left the land bare, trodden down, and burned. Before them were cities, strong and sturdy; behind them they left only the blackened smoke of ruins. As they marched onward to Jerusalem, Hezekiah was biting his fingernails. But with his spirits lifted by the messages of the prophet Isaiah, Hezekiah refused to comply with the Assyrians' demand. God would be his *refuge*, which means "a place of shelter."

This psalm teaches us three things. First, when we are in a treacherous place, we need a *superior* shelter. Many places that are more susceptible to windstorms will have storm cellars. These are dug in the ground for protection from the storm. As a shelter it is superior to a normal residence. In the perilous circumstances of our life, we need superior protection. No wonder the psalmist said, "God is our refuge."

Second, when we are in a tight place, we need a *strong* shelter. God is not only our refuge but also our "strength, a very present help [not a distant help!] in trouble." The word *trouble* here refers to a tight place. The tight places we find ourselves in can become a breeding ground for God's strength to be demonstrated. Just ask the three Hebrews in the fiery furnace; they knew something about a tight place (Daniel 3)!

Third, when we are in a threatened place, we need a *secure* shelter. The hymn writer declared, "A mighty fortress is our God, a bulwark never failing"; therefore, there is nothing to fear! The Enemy will send his threats, but in Christ, our refuge is superior, strong, and secure!

 We thank You, oh Lord, for You turn our distress into delight. In Jesus' name, Amen.

ARDEN TAYLOR, GRAY, TN

WEEK 26—DAY 5

Reflection and Prayer

What struggles and issues must you deal with if God's will is to prevail over your will?

_____

_____

_____

_____

_____

_____

_____

What is the Enemy throwing at you right now to threaten you? What is it that is making it hard for you to sleep, or is like a dark cloud hanging over you? How will you respond to this in faith?

_____

_____

_____

_____

_____

_____

_____

_____

WEEK 27—DAY 1

What Is the Benefit of Stillness before the Lord?

Be still, and know that I am God; I will be exalted among the nations, I will be exalted in the earth!

Psalm 46:10

There is no substitute for time alone with God. Stillness before the Lord prepares you for the unexpected challenges and opportunities of life. Rather than allowing our mind to race from one problem to another, trying to figure out every possible solution, wondering what will come next, or grieving about the past, we are simply to "be still." This phrase literally means, "Take your hands off! Relax." He is in control. He is God and He has got everything covered. You can put your trust in Him. Let there be no doubt whatsoever that He has a perfect plan for all of us.

Sometimes we just need to wait quietly and simply let Him work in us so He can work through us. Being still is a challenge at times . . . but is it not reassuring to know that He is God and He has everything under control? He will keep in perfect peace all those who trust in Him, whose thoughts turn often to Him.

If you have not developed the habit of daily prayer and Bible study, why not begin now, so you will be prepared for whatever life brings your way?

 Father, You are God and even when I do not see Your plan, I know You have everything under control. I praise You today for the care and attention You give to my life. I exalt You, for Your grace is enough. Amen.

CHRIS DIXON, DUBLIN, GA

WEEK 27—DAY 2

When You Listen, God Will Meet Your Need

I am the LORD your God, who brought you out of the land of Egypt;
open your mouth wide, and I will fill it.

Psalm 81:10

Do you believe God can meet your needs? The Word of God teaches that you will never face a need for which God cannot provide the supply. This promise appears over and over again in the Bible. If we are not experiencing God's provision, where is the problem? Is the problem with God? Or could the problem be our lack of faith in the promise that God can meet our every need?

Every resource of God is available to Christians who will listen to Him and put their trust in Him. No one who has ever placed their life in His hands and trusted in His promises and provision has ever been let down. Just as He provided a way for the children of Israel out of the bondage of Egypt, He can provide a way for you. Philippians 4:19 says, "God shall supply all your need according to His riches in glory by Christ Jesus." Today, live in confidence knowing that the God who made a way for Israel is the same God who is going to provide a way for you.

 Father, You have provided for me and met my greatest need through Your Son, Jesus Christ. Thank You for the wonderful forgiveness and the intimate relationship You have made available to me. Today, I have confidence that You will supply all my needs as I seek to follow Your will for my life. Amen.

WEEK 27—DAY 3

Boldness for God Has Its Rewards

The LORD said to Joshua: "Get up! Why do you lie thus on your face? . . . Get up, sanctify the people, and say, 'Sanctify yourselves for tomorrow, because thus says the LORD God of Israel: "There is an accursed thing in your midst, O Israel; you cannot stand before your enemies until you take away the accursed thing from among you."'"

Joshua 7:10, 13

The children of Israel were moving into the Promised Land. They had witnessed an amazing victory over the city of Jericho, and were continuing toward their next victory. To their surprise, they met defeat as they attempted to capture the town of Ai. When they asked for God's explanation for their defeat, He responded by revealing that someone in their camp had disobeyed His command not to keep any possessions from Jericho. The disobedience of one man and his family had paralyzed an entire nation! Achan thought he could conceal his sin and it would not affect anyone else. One act of disobedience cost Achan and his family their lives. His sin had serious repercussions for others, denying them the blessings, power, and victory of God. Our sin makes an impact on others.

However, as we look at Joshua, we realize that obedience to God can also have effects far beyond our own individual lives. Joshua's willingness to respond to God and walk in obedience changed the outcome for an entire nation. David wrote in Psalm 37:25, 26, "I have been young, and now am old; yet I have not seen the righteous forsaken, nor his descendants begging bread. He is ever merciful, and lends; and his descendants are blessed."

Always remember, disobedience leads to defeat. Obedience leads to victory. Diligently seek to obey every word from God! Scripture promises that if you will obey the Lord, He will not only bless your life but also use your life as a channel of blessing to others.

Father, examine my heart and reveal to me any area of disobedience. Make Your way clear to me so I can walk according to Your will. Allow my life to be a channel of blessing to others so the world can see what a great and awesome God You are. Amen.

CHRIS DIXON, DUBLIN, GA

WEEK 27—DAY 4

How Listening to God Spares Us Pain

I was forty years old when Moses the servant of the LORD sent me from Kadesh Barnea to spy out the land, and I brought back word to him as it was in my heart. Nevertheless my brethren who went up with me made the heart of the people melt, but I wholly followed the LORD my God.

Joshua 14:7, 8

Caleb's faith in God never wavered even though nearly everyone around him doubted. All his life he had been taught about the land God had promised the Israelites. I cannot even begin to imagine the excitement he felt when at the age of forty he looked over the land God had prepared for His people. Caleb was convinced God would give the land to the children of Israel, but the people were afraid of the protected cities and the giants that had been reported in the land. Their lack of faith in God cost them the opportunity to experience God's blessing and forced Caleb to wait forty years in the wilderness. But God ultimately brought Caleb into the Promised Land because he listened to and wholly trusted in God's promise.

Take inventory of your life and the decisions you are presently facing. Have you chosen to believe the promises of God and trust Him wholeheartedly? The same God who provided for Caleb is just as capable of working through your life. If you will proceed with what He has told you, no matter how incredible it might seem, you will experience the joy of seeing God work in your life.

    Father, I want to thank You for Your wisdom and guidance in my life. I acknowledge that Your plan for my life involves peace and prospering, not evil; You desire to give me a future and a hope. Today, give me the courage and the strength to be wholly committed to You. In my words and deeds, may my life be a testimony to Your faithfulness and goodness. Amen.

WEEK 27—DAY 5

Reflection and Prayer

In what areas of your life do you need to "be still" and trust God to work? Be specific and list out the things you need to surrender to God's plan.

_____

_____

_____

_____

_____

_____

_____

_____

_____

Are there any areas of disobedience in your walk with God? Remember, you will never experience victory apart from obedience. Write out a prayer of confession and allow God to lead you into victory.

_____

_____

_____

_____

_____

_____

_____

_____

_____

CHRIS DIXON, DUBLIN, GA

Week 28—Day 1

God Desires to Communicate with Us

O Lord, You have searched me and known me. You know my sitting down and my rising up; You under-stand my thought afar off. You comprehend my path and my lying down, and are acquainted with all my ways. For there is not a word on my tongue, but behold, O Lord, You know it altogether.

Psalm 139:1–4

Few passages in the Bible tell us more about the character of God as it applies to His relationship with us. This psalm can be simply outlined as follows: 1) How well does God know me? (vv. 1–6); 2) How close is God to me? (vv. 7–12); 3) How carefully has God made me? (vv. 13–16); 4) How well does God protect me? (vv. 17–24).

God knows all there is to know; therefore, He knows all our past, all our present, and even our future. Yet, knowing everything, He still desires to have an intimate relationship with us. Revelation 3:20 says, "Behold, I stand at the door and knock. If anyone hears My voice and opens the door, I will come in to him and dine with him." Jesus desires above all to "dine" with us, that is, to have times of intimate fel-lowship—to communicate with us on a deep spiritual level.

Hebrews 1:1, 2 says, "God, who at various times and in various ways spoke in time past to the fathers by the prophets, has in these last days spoken to us by His Son." All through history God has spoken in different ways; now He speaks through His Son. Before Christ's death on the Cross, we were separated from God. The veil in the Jewish temple separated people from the Most Holy Place, the place where God dwelt. Only the high priest could go behind the veil once a year in order to make sacrifices to God. After the sacrifice of Jesus dying on the Cross, the veil of the temple was torn in half by the hand of God (Matthew 27:51). This signified that through receiving Jesus, we can now have fellowship with Him, twenty-four hours a day, seven days a week. He still stands at your heart's door and knocks. Open the door and "dine" with Jesus.

Lord Jesus, I need to hear from You today. I sense that You are knocking on my heart's door. Please come in and help me to know Your love and Your direction for my life. I do not wish for a normal, everyday devotional time. I desire to hear from You, to sense Your touch, to know Your fellowship. Amen.

WEEK 28—DAY 2

Human Life Was Formed by God in the Beginning

You formed my inward parts; You covered me in my mother's womb. I will praise You, for I am fearfully and wonderfully made; marvelous are Your works, and that my soul knows very well.

Psalm 139:13, 14

It is said that no one is irreplaceable. However, as far as God is concerned, everyone is irreplaceable. Earlier in Psalm 139, the psalmist declared that God knows everything (vv. 1–6) and that He is everywhere (vv. 7–12). In verses 13 and 14 he declares that God created him in His wisdom. God's wisdom is seen in His creation of his innermost parts. God's love is demonstrated in that He made him special—one of a kind. Of course, the same is true for every human being. You were particularly formed by God while you were in your mother's womb. The Hebrew wording here has a sense of "embroidering," meaning that you were sewn together by the hand of the Lord for a particular purpose. You are "fearfully and wonderfully made."

What can we see from this passage? First, that God gave us life the moment we were conceived (Jeremiah 1:5; Luke 1:41). Second, that God knew we would be here and that He is not surprised at our strengths or our weaknesses (Psalm 139:16). Third, that we are special. We have our own DNA, our own fingerprints, and our own purpose in life. Jeremiah 29:11 reads, "I know the thoughts that I think toward you, says the LORD, thoughts of peace and not of evil, to give you a future and a hope."

Even our weaknesses are woven into God's plan. Years ago, a friend of mine related to me how God had used a facial deformity in his life. He said, "I know that I am so prideful that if God had not given me this challenge, I do not believe I would ever have been humble enough to receive Christ."

God has a plan for you. You are special to God and to the world. You are irreplaceable.

 Lord Jesus, thank You that You knew us even before we were born. Thank You that even with all our challenges, You can bring forth something great for our lives. Help me to draw close to You today. Help me feel Your touch on my life and lead me to touch the lives of others. Make me irreplaceable today. Amen.

DR. DWAYNE MERCER, OVIEDO, FL

WEEK 28—DAY 3

How Does God Get Our Attention?

Ask now concerning the days that are past, which were before you, since the day that God created man on the earth, and ask from one end of heaven to the other, whether any great thing like this has happened, or anything like it has been heard ... To you it was shown, that you might know that the LORD Himself is God; there is none other besides Him.

Deuteronomy 4:32, 35

It's been said the quickest way for a mother to get the attention of her children is to sit down and look comfortable. In the Book of Deuteronomy, the knowledge of God sprang from God revealing Himself through events. Without the Bible, the Israelites were dependent upon God's revelation through miracles. Two such miraculous events were the Exodus and the giving of the Law on Mount Sinai. These two events became the framework for Israel's early theology. Moses declared that through all history (to that point) there had never been a greater and more observable miracle than what happened on Mount Sinai. God performed this great miracle so that Israel would know that Yahweh was the one true God. This was a one-time event. It was not normal. Otherwise, it would not have received Israel's attention.

God often uses the extraordinary to speak to us today. These include a special word from the Bible—perhaps a particular verse that grips you. It may be through a sermon from your pastor. Sometimes it's a rebuke from a loved one. If you are like me, it is quite often through times of adversity. I remember a few years ago, I was taking my wife to the doctor for a report on her biopsy. The doctor called Pam to give her a warning that the tumor was cancerous. When she told me, I drove the car in silence for twenty minutes. I was shocked. You never think it will happen to you or someone you love. God had my attention. Thankfully, as I write this, she is cancer-free.

Is God trying to get your attention? If so, why? What do you need to correct? Have you been taking your fellowship with God for granted? Is there something you need to change?

 Lord Jesus, help me to live in such a way that You always have my attention. I pray You will not need to place adversity in my path. However, when You do need to get my attention, please do what You must do. I do not want to stray from Your will. Amen.

WEEK 28—DAY 4

The Promise of God's Blessing Requires Obedience

Know this day, and consider it in your heart, that the LORD Himself is God in heaven above and on the earth beneath; there is no other. You shall therefore keep His statutes and His commandments which I command you today, that it may go well with you and with your children after you, and that you may prolong your days in the land which the LORD your God is giving you for all time.

Deuteronomy 4:39, 40

As Moses was about to reintroduce the Israelites to God's Law, he remembered what God had done. He said there is no one like God. No one has done the things that God has done. He looked at creation (Deuteronomy 4:32); God speaking from a fire (v. 33); taking a nation—Israel—from the midst of another nation—Egypt (v. 34). Why? So that the people would know that the Lord is God (v. 39). The question then is, how do we receive blessings from this almighty God? The answer is *obedience* (v. 40).

I like to think of God's will for our lives as a path of blessing. When we stay on this path, we receive all the blessings God has for us. If we veer off into the wilderness, we will miss those blessings.

Obedience is required to walk the path of blessing. Obedience always grows in an atmosphere of struggle. The key is to realize that every step of obedience is a step of faith. God speaks to us through His Word. We then either believe it or disbelieve it. If we truly believe, we take action to obey. Each time God asks us to do something, a question arises in our hearts: "Am I better off obeying God than going my own way?" The answer to that question will determine if we enter (or stay) on God's path of blessing for our lives or if we wander from that path. Never be offended by God's Word. Always receive it. The promises for obedience are countless. It is all dependent on us listening, believing, and responding in obedience.

The next time God convicts your heart to act, just trust Him and obey.

Lord Jesus, help me be sensitive to Your Spirit today. I know I have not arrived. I know You want to speak into my life as I read Your Word. Help me love You enough to listen and trust You enough to obey. Amen.

DR. DWAYNE MERCER, OVIEDO, FL

WEEK 28—DAY 5

Reflection and Prayer

You are indeed fearfully and wonderfully made. Is there something about yourself you have difficulty accepting? How can this be turned into a signature of God's love in your life?

_____

_____

_____

_____

_____

_____

_____

_____

What tool has God used in your life to get your attention? What is He trying to tell you as He speaks to your heart?

_____

_____

_____

_____

_____

_____

_____

_____

_____

WEEK 29—DAY 1

Learning to Hear God's Voice

The LORD called Samuel again the third time. So he arose and went to Eli, and said, "Here I am, for you did call me." Then Eli perceived that the LORD had called the boy. Therefore Eli said to Samuel, "Go, lie down; and it shall be, if He calls you, that you must say, 'Speak, LORD, for Your servant hears.'" So Samuel went and lay down in his place. Now the LORD came and stood and called as at other times, "Samuel! Samuel!" And Samuel answered, "Speak, for Your servant hears."

1 Samuel 3:8–10

There are many voices screaming for our attention today. One of the greatest needs in a Christian's life is to have the ability to recognize the voice of God. God's voice comes in various forms: comfort, warning, rebuke, salvation, and repentance, to name a few. However, the real test in believers' lives is how they respond to God's voice.

Although God's voice came to Samuel four different times, Samuel misunderstood the first three times (1 Samuel 3:2–8). He confused God's voice with that of Eli's. Each time Samuel went to Eli and replied, "Here I am." Each time Eli instructed Samuel to go back to sleep. Samuel did not respond to God's voice for the same reason many people today do not respond; he did not yet know the Lord. He ministered in the flesh and not the Spirit.

The call of God demands a positive response. We must be careful not to reject it. Our response must be the same as Samuel's: "Speak, for Your servant hears."

Take joy in knowing that the Lord loves you enough to call you to faith and repentance. Heeding God's voice always brings joy; dismissing God's voice always brings regret.

   Lord Jesus, thank You for calling me to salvation. Thank You for calling me to spread Your glorious gospel. I am so grateful You call me to repentance each day of my life. Amen.

TIM ANDERSON, ATHENS, AL

Week 29—Day 2
We All Need God's Wisdom

Trust in the LORD with all your heart, and lean not on your own understanding;
in all your ways acknowledge Him, and He shall direct your paths.

Proverbs 3:5, 6

We have all faced major decisions. Should I change jobs? Should I buy this house? Should I buy this car? Should I invest in this retirement plan or another one less risky? Life is all about choices. I have learned that the will of God for my life is found in the Word of God—every time! That is why a daily intake of the Word of God is essential if we are to live victoriously in this life.

It isn't enough for us just to own a Bible; we must allow the Holy Spirit to write it upon the tablet of our heart. Obedience to the Word not only enriches our lives, it gives us direction and safety. The psalmist said, "How can a young man cleanse his way? By taking heed according to Your word" (Psalm 119:9).

The word *trust* can mean "to lie helpless or face down." This is the image of a defeated soldier yielding his rights in total submission. The danger we all face is leaning on our own understanding and rushing toward disaster and ruin. Who among us hasn't been guilty of that?

Many times in my life I have stood at the intersection of decision and doubt. At those times the Word of God has reminded me that "a double-minded man" is "unstable in all his ways" (James 1:8). Nothing less than total surrender and commitment will yield the wisdom of choosing the right path. Solomon's words in Proverbs 1:7 still ring true: "The fear of the LORD is the beginning of knowledge, but fools despise wisdom and instruction."

 Lord Jesus, I confess to You today that I am totally dependent upon Your wisdom and instruction. I pray that I never take another step toward human wisdom, but always trust in You and Your direction. Thank You for Your mercy and amazing grace. Amen.

WEEK 29—DAY 3

How Important Is Waiting on God?

Since the beginning of the world men have not heard nor perceived by the ear,
nor has the eye seen any God besides You, who acts for the one who waits for Him.

Isaiah 64:4

Who in their right mind likes to wait? My life's philosophy is this: "I am in a hurry, even when I am not in a hurry." But the Lord has shown me that waiting is a virtue as well as a discipline. Any serious disciple of the Lord Jesus knows that patience and waiting are lifelong pursuits that nobody ever masters.

Isaiah's message here is simply this: our senses of seeing and hearing will never be able to comprehend the beauty of God's reward for those who wait upon Him. God is patient with us because that is His nature, and as we live in His patience we are to build longsuffering and discipline into our lives as well. Never let us forget the prophet Isaiah's words in an earlier chapter: "Those who wait on the LORD shall renew their strength; they shall mount up with wings like eagles, they shall run and not be weary, they shall walk and not faint" (Isaiah 40:31).

The word *wait* in today's text is a very interesting word. Isaiah is not suggesting that the children of God should just sit around and do nothing. No, we are to work while there is still light because, as Jesus said, a time is coming "when no one can work" (John 9:4). Isaiah is teaching us to hope and trust in God, to look to God for all the provisions in life. I would rather wait and walk with God than run ahead without Him. I have often been sorry for rushing, but seldom have I been sorry for waiting.

Lord, it is my prayer that I would no longer run ahead of You, but instead, wait upon You and see the mercy given to those who trust You. As I walk by faith and not by sight, may I bring You glory with an obedient life. Amen.

TIM ANDERSON, ATHENS, AL

WEEK 29—DAY 4

The Process of Spiritual Growth

---

*The vessel that he made of clay was marred in the hand of the potter; so he made it again
into another vessel, as it seemed good to the potter to make. Then the word of the LORD
came to me, saying: "O house of Israel, can I not do with you as this potter?" says the LORD.
"Look, as the clay is in the potter's hand, so are you in My hand, O house of Israel!"*

Jeremiah 18:4–6

Spiritual growth is a lifelong process of discipline and devotion. Although none of us will fully be
what we should be in this life, one thing is for sure: we are to grow in the grace and knowledge of the
Lord Jesus. The sad truth for many Christians is that they are no further along in their Christian walk
than they were ten years ago. There are few things worse than unproductive Christians. Simply put, the
only way to grow in our faith is to spend time with the One who made us.

God told Jeremiah to go to the potter's house. When he arrived he saw the potter working at the
wheel, molding clay into a vessel. When the potter noticed a flaw in the vessel, he mashed it into a lump
of clay, then reworked it until it was to his liking. God impressed upon Jeremiah's heart that the Lord is
sovereign and He can do what He wills with His people.

From the very beginning, when the Lord breathed us into existence, He had a master plan for our
lives. However, it is up to us to spend the rest of our lives developing into the disciples He desires us to
be. God did not make us into robots; rather, He made us free moral agents that have the ability to choose
whether to worship Him or to reject Him. Ask God to help you become malleable clay in His hands,
freely surrendered to His purposes as He forms you into Christ's likeness.

 *Lord Jesus, You gave me eternal life with salvation. I desire to give my life
back to You and allow You to rework me as You see fit, so that I may grow
to be more Christlike. Thank You for loving me and repeatedly forgiving
me. Amen.*

WEEK 29—DAY 5
Reflection and Prayer

Responding to God's voice brings joy and dismissing God's voice brings regret. What are the distracting voices in your life that are keeping you from victory today? Are there any that even have you on the brink of disaster?

_____

_____

_____

_____

_____

_____

_____

_____

_____

Are you about to make a decision without making God's will and timing the primary consideration? Will the decision you are about to make bring you closer to God or lead you further away from Him?

_____

_____

_____

_____

_____

_____

_____

_____

_____

_____

TIM ANDERSON, ATHENS, AL

WEEK 30—DAY 1

What Can I Do to Become More Spiritually Responsible?

Moses said, "I will now turn aside and see this great sight, why the bush does not burn."
So when the LORD saw that he turned aside to look, God called to him from the midst of the
bush and said, "Moses, Moses!" And he said, "Here I am." Then He said, "Do not draw
near this place. Take your sandals off your feet, for the place where you stand is holy ground."

Exodus 3:3–5

Is there any room for improvement in your walk with Jesus? I don't believe I have ever met anyone with an ounce of honesty who doesn't see the opportunity for improvement in his or her spiritual journey. Being spiritually responsible with all that we are and all we possess is a challenge we wake up with every morning. Improvement in our walk with Jesus and spiritual responsibility is not simply a decision we make—it is a lifestyle we live! The big question is, "How do we begin to take steps in the right direction?"

What God called Moses to do on the mountain in Exodus 3 provides us with some clear footprints to follow. The everyday demands of ordinary life have a tendency to occupy our time and thoughts, and we forget to look God's way. Moses was going about his normal routine when God got his attention. What Moses saw that day changed his life. The first step to real improvement in our journey with Jesus is the willingness to step aside from the normal to encounter the supernatural. When we turn our eyes God's way, it doesn't take a burning bush to change our lives. When we see what God is doing and hear what God is saying, our lives ignite to burn brighter and brighter.

It would seem that shoes are necessary for a more responsible walk with Jesus, but what is needed most are bare feet—feet that acknowledge the holy nature of an encounter with our Savior and God. The more we recognize the grace-filled privilege we have to meet with the God of all creation, the more we will turn aside from the ordinary to meet with Him. He is the One who changes everything!

    Oh Lord, there is nothing like hearing You speak from Your Word and
seeing You work in Your world through my life. Draw me close to You each
day so that I may live Your way. Thank You for hearing my voice and saving
my life! Amen.

WEEK 30—DAY 2

How Does God Teach Me Patience?

May the Lord direct your hearts into the love of God and into the patience of Christ.

2 Thessalonians 3:5

Growing up in the South, I have become used to hearing and using expressions that add flavor to ordinary conversation. Expressions like, "Go whole hog," "You're barking up the wrong tree," and "That just takes the cake," are just a few. One expression I have heard all my life to describe a person with amazing patience is, "That man has the patience of Job." After reading the story of Job's life, his measure of patience does seem very unusual, almost unachievable. However, Paul raises the expectations when he prays that God would guide the hearts of believers "into the patience of Christ." Wow! Now that's really raising the bar!

Patience is a virtue that most people, even believers, would say they possess in small amounts, if at all. So when we read this kind of challenge, we almost want to give up at once because it seems like an impossible task. However, there are two facets of this passage that offer hope. Commentators are divided on whether this verse is just teaching Christ as our model for the patience we are to display, or if He is the One who gives us the patience we are to display. I believe the answer is both. Jesus is the One who walks ahead of us, displaying patience in unmistakable fashion as an inspiring example, and He is the One who gives us the strength to exhibit real patience.

Another expression we have in the South is, "To run fast, you just need to run fast." To apply that same logic to patience, some might be tempted to say, "To have patience, you just need to have patience." However, this kind of patience isn't obtained through practice, but rather through daily participation in a relationship with Jesus. Chasing patience will never get you where you want to go, but pursuing a life with Jesus will take you beyond your greatest expectations.

 Oh Lord, I desire to live like You, especially when I need to be patient and loving. Give me the strength and heart to be grace on display every day. Amen.

TIM DOWDY, MCDONOUGH, GA

WEEK 30—DAY 3

What Is God's Forever Love?

Love suffers long and is kind; love does not envy; love does not parade itself, is not puffed up;
does not behave rudely, does not seek its own, is not provoked, thinks no evil; does not rejoice in iniquity,
but rejoices in the truth; bears all things, believes all things, hopes all things, endures all things.

1 Corinthians 13:4–7

For some love is fickle, but with God it is forever! As I read again the words of the apostle Paul in the great Love Chapter of the New Testament, I am challenged to love more and love better. I am also reminded that God always possesses and displays every characteristic on Paul's list. God is never lacking in the love department. He never acts in a way that contradicts the noble characteristics of real love. Why? The answer might surprise you.

The reason God's love is a forever kind of love is because it is not something He possesses; rather, it is who He is. First John 4 paints the picture of the nature of God's heart in this way: "He who does not love does not know God, for God is love"(v. 8). The way the apostle John describes love in this passage reveals that apart from God, there is no love, because "God is love." In fact, he repeats that claim later in the same chapter, "We have known and believed the love that God has for us. God is love, and he who abides in love abides in God, and God in him" (v. 16).

If God is love, how much does He love, and for how long? John answers both questions in one encouraging sentence: "In this the love of God was manifested toward us, that God has sent His only begotten Son into the world, that we might live through Him" (1 John 4:9). In Christ—and in the eternal life we can have through His life, death, and Resurrection—we see the full measure of God's love.

 Oh Lord, thank You for Your love. I know there is nothing in me that deserves Your attention, and there is nothing lacking in You so that You need to love me. You love because You are love, love that lasts forever. Help me love others the way You have loved me! Amen.

WEEK 30—DAY 4

Why Does God's Love Never Fail?

Love never fails. But whether there are prophecies, they will fail; whether there are tongues, they will cease; whether there is knowledge, it will vanish away. For we know in part and we prophesy in part. But when that which is perfect has come, then that which is in part will be done away.

1 Corinthians 13:8–10

*F**ailure is not an option.* This inspirational quote usually stands between a determined individual and a very difficult challenge. The hope is that these words will serve as the motivation needed to overcome any challenge and bring victory. The key word in the previous sentence is *hope*. In this kind of scenario there are no guarantees and failure often claims another victim. However, when you apply this quote to God and His great love, it is a statement of fact rather than hope. God's love is a guarantee and it never fails.

Paul follows his inspirational description of love in 1 Corinthians 13 with a statement of promise. Interpreters debate about the exact time when prophecies, tongues, and knowledge will cease, but no one is confused about when love will fail . . . never! As we learned yesterday, "God is love" (1 John 4:8, 16). Because God is a forever God, God's love is a forever love. There is never a time when God doesn't love you, and there never will be. Even when we face the most difficult circumstances, God's love is not overwhelmed. When our adversaries seem to be stronger than we are and cause us to be afraid, we should confess with the psalmist, "Why do you boast in evil, O mighty man? The goodness of God endures continually" (Psalm 52:1). God told His people, "I have loved you with an everlasting love" (Jeremiah 31:3). Paul said, "I am persuaded that neither death nor life, nor angels nor principalities nor powers, nor things present nor things to come, nor height nor depth, nor any other created thing, shall be able to separate us from the love of God which is in Christ Jesus our Lord" (Romans 8:38, 39). Always remember, there is no challenger in this life that can tear us from the grip of God's mighty love.

At some point, priceless treasures like tongues and prophecies will fade into the pages of history; in a sense they will "fail" the test of time. But for the amazing, indescribable, eternal love of God, "failure is not an option," and that's a fact.

 Oh Lord, thank You for Your steadfast, everlasting love that never fails. Your love fills a place in my life that remains alive only because of Your love. Help me always to trust in Your unfailing love! Amen.

TIM DOWDY, MCDONOUGH, GA

Week 30—Day 5

Reflection and Prayer

Spending time with the God of all creation and of your salvation is the most important encounter you can have each day. Given the fact that God desires to meet with you, how can you spend more time with your shoes off (remember Moses) in the presence of your King?

_____

_____

_____

_____

_____

_____

_____

_____

_____

_____

How can you engage the world you live in with the love of God so that those you meet see Him?

_____

_____

_____

_____

_____

_____

_____

_____

_____

_____

Week 31—Day 1

Repentance Is Necessary for Genuine Service

Thus says the Lord: "If you return, then I will bring you back; you shall stand before Me; if you take out the precious from the vile, you shall be as My mouth. Let them return to you, but you must not return to them. And I will make you to this people a fortified bronze wall; and they will fight against you, but they shall not prevail against you; for I am with you to save you and deliver you," says the Lord.

Jeremiah 15:19, 20

One of the greatest misconceptions in the Christian faith is that God brought us into a relationship with Himself so that we could *live for Him*. It sounds so spiritual, doesn't it? But the truth is He never expected us to be able to live for Him. In reality it's not *our lives* He is interested in at all. Jesus Christ brought us into a relationship with Himself so that He might live *through* us. The only life in us that pleases the Father at all is the very life of Christ being expressed in our lives. Paul said, "I have been crucified with Christ; it is no longer I who live, but Christ lives in me; and the life which I now live in the flesh I live by faith in the Son of God, who loved me and gave Himself for me" (Galatians 2:20).

When we understand this powerful truth, two things happen. First, there is an overwhelming sense of freedom. That only makes sense, right? Jesus said, "You shall know the truth, and the truth shall make you free" (John 8:32). We are free from trying to live autonomously, and free to depend on Him to live through us. Second, it establishes a new focus—it shifts from what we are to do for Him to what He desires to do in and through us. Everything He desires to do through our lives He will do out of the overflow of what He is doing in our lives. This puts the focus on intimacy with Him instead of activity for Him.

As we daily seek Him relationally and live a life of repentance—turning from self to His life in us—He then accomplishes His purpose through us, bringing glory to Himself in and through our lives. Repentance is not an event; it is a lifestyle of denying self so that His life may be lived through us.

 Lord Jesus, thank You for the freedom that is found in knowing You! I acknowledge my absolute and utter dependence on You for anything and everything in my life. May I live a life of repentance. May I constantly turn away from myself and trust in You to live through me a life that is pleasing to the Father and accomplishing His purposes locally and globally. Thank You that You not only died for me, but that You also seek to live in and through me! Praise Your glorious name! Amen.

VANCE PITMAN, LAS VEGAS, NV

WEEK 31—DAY 2

The Benefits of Prayer and Fasting

Go, gather all the Jews who are present in Shushan, and fast for me; neither eat nor drink for three days, night or day. My maids and I will fast likewise. And so I will go to the king, which is against the law; and if I perish, I perish!

Esther 4:16

We are absolutely desperate for God. Jesus said, "Without Me you can do nothing" (John 15:5). The problem is we don't believe that is what He meant. We think He meant, "Without Me you can't do *big* things." Ask yourself this question: "When do I pray the most?" Probable answer: "I pray the most when I'm the most desperate. If it is just an ordinary day, I might spend time with God in prayer. I might fast. But when a *big* thing comes up in my life, I become a prayer warrior. I spend every waking moment seeking God."

Prayer and fasting are in some ways a great barometer for our desperation for God. When we pray and fast, we deny physical gratification in order to focus on our relationship with God. We acknowledge our great need for God and invite His activity into our lives. At our church we say it this way: "We don't pray before we work. Prayer is the work; then God works." When we live a life of prayer and fasting, we are walking in humility before God and always inviting His blessing and favor into our lives and the lives of those in our circle of influence.

It is true that without Jesus we can do nothing. But it is also true that we can do all things through Him who gives us strength. As our lives demonstrate dependence on Him, He will accomplish through us more than we could ever ask, think, or imagine.

Father I know I am desperate for You! I also know that I am tempted to try to live independently of You. Give me the grace today to be aware of my dependence on You. Give me the faith to seek You constantly. May You use the disciplines of prayer and fasting as instruments to draw me intimately close to You. Help me cultivate dependence on You. May You capture my heart and conform me to Your image. Thank You for Your patience and grace in my life! Amen.

WEEK 31—DAY 3
God's Hatred of Human Pride

Pride goes before destruction, and a haughty spirit before a fall.

Proverbs 16:18

I have four amazing kids. Honestly, I had no idea fatherhood would teach me as much about my personal relationship with God as it has. Life lessons have been hiding out for me at every stage of their development, in places I never imagined.

For example, when each of my kids was about three or four years old, we went through that stage of learning to tie a shoe. Daily we would walk through the process together, until finally the day came when they declared, "No, Daddy, I'm gonna do it myself!" At that point, I would humbly remove myself from the process and say, "Go ahead! Help yourself." I would sit back and watch as they attempted in every way possible to tie that shoe. Laces flying, tongue hanging out of the mouth, arms twisting—they were passionately engaged. At a certain point, my kid would come to me completely frustrated and say, "Daddy, would you help me?" I would take their little hands in mine, tie the shoes, and then let go of their hands and declare, "Look, you tied your shoes!" Of course, I knew that I had tied their shoes. I had simply done it through them. In that moment, I saw an ugly picture—*my pride!* How many times I had said, "God, I'll do this myself!" Maybe not aloud, but with my lack of dependence on Him, I said it nonetheless. And every time I failed. I fell flat on my face. In every instance, He was waiting patiently for me to cry to Him for help. Then and only then would He manifest His life through me.

Pride says, "God, I don't need you." Humility says, "God, I'm desperate for you," and humility is the defining characteristic of the life of Christ in us.

    Lord, I confess my arrogance. I know that my natural tendency is to depend on myself and to look to myself for strength to live each day. I acknowledge the truth that living that way will always lead to failure. I can do absolutely nothing apart from You. I need You more than I need air to breathe. I need You today; I need You right now. Fill me with Your Spirit and do through me what only You can do. Thank You that through You I can do all things. I love You, Lord. Amen.

VANCE PITMAN, LAS VEGAS, NV

WEEK 31—DAY 4

How to Handle Feelings of Guilt

There is therefore now no condemnation to those who are in Christ Jesus,
who do not walk according to the flesh, but according to the Spirit. For the law
of the Spirit of life in Christ Jesus has made me free from the law of sin and death.

Romans 8:1, 2

*S*inner *saved by grace.* "Forgiven, not perfect." Have you ever used one of those phrases in reference to yourself? Statements like these permeate church language. The problem is they are not a complete understanding of our true identity according to Scripture. When we do not understand our true identity, we are prime candidates to be deceived, misled, and defeated by the Enemy on a daily basis.

Paul's favorite phrase to refer to believers in the New Testament is "in Christ." Through the miracle of salvation, we have been placed in Christ. This means that when God sees me, He no longer sees me as a sinner simply saved by grace; He sees me as righteous as the very Son of God Himself. Is that because I am that righteous? Absolutely not! It is because that righteousness is what I have been given by the grace of God. That is who I am now in Christ! That is my true identity.

Ponder this staggering truth: when you have been in heaven for ten thousand years, you will not be any more righteous in the sight of God than you are right now as you are reading this paragraph. You might ask, "How is that possible?" It is possible in Christ! My righteousness before God is not based on my performance for Christ, but my position in Christ. Because I am in Him, there is *no* condemnation. Any condemnation that I sense is the Enemy trying to lay accusation where it doesn't belong, and the only reason I fall for his ploys is that I do not understand who I am in Christ. The greatest thing you could do today is read what the Bible says about you and by faith believe it. Let the truth sink in, my fellow saint!

Precious Jesus, I am amazed at the grace that You have displayed in my life. I am chosen, adopted, forgiven, redeemed, reconciled, filled with Your Spirit, raised with Christ, and seated in the heavenly places with Him. There is absolutely no condemnation in my life because of Your amazing grace. I pray that today You would help me live out of the resources of who I am in You. I am Your child. I am holy and blameless. I am a new creation in Christ. May Your grace transform my life today for Your glory. Amen.

Week 31—Day 5

Reflection and Prayer

Are you trying to live the Christian life or are you passionately pursuing Christ to live His life through you? Are you focused on intimacy with God or activity for God? Examine your life to see how much time you spend with God and how much time you spend for God.

_____
_____
_____
_____
_____
_____
_____
_____

How do you see yourself? Do you have a problem with being called a saint—holy, righteous, and perfect? Spend some time reading through the letters of Paul in the New Testament and underline the words that refer to your identity as a follower of Christ. As you read, acknowledge by faith that the Word of God is true.

_____
_____
_____
_____
_____
_____
_____
_____

VANCE PITMAN, LAS VEGAS, NV

WEEK 32—DAY 1

Brokenness, the Way to Blessing

"Now, therefore," says the LORD, "turn to Me with all your heart, with fasting, with weeping, and with mourning." So rend your heart, and not your garments; return to the LORD your God, for He is gracious and merciful, slow to anger, and of great kindness; and He relents from doing harm.

Joel 2:12, 13

Brokenness sounds as foreign to our culture as Chinese Mandarin would be to a cocker spaniel. In our day and age, Donald Trump puts his index finger in the "locked and loaded position" and triumphantly says, "You're fired," an entire government is exploding with debts and deficits of formerly unheard of amounts, and some couples perform their wedding nuptials in the nude. While our culture has a hard time understanding brokenness, to God it is the prerequisite to blessing.

Brokenness is a part of the fabric of life that makes even our existence possible. Unless the soil is broken, no seed can be sown nor can a harvest be gleaned. Unless the clouds are broken, no rain will come to water the crop. Unless the grain is broken, the bread cannot be gathered.

I recently learned that doctors are being trained to deliver super-sized babies —infants that are so big their shoulders get stuck during labor. In extreme cases doctors have to break their collarbones to free them and save their lives! In other words, some babies have to come into this world literally "broken." We see this emphasis on brokenness throughout the Bible. Unless the alabaster flask had been broken, no perfume would have been available for the preburial anointing of Jesus (Mark 14:3, 8). Unless Jacob had been broken in history's greatest wrestling match, he would have never known the power and favor of God (Genesis 32:24–32). God still desires sacrifices from His people on a daily basis. As David said, "The sacrifices of God are a broken spirit, a broken and a contrite heart—these, O God, You will not despise" (Psalm 51:17).

  Dear God, please show me the way to brokenness. Remind me daily that brokenness is the path to true prosperity, wisdom, success, and blessing. Break me and mold me into all that You want me to be. May my brokenness bring blessing to others in every way You choose. Even now accept my brokenness over all my faults, flaws, and failures, and may my contrite spirit be a foundation You can use to bring me to greater heights for Your great glory. Amen.

DR. JAMES MERRITT, DULUTH, GA

WEEK 32—DAY 2

Repentance and Renewal Are Necessary for God's Blessing

*Let the priests, who minister to the LORD, weep between the porch and the altar; let them say,
"Spare Your people, O LORD, and do not give Your heritage to reproach, that the nations should
rule over them. Why should they say among the peoples, 'Where is their God?'" . . . The LORD
will answer and say to His people, "Behold, I will send you grain and new wine and oil,
and you will be satisfied by them; I will no longer make you a reproach among the nations."*

Joel 2:17, 19

There is little difference between most people who go to church and most people who don't. Why is that the case? I believe the answer can be given in one word—*repentance*.

Repentance has become the missing note in the music of most preaching. Yet Jesus said, "Unless you repent you will all likewise perish" (Luke 13:3). That statement means that the death of Jesus, the blood of Jesus, and the Cross of Jesus are absolutely worthless to you if you do not repent.

Repentance is more than regret. Repentance is more than remorse. Repentance is not the shoplifter who wrote an anonymous letter to a department store saying, "Dear Sir, I have just become a Christian and I can't sleep at night because I feel guilty. So here's one hundred dollars that I owe you." He signed only his first name and wrote at the bottom of the letter, "PS If I still can't sleep, I'll send you the rest."

Repentance is literally a complete about-face. We turn away from self and sin, and totally surrender to the Savior. Have you truly repented?

   Father, my sin calls for nothing less than my complete and total repentance. I repent of sin and selfishness. Reveal to me even the secret sin in my life, and lead me to repentance so that I may in all my ways please You today. May others see in me the fruits of repentance, for I know that repentance is Your pathway to peace, in my relationship with You and in my relationships with others. So, Lord, I repent from all known and unknown sin today. In the mighty name of Jesus, Amen.

DR. JAMES MERRITT, DULUTH, GA

WEEK 32—DAY 3

How God Uses Adversity

As he journeyed he came near Damascus, and suddenly a light shone around him from heaven.
Then he fell to the ground, and heard a voice saying to him, "Saul, Saul, why are you persecuting Me?"
And he said, "Who are You, Lord?" Then the Lord said, "I am Jesus, whom you are persecuting."

Acts 9:3–5

Call it whatever you want—trials, troubles, tribulations. "Adam had 'em" and every human being has faced his or her share ever since. Adversity plays no favorites, exempts no races, skips no gender, passes over no nationality. It can't be avoided or bribed. Troubles come in all shapes, sizes, and colors. There are physical troubles, financial troubles, marital troubles, psychological troubles, and spiritual troubles. Adversity comprises the most difficult and toughest test of faith—when life goes south and things go sour. The question is not, "Will I experience adversity?" Rather, the question is, "How does God use adversity in my life?" There are always at least two things God is doing when the waves of adversity rush over the side of our boat.

First, He is testing our faith. Every trial is a test that is made up of two questions. You need to remember that God is asking you these two questions every time you are T-boned by trouble: 1) Do you trust Me or not? 2) How much? Second, He is toughening our faith. Remember this: God is in the faith-growing business. Faith grows the most in times when it is most difficult to exercise it, because faith is like a muscle. In order to grow, it has to be stressed, stretched, and strengthened. So many times we want to avoid or escape trials when those trials are actually what we need the most.

Real faith says, "When everything comes up snake eyes, when all that could be lost is lost, and everything that could go wrong does go wrong, I will still trust You, love You, worship You, and serve You." No matter what happens, real faith remains steadfast. Through every trial, real faith grows.

> *Lord, I am reminded today that life is a test; each day is full of them. As these tests come, may this be my response: "Lord, I can't handle this situation. I don't understand why it is happening to me. I need wisdom to see this from Your point of view so that my faith will be strong. Use this test to toughen me in areas where I am weak and soften me where I am rough. Take me not where I want to go but where You know I need to go." In Jesus' name, Amen.*

WEEK 32—DAY 4
How Does God Deal with Disobedience?

The word of the LORD came to Jonah the second time, saying, "Arise, go to Nineveh, that great city, and preach to it the message that I tell you." So Jonah arose and went to Nineveh, according to the word of the LORD. Now Nineveh was an exceedingly great city, a three-day journey in extent. And Jonah began to enter the city on the first day's walk. Then he cried out and said, "Yet forty days, and Nineveh shall be overthrown!"

Jonah 3:1–4

There was once a strong-willed four-year-old girl who kept trying to go AWOL on her tricycle. Her mom tired of her disobedience and said, "You can ride your tricycle on the sidewalk in between our driveway and that tree over there. If you go past that, you are going to get a spanking. I've got to go inside, but I'm going to be watching you." The little girl looked at her mom for a moment, got off her tricycle, backed up to her, pointed to her posterior and said, "You might as well spank me now, because I've got places to go."

This story is actually the story of the human race. God sets boundaries, we break them, and then He pulls out the rod. Disobedience always follows the pattern of the prophet Jonah. First, God *demands*. God commanded Jonah to go to Nineveh. Second, we *decide*. Do we say yes or no? These are always the only two answers you can give God. Third, we *disobey*. We say no to God's "Will you?"

How does the God of the universe respond? Always the same: He *disciplines*.

When God demands and you disobey, He doesn't merely ignore or punish you—He's ultimately interested in restoring you. He doesn't just leave you and say, "OK, I'll get someone else." God is going to do whatever He can to turn you around, because God is not interested in turning His back or paying us back. He is interested in bringing us back.

 Dear God, I know that far too many times I have said no to Your "Will you?" Thank You for loving me enough to discipline me when I rebel and refuse. Help me say yes to Your every demand, regardless of how uncomfortable, inconvenient, or costly it may be for me to obey You. Help me remember that the blessing of obedience is always greater than the burden of disobedience. Amen.

DR. JAMES MERRITT, DULUTH, GA

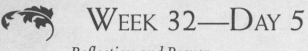

Week 32—Day 5

Reflection and Prayer

What is one sin that you have difficulty letting go of?

_____

_____

_____

_____

_____

_____

_____

_____

Where in your life are you saying no when God is looking for a yes?

_____

_____

_____

_____

_____

_____

_____

_____

WEEK 33—DAY 1

What Does It Mean to Do Spiritual Battle?

I know that in me (that is, in my flesh) nothing good dwells; for to will is present with me, but how to perform what is good I do not find. For the good that I will to do, I do not do; but the evil I will not to do, that I practice. Now if I do what I will not to do, it is no longer I who do it, but sin that dwells in me.

Romans 7:18–20

Are you aware that battles and wars have been taking place every day all over the earth for thousands of years? You may be thinking, *Wow, I'm glad I'm not living in a dangerous war zone.* The truth is, you are; there is a battle being waged every day in your life. It's an unavoidable spiritual battle that affects every area of your life. Tragically, many Christians are totally unaware of the clashing forces within them.

This inner war is a conflict between the flesh and the Spirit. Every believer has two natures. You have an old nature, the Adamic nature you received at birth—it's in your genes. You also have a new nature, the spiritual nature that was given to you when you were born again. These two natures are in constant conflict because they are incompatible and irreconcilable. "For the flesh lusts against the Spirit, and the Spirit against the flesh; and these are contrary to one another, so that you do not do the things that you wish" (Galatians 5:17).

The godly apostle Paul knew about this conflict. Do you? Much of the battle is won just by realizing that the struggle exists. The moment you are born again, sin becomes like an exiled ruler. It is no longer king! However, sin still manages to survive and dwell in our unredeemed flesh. We look forward to the day when we will experience glorification and the absence of sin. In the meantime . . . to your battle stations! God has given us a plan for victory: "walk in the Spirit, and you shall not fulfill the lust of the flesh" (Galatians 5:16).

 Lord Jesus, thank You for being the Captain of our salvation. I ask You this moment to give me a fresh supply of the power of Your Spirit. Please strengthen me in my inner person. In Your strong name I pray. Amen.

JEFF CROOK, FLOWERY BRANCH, GA

WEEK 33—DAY 2

There Is Victory in Jesus

I delight in the law of God according to the inward man. But I see another
law in my members, warring against the law of my mind, and bringing me
into captivity to the law of sin which is in my members. O wretched man that I am!
Who will deliver me from this body of death? I thank God—through Jesus Christ our Lord!

Romans 7:22–25

What do you think about most often? Do you think about all that you are and all that you have in the Lord Jesus Christ? He has saved us. He has healed us. He has filled us. We were dead in sins, but He has made us alive. We were living in darkness, but He has brought us into the light. We were shackled in sin, but He has set us free. Now we can say, "Thank You, Jesus! Lord, You're worthy of all the glory and all the honor and all the praise!"

How often do you think about the Lord? As we move toward Jesus, we move away from our sin. And the closer we get to Jesus, the more we see our wretchedness and our desperate need for Him. Our self-determination and willpower are worthless. Living the Christian life and overcoming sinful desires is not just hard; it's impossible. Impossible for us, that is. We need Jesus. We need His life and power to flow through us. We need an *exchanged* life, trading our limping, sin-crippled life for His limitless power.

The apostle Paul was thinking about this when he wrote, "I have been crucified with Christ; it is no longer I who live, but Christ lives in me; and the life which I now live in the flesh I live by faith in the Son of God, who loved me and gave Himself for me" (Galatians 2:20). Today, think about the Lord and give Him thanks for being the sole provider for your victory in the spiritual battle: "we are more than conquerors through Him who loved us" (Romans 8:37).

 Lord, I want to think about You all day long. I thank You for the victory
I have in and through You. May my heart and mind be saturated with You,
and may I be both grateful for and overwhelmed by the life-giving power
that is found only in You. Amen.

WEEK 33—DAY 3

David: A Case Study in Repentance

David said to Nathan, "I have sinned against the L ORD." And Nathan said to David,
"The L ORD also has put away your sin; you shall not die."

2 Samuel 12:13

It was a miserable year for King David. Many scholars suppose that the time between David's great act of sin and his defining moment of repentance was twelve months. During this time David described his emptiness by saying, "My sin is always before me" (Psalm 51:3). David was reminded every day that joy and peace had vanished from his life. But everything changed when the heartfelt words from today's verse came from David's lips, "I have sinned." As Charles Spurgeon said, "The Lord does not allow His children to sin successfully." Instead, He leads us to repentance. David repented, and God responded with incredible grace and mercy: "The L ORD also has put away your sin; you shall not die."

What is repentance? It means to change one's mind. It is a word that describes not only what we say with our lips but also how we live our lives. Repentance is honest confession. It's not minimizing, rationalizing, or generalizing. It does not place blame; it takes the blame. It's a complete break, putting away the desires and deeds of sin. It's turning around and going in God's direction.

God is serious about repentance. His infinite grace and mercy are exhibited in these words: "You have cast all my sins behind Your back" (Isaiah 38:17). How serious are you about repentance? Repentance is returning to God, and what returns to you in the process of repentance is priceless. Just as David received back his joy and peace, God will restore you when you repent. First John 1:7 says, "If we walk in the light as He is in the light, we have fellowship with one another, and the blood of Jesus Christ His Son cleanses us from all sin." God responds to our repentance. How do you need to respond to today's devotional? Do you need to repent?

 God, thank You for Your everlasting love, infinite grace, and great mercy.
I praise You for the fact that You are faithful and just to forgive me of all my
sin. I praise and glorify You, my Redeemer. Amen.

WEEK 33—DAY 4

Serving God Is a Choice

When Daniel knew that the writing was signed, he went home. And in his upper room,
with his windows open toward Jerusalem, he knelt down on his knees three times
that day, and prayed and gave thanks before his God, as was his custom since early days.
Then these men assembled and found Daniel praying and making supplication before his God.

Daniel 6:10, 11

Every day is filled with choices and decisions. Some are small issues, such as what you will have for breakfast or what clothes you will wear. There is another choice that confronts you daily, and it's no trivial issue. In fact, your decision on this issue will clarify all the other choices you will make. Here's the question: will I or will I not acknowledge God by seeking Him in prayer today?

The Old Testament prophet Daniel is a towering personality in the Bible. He is one of the very few of whom the Bible records no bad report. God so favored Daniel that He entrusted him with visions of the end of time and the return of Jesus Christ. Why Daniel? Because Daniel chose to be a man of prayer. He kept daily appointments with God that resulted in God's divine favor on his life. Daniel's success is really no secret. He left his windows open for us to watch him! The biblical account records Daniel kneeling to talk to God three times a day. You may be thinking, *I am just too busy to do that*. Remember Daniel's vocation? He was a high-ranking official in the Persian Empire. Daniel was extremely busy, yet he chose each day to bow in God's presence.

How deceived we are to view prayer as wasted time. Prayer is actually a time-saver. Think about it: instead of spending time in worry and turmoil, we can run to God in prayer and receive peace. Will you choose this day to come into God's presence? It's always the best choice when we get on our knees and seek God. It's the most significant choice we make all day.

 Lord, what a privilege it is to come into Your presence in prayer through-
out this day. I thank You for hearing my praises and petitions. You are wor-
thy of all my praises, and You are able in all my petitions. I bless Your strong
name! Amen.

We've talked this week about being engaged in spiritual battle. List some ways that you can prepare for battle with sin and commit to follow your battle plan (Ephesians 6:10, 11).

_____

_____

_____

_____

_____

_____

_____

_____

David fell, but he repented and got back on track. When we fall, what must we do to get back into the race set before each of us (Hebrews 12:1, 2)?

_____

_____

_____

_____

_____

_____

_____

_____

WEEK 34—DAY 1

How to Pray with Authority

We do not have a High Priest who cannot sympathize with our weaknesses, but was in all points tempted as we are, yet without sin. Let us therefore come boldly to the throne of grace, that we may obtain mercy and find grace to help in time of need.

Hebrews 4:15, 16

The author of Hebrews reveals to us the high privilege and great power of prayer. Immediately preceding these verses, we learn of our responsibility and accountability before a holy God: "There is no creature hidden from His sight, but all things are naked and open to the eyes of Him to whom we must give account" (v. 13). One day we will all give an account before God. Commenting on this passage, Martin Luther said, "After terrifying us, the apostle now comforts us." That comfort comes from hearing that through Jesus Christ, we have been given what the military calls "permission to speak freely." We are welcomed into the presence of God through our High Priest who can sympathize and identify with us.

In the days of the tabernacle and temple, the Jews had a high priest. This priest was appointed by God to act on behalf of the people in their relationship with God. One day each year, he was required to make sacrifices for his own sins and the sins of the people. Jesus Christ is our Mediator who alone possesses the proper credentials to be both the perfect sacrificial offering for sin and the Great High Priest interceding on our behalf. His death satisfied the just demands of a holy God and paid the price for our sins. Now we have been granted access into God's presence through Christ's atoning work!

You've heard of the Great Commission given to the followers of Christ in Matthew 28:19, 20. We can think of these verses from Hebrews as "The Great Permission." We are permitted and welcomed to come into the presence of God through the sacrifice of Jesus Christ upon the Cross. Now we "obtain mercy and find grace to help in time of need." Remember, our Great Intercessor lives—we have no excuse for lifeless prayers!

Gracious Father, thank You for Christ's death on the Cross and His continual intercession on my behalf. Thank You that the atoning sacrifice for sin has been received and accepted, and that now I can "come boldly to the throne of grace." Thank You that Jesus is both the perfect sacrifice for sin as well as the Great High Priest who can identify with my weaknesses. I rest on His atoning work and rejoice in His intercession. In His great and glorious name, Amen.

Week 34—Day 2

What Is the Purpose of Confession in Prayer?

I acknowledged my sin to You, and my iniquity I have not hidden. I said,
"I will confess my transgressions to the LORD," and You forgave the iniquity
of my sin. For this cause everyone who is godly shall pray to You.

Psalm 32:5, 6

The earliest African converts to Christianity were earnest and regular in their private devotions. Each one reportedly had separate spots in the thicket where he poured out his heart to God. The several paths to these places of prayer became distinctly marked; when anyone began to decline in devotions, it was soon apparent to others. They would then kindly remind him, saying, "Brother, the grass grows on your path yonder." Have you forgotten the great privilege of prayer and confession? Are you allowing your pathway to prayer to be covered up by the cares of this world?

The verses prior to today's passage describe how David's unconfessed sin weighed heavily on his heart and mind, and crowded out his relationship with God. David used three words to describe his disobedience to God: *sin*, *iniquity*, and *transgression*. David confessed it all, holding nothing back. Literally, *confession* means saying the same thing that God says about sin. It is agreeing with God about your condition—not excusing it or minimizing it. Confession cleans the slate for God to begin to speak to you and work in your life as He desires. It removes the barriers of communication created by sin and disobedience.

As a father of small children, I'm amused when one of them comes to me and asks me to guess what's behind their back. I almost always know what's behind their back because I saw them put it there. But, just for fun, I play the guessing game. Why do we as adults play games with God in confession? What are you hiding from God? Whatever it is, He already knows about it—He can see behind your back. Follow David's example and break down any walls unconfessed sin has built between you and God. Like the early African believers, walk that path once again to your place of prayer in the thicket. Offer God an open, humble, repentant heart in prayer.

 Dear Lord, thank You for the privilege of confession. I I agree with You about my sin; I turn from it and trust You to guide my life each day. Remove the barriers of communication created by my sin and enable me to follow Your will. In the matchless name of Jesus, Amen.

DR. JIM PERDUE, MILLINGTON, TN

Week 34—Day 3

When We Pray About Everything, God Answers

Be anxious for nothing, but in everything by prayer and supplication, with thanksgiving,
let your requests be made known to God; and the peace of God, which surpasses
all understanding, will guard your hearts and minds through Christ Jesus.

Philippians 4:6, 7

What do you do when you worry? Do you lose sleep? Is your mind dominated by anxious thoughts? Do you think of the worst possible scenarios that might occur? Does your stress level go through the roof? The Bible tells us that we should "be anxious for nothing." It seems that it's easier to worry about our circumstances than to trust God with them.

The Bible assures Christians that when we pray, God hears us (1 John 5:15). The difficult situations you encounter and problems you face do not come as a surprise to Him. So when troubles come your way, instead of wasting your time in worry, invest some time in prayer. Worry is a nasty weed that is killed only through prayer. Prayer eliminates worry. Remember, if you are God's child, you're in good hands. Prayer reminds you that no matter what you face, God can handle it. An old Jamaican proverb does a good job of summarizing the biblical view of worry and prayer. It simply states, "If you're going to pray, don't worry; if you're going to worry, don't pray."

Worry begins to dominate our lives when we take our eyes off God and focus on our circumstances. In contrast, when we pray, we take our eyes off our circumstances and focus on God. The promise found in today's passage is comforting: "The peace of God . . . will guard your hearts and minds through Christ Jesus." God's answer is always peace when we trust Him. The next time you start to feel anxious, turn to God in prayer and experience His peace filling your heart, leaving no room for worry.

Dear Lord I pray that when problems come my way, my natural inclination will be to trust You instead of worrying. I am blessed to know that every time I pray Your answer is peace. I know there's nothing that will come my way that You cannot handle. Teach me to trust You, believe You, and depend on You in prayer. Amen.

WEEK 34—DAY 4

God Always Has a Plan

The children of Israel shall abide many days without king or prince, without sacrifice or sacred pillar, without ephod or teraphim. Afterward the children of Israel shall return and seek the LORD their God and David their king. They shall fear the LORD and His goodness in the latter days.

Hosea 3:4, 5

This section of Scripture provides us with an intimate glimpse into the faith and life of Hosea. God had chosen this godly man to become a living example of His grace by commanding him to take a wife given to harlotry, much like Israel was given to spiritual harlotry. Unlike Israel, Hosea was committed to God's will, regardless of how much it would cost or how much it would hurt. In this particular text, God offers the example of Hosea's longsuffering and loving grace toward his adulterous wife, Gomer, as a picture of His plan to redeem His people out of their bondage to sin.

Like Hosea, we must be committed to God's will regardless of how it might make us feel. Prayer, in its most basic form, is an expression of either our dependence on God or our independence from God. In prayer, we either demonstrate that we trust God's will for our lives and desire to follow His plan, or that we trust our own will for our lives and are merely seeking God's stamp of approval on our plans.

Christ's prayer in the Garden of Gethsemane provides a helpful model for surrendering our will to God's. He was committed, above all things, to fulfill the will of God regardless of the great cost that would be required. Luke 22:42 records this prayer: "Father, if it is Your will, take this cup away from Me; nevertheless not My will, but Yours, be done." There are two ways to pray—"Lord, my will be done" or "Lord, Thy will be done." We either trust in our own abilities, knowledge, and intellect, or we trust the One who is perfectly wise and all-powerful, knowing that He always has a plan for us that is far better than anything we could imagine.

Faithful God, thank You that Your plans are perfect and they never fail. Teach me to desire Your will instead of depending on my wisdom. I pray that I will follow Your plan for my life regardless of the cost or consequences. Help me know that no matter what I face, I can have confidence that You are always working behind the scenes to bring good to my life and glory to Your name. Amen.

DR. JIM PERDUE, MILLINGTON, TN

WEEK 34—DAY 5

Reflection and Prayer

Have you allowed worry to crowd out your faith in God? What practical steps can you take right now to fight worry with effective and fervent prayer?

_____
_____
_____
_____
_____
_____
_____
_____

How can you adjust your prayer life to focus less on a "my will" kind of praying and more on a "Thy will" kind of praying?

_____
_____
_____
_____
_____
_____
_____
_____

WEEK 35—DAY 1
The Destiny of Satan

The devil, who deceived them, was cast into the lake of fire and brimstone where the beast and the false prophet are. And they will be tormented day and night forever and ever.

Revelation 20:10

Like a deer hunter hiding in the woods, Satan has his crosshairs on us. His objective is to keep us from the only way to God—the truth of Jesus Christ. Satan's favorite bait? The deception of religion, humanity's own ways to God.

We were created in God's own image, but, thanks to Adam's original sin, everyone enters this life separated from God. We are born to be wild. God's plan for us is that we be reborn to be blessed. Remember, Satan doesn't have to *get* us; all he has to do is *keep* us from the Way, the Truth, and the Life, Jesus Christ.

Everyone is born sharing Satan's destiny—eternal separation from God. Satan rejected God's Word as the truth, so God, the righteous Judge, sentenced him to the eternal lake of fire, where he and all who reject God's Word will stay forever. I believe that Satan knows he's going down, but he wants to bring as many souls down with him as he can. I think he hopes that when he faces God, God will change His mind when He sees so many who rejected Him. I can imagine Satan saying, "Lord, how can a loving God cast this many into the lake of fire?" And God's reply? "Just like this. Depart from Me. I never knew you!"

Satan chose his destiny, and you are choosing yours. Have you ever chosen, by faith, to receive God's Son as your only way to God—the only way out of Satan's family? Flee Satan's deception, doom, and destiny. Believe in Jesus Christ, and encourage others to do the same.

 Father God, I come to You confessing my sins. Thank You that You loved me enough to forgive all my sin—past, present, and future. Help me show my love for You by learning and living by Your Word. Help me daily learn Your Word of truth so I will not be deceived by Satan's attractive, addictive lies. I pray in Christ's name. Amen.

BOBBY JOINER, LEESBURG, GA

WEEK 35—DAY 2

Does God Allow Adversity?

Joseph's master took him and put him into the prison, a place where the king's prisoners were confined. And he was there in the prison.

Genesis 39:20

According to Scripture, our real enemies are divided into three categories: the world (its temporary pleasures and treasures), the flesh (our sinful nature acquired at birth), and the devil (the temporary god of this world). Satan tries to deceive us into blaming God or others for most of our problems. He also knows how to control and use the world to tantalize our flesh and our five senses. He tempts us to treat symptoms rather than the root cause of our real problem—sin.

From Genesis through Revelation, God's Word teaches us that God often uses adversity to turn us to Himself and prompt us to confess our sin and receive by faith an eternal relationship with Him through Jesus Christ. Unlike all other religions, only Christianity offers its followers an irrevocable, eternal relationship with God. When we sin, we can't lose our relationship with our Father. We do, however, lose fellowship with Him as a result of sin. Often our Father uses adversity to convict us to repent or discipline us for our sin. We must rely on the truth of 1 John 1:9, which says, "If we confess our sins, He is faithful and just to forgive us our sins and to cleanse us from all unrighteousness." Our Father responds to our confession, immediately restoring us to fellowship with both Him and all other believers. Only then can we correctly employ God's Word and Spirit to enjoy victory in adversity.

Other adversity is simply the ripple effect of humanity's sin in the garden. Remember, humans, not God, spawned evil. This is why God chooses not to put an end to evil or adversity yet. God is using all of the world's evil (the good, the bad, and the ugly) to demonstrate His glory and prove to Satan, demons, and "the many" of Matthew 7:13, 14 that God wins in the end! Adversity will occur in every person's life, but only the Christian is divinely equipped to triumph in it.

 Father God, I come to You confessing my sin. Thank You for allowing Your Son to go through all the adversities He did to demonstrate for us how we are to handle our own adversities. Help me remember that Jesus did His best work in the worst adversity any human has ever experienced. Help me always to focus on You and not my adversities, knowing I will receive Your best when it is all over. I pray in Jesus' name. Amen.

How Can I Endure in My Faith?

The Lord your God in your midst, the Mighty One, will save; He will rejoice over you with gladness, He will quiet you with His love, He will rejoice over you with singing.

Zephaniah 3:17

The moment we place our ever-changing, unfinished faith in the finished work of Jesus Christ, God grants us an eternal relationship that we can't lose. We don't have to add to this salvation faith to ensure we will be saved; that's God's job. He saves us. But our weak salvation faith must grow into strong Christian faith in order to receive all the family benefits and blessings of being a much-loved child of God.

About twenty-five years ago, I began going into prisons using R&B music loaded with God's Word to present God's forgiving love and plan to bless all sinners. On one of my visits I met David, a muscular, mean-faced guy who stood about six-foot-plenty. He had no family, and he was a hurt soul. Another prison minister once said, "Hurt people hurt people; loved people love people." David went around hurting others and himself.

I sang and spoke about God's unconditional love for sinners. I explained that it is the object of our faith (Jesus), not our own strength, that saves us. God's Spirit motivated David to approach me afterwards and say, "You mean to tell me that God loves me?" I replied, "David, that's all I came to tell you." Suddenly, tears streamed down his face. He reached through the bars and grabbed my hand, and Jesus. And his smile? Wow!

I always encourage believers to start each day fellowshiping with our Father, and David followed through on that. Over the next months, his weak faith grew strong. Soon, David's mean face became a sweet face, and God used David to draw many hurting souls to Himself.

 Father God, I come to You confessing my sin. Today, and every day You choose to leave me here in the game of life, help me grow my faith in Your Word. I want to practice relying upon what You have already said and done, not what I have to do. All I have to do to be blessed is to learn to rest in Your Word. Help me remember that Your Word is better known as Jesus! I pray in Jesus' name. Amen.

BOBBY JOINER, LEESBURG, GA

Week 35—Day 4
The Results of a Life Wasted

Woe to you who put far off the day of doom, who cause the seat of violence to come near ... They shall now go captive as the first of the captives, and those who recline at banquets shall be removed.

Amos 6:3, 7

Jesus said that few people enter by the narrow gate, which leads to life, while many take the way of the wide gate, which leads to destruction (Matthew 7:13, 14). Christ took the challenge of taking the narrow path. He died painfully so we could live gainfully.

Living with Christ in us is the only way to live a life of purpose. He came to demonstrate love and joy. He said, "I came so your joy may be full" (John 15:11), and taught that this involves seeking first the kingdom of God (Matthew 6:33). This teaching is very similar to God's command to Israel never to put anyone or anything ahead of Him (Exodus 20:3). Colossians 1:18 says that "in all things" Christ is to "have the preeminence"; He is to be first in everything. Even the very first words of Scripture point to God's superiority, and thus, His secret to a blessed life: "In the beginning, God," from which we can understand, "First—God!" Throughout His Word, He continually reminds us of this foundational truth.

Those who spend their time and talents using any other priority system will eventually experience a wasted life. Jesus warned people not to do this when He said, "What will it profit a man if he gains the whole world, and loses his own soul?" (Mark 8:36). So how do we keep from living this wasted life? By reordering our priorities according to God, the Creator of life, as He reveals Himself through His Word.

Remember why God leaves us on earth after He gives us salvation through Christ—for the purpose of conforming us to the image of Christ (Romans 8:29). God designed us to become like those we hang around, and He wants us to hang out, or fellowship, with Him. He blesses those who do. We must discipline ourselves to invest daily time with God. Start by reading the Book of John over and over. Marinate in the Book of Psalms. Wear out 1 John 1:9! Becoming Jesus' devout disciple will result in a blessed, purpose-filled life here on earth, and a rewarded life in heaven forever! After our time on earth, will there be anything more important than God taking us in His arms and saying, "Well done, My child"?

 Father, help me use my time and talents to represent You instead of my own desires, and to live each day with a focus on eternal, not worldly, things. Amen.

WEEK 35—DAY 5

Reflection and Prayer

We learned this week that God allows adversity. Write down the adversity you are facing and ask God to help you understand its purpose in your life. Write out at least one truth from God's Word you want to dwell on as you walk through this adversity with Him.

_____

_____

_____

_____

_____

_____

_____

_____

Are there areas of your life that are being wasted? Write down a few ways you can imagine using your time and talents for God in the coming weeks. Ask God for the wisdom required to live purposefully for Him.

_____

_____

_____

_____

_____

_____

_____

_____

_____

WEEK 36—DAY 1
How Do I Deal with Discouragement?

I know the thoughts that I think toward you, says the LORD,
thoughts of peace and not of evil, to give you a future and a hope.

Jeremiah 29:11

If anyone in the Bible knew about discouragement, it was Jeremiah. His prophecy is filled with tears and sorrow. His companion poem, the Book of Lamentations, is the Wailing Wall of the Bible. For years Jeremiah attempted to call his people and his nation back to God. No one seemed to listen to him, and the situation grew worse and worse. Eventually, Jeremiah witnessed the destruction of Jerusalem. As he saw it burn, he sat down in the ashes and hot tears streamed down his face. He was the picture of discouragement. But in his darkest days, Jeremiah knew that a loving, sovereign God was in charge of his future, and that peace and hope were planned for him.

Every day there are new frustrations, new challenges, new needs, new discouragement, new fears, new worries, new sins. The troubles never cease. There once was a farmer and his wife who were driving home from church, minding their own business, and they hit an elephant! Isn't that the way it is? You're cruising along through life and suddenly you hit an elephant—something unexpected, some problem you've never run into before, something that discourages you.

If you are discouraged today, take heart. Tomorrow morning there may be a new set of problems waiting at your doorstep, but there will also be new hope waiting for you. You may have failed the Lord yesterday, but today is a brand new day, and His mercy is new every morning. You may feel as if you are going through the darkest night of your life, but take heart—the sun is about to rise, and there is new love, new hope, and new provision for you. Go ahead, get your hopes up! Romans 9:33 says, "Whoever believes on Him will not be put to shame."

 Lord, life can be discouraging. Teach me to focus on Your faithfulness, not my frustrations. Grant me the ability to face this day with courage and confidence as I trust in You. Give me an opportunity today to share my hope in You with someone who is discouraged. Amen.

Why Doesn't God Keep Us from Tests and Trials?

The king gave the command, and they brought Daniel and cast him into the den of lions.
But the king spoke, saying to Daniel, "Your God, whom you serve continually, He will deliver you."

Daniel 6:16

When Daniel hit the floor of that lions' den and heard this statement from the king, I wonder what went through his mind. I might have thought, *If God loves me, why didn't He deliver me before I was thrown to the lions?* But Daniel must have understood that sometimes God allows us to go through tests and trials in order to set the stage for a miracle. Sure, God could have delivered Daniel *from* the lions' den, but He chose to deliver him *in* the lions' den. This more powerful, dramatic intervention caused a king and a nation to take notice of God's power and Daniel's faith.

Those words may have a hollow ring if you have just gotten some bad news from the doctor, if you are staring at a bill you can't pay, if you have just argued with a rebellious child, or if you are fighting through another bout of depression. But understand that God often allows us to go through tests and trials in order to perfect our faith. The truth is that God is more concerned about our character development than our contentment.

Sometimes, for reasons related to His sovereign plan, God allows the suffering of His people. But remember the truth of Romans 8:28: "We know that all things work together for good to those who love God, to those who are the called according to His purpose." It doesn't say that all things are good—some things (lions' dens, for instance) are very bad; but it does say that God works all things together for your good and for His glory. He certainly did that with Daniel. Take a cue from Daniel and trust God today, *no matter what.*

 Father, Daniel did not whine, complain, or question You when he was faced with certain death. He did not know Your plan, but He trusted You. I want to be like that, facing every challenge and adversity with unwavering faith. Teach me to trust You like Daniel did. As I do, make my life a witness to Your saving power. I rest in Your love today. Amen.

WEEK 36—DAY 3

Trusting in God Is a Choice

I know that my Redeemer lives, and He shall stand at last on the earth; and after my skin is destroyed, this I know, that in my flesh I shall see God, whom I shall see for myself, and my eyes shall behold, and not another. How my heart yearns within me!

Job 19:25–27

Down through the centuries, God has used the character of Job and the message of the book that bears his name to encourage people who are suffering. Many times people have told me, "Pastor, I never paid much attention to the Book of Job until life had knocked me flat on my back, but now I understand it. God used that book to inspire my faith." Job chose to trust God in the face of overwhelming difficulty.

Scripture reveals that Job was blameless and upright. He feared God and shunned evil. He was right with himself, with others, and with God. Job was a blessed man: he was healthy, wealthy, and godly. But oh, how quickly things can change. By Job chapter 2, Job's life had fallen apart: his family, his possessions, and his health were all gone. He was at the lowest point of his life, and he had no idea why any of it was happening. Job had it all, and then he lost it all—except for a nagging wife who told him to curse God and die! But Job demonstrated extreme faith, trusting God the same when He poured out blessings and when He took away those blessings. To Job, faith meant waiting in confident expectation that God is in control and whatever He does is right.

Having read the end of the Book of Job, we know that God was proving Job's faith, and that He would eventually restore everything . . . but Job didn't know that. He didn't know the happy ending. Job didn't have the Book of Job when he was living through this! But he stood firm and he chose to trust God. You can trust Him, too. You may be stuck between the tragedies and the happy ending—just enduring, waiting on the Lord. But learn from Job today: you can trust God's providence. You can trust God's plan. You can trust God's character.

    Lord, I choose to trust You today. I may not understand everything that is going on in my life, but I understand that You are in control, You are working out Your will for my life, and You love me with an undying love. I thank You that no matter what I go through, I don't go through it alone, because You are with me every step of the way. Be near me today, Lord. I need You. Amen.

How Can I Comfort a Believer Who Has Fallen Spiritually?

Brethren, if a man is overtaken in any trespass, you who are spiritual restore such a one in a spirit of gentleness, considering yourself lest you also be tempted.

Galatians 6:1

Remember the first brothers, Cain and Abel? In his anger, Cain lured his brother out into the fields and killed him in a fit of rage. It was a terrible crime, the first murder. God asked Cain a question to which He already knew the answer: "Where is Abel your brother?" Cain answered with a question of his own: "I do not know. Am I my brother's keeper?" (Genesis 4:8, 9). What he was really saying was, "He's my brother, but he's not my responsibility!"

We may not have committed murder like Cain, but I wonder how many times we sit idly by as people are overtaken by the pull of the world and the deception of the devil, and use the excuse of the world's first murderer: "It's not my responsibility. Am I my brother's keeper?" But the Bible says that you are.

As a Christian, I am called to be my brother's/sister's keeper. We live in a dangerous world. There are all kinds of opportunities for falling into sin. The devil is prowling around like a roaring lion looking to bring us down (1 Peter 5:8). Many Christians have fallen into sin and out of church, and our responsibility is to do something about that. All of us have had times when we needed correction and a stern, loving rebuke from another Christian to get us back on track. It's not an issue of one person being superior to another person; it's an issue of one who is standing on solid ground reaching out a hand to help someone who has stumbled.

It shouldn't be so hard for one Christian to say to another, "Brother/sister, God loves you and I love you, but you're not living right, and I want to help you get back on track." You can do it.

 Father, thank You for not giving up on me. You came seeking me like a shepherd seeks for a lost sheep. I want to be like You in that way, seeking after those who have been overtaken by sin and restoring them in a spirit of gentleness. Bring to my mind someone who has wandered away and needs me to love them back into the fellowship of Your family. Give me grace to have that first conversation and open up a line of communication. Use me as an instrument of restoration. Amen.

DAN SPENCER, THOMASVILLE, GA

WEEK 36—DAY 5

Reflection and Prayer

Make a list of your greatest challenges, problems, or discouragements. Write a prayer expressing your faith in God to see you through all of them.

_____

_____

_____

_____

_____

_____

_____

_____

_____

Do you know anyone who has fallen into sin or wandered away from the fellowship of your church? Write down this person's name and how you will take action to restore him or her to fellowship.

_____

_____

_____

_____

_____

_____

_____

_____

_____

WEEK 37—DAY 1

What Value Could There Possibly Be in Weakness?

He said to me, "My grace is sufficient for you, for My strength is made perfect in weakness." Therefore most gladly I will rather boast in my infirmities, that the power of Christ may rest upon me.

2 Corinthians 12:9

What are your strengths, the things people regularly compliment you on, areas in which you are accomplished or talented? We are affirmed in our successes, not our failures. But personally, I've learned more from my struggles than from the things that come easily to me. My self-confidence is strengthened when I reach a goal, but I learn more and depend on God more when I am seeking wisdom during the struggle toward achievement.

Failure is not an option in life—it's a guarantee. Daily, we could learn dozens or even hundreds of lessons from our errors. The race to perfection leads to a dead end of missed fulfillment. There's never been a trophy big enough to fill the heart of any person. The only real void-filler is a personal relationship with Jesus.

It's not our strengths, smarts, or strategies that can make the life-changing difference. The power of God's orchestrations is what brings real hope in life. We are His vessels. It's ultimately by His grace, which is sufficient. In our admission that we are not the source of strength, we find a greater power in God's might.

Today, yield to the power of God to make a way. Put your hope in God to lead you to a divine appointment. Rejoice in your weakness because you have a refuge in your Lord and Savior. Rest in the blessed assurance that Jesus is your source of strength. When in doubt, ask God for wisdom. When you face fear, call upon the name of the Lord. When you fail, thank Him for grace and then reach for a new lesson, a new opportunity to grow in your love for your Savior.

Dear God, keep me focused on You as the source of strength. May my self-confidence not be the driving force for getting things done. I want to yield to Your will and Your power. My best ideas are just the start. Your strategies are the only way to go and I want to step forward in Your will. When I fail, help me embrace Your grace and remain thankful for Your endless love. You are my strength. Amen.

TIM DETELLIS, ORLANDO, FL

WEEK 37—DAY 2

What's the Fruit of the Spirit?

The fruit of the Spirit is love, joy, peace, longsuffering, kindness, goodness,
faithfulness, gentleness, self-control. Against such there is no law.

Galatians 5:22, 23

When people hear the words "radical" and "Christian" in the same sentence, they often think of the phrase "Jesus freaks"—referring to people so sold out to God that they can think of little else. Nothing, however, could be further from the truth. On the contrary, the word *radical* is derived from the same word as "root," as in "of or going to the root or origin." Therefore, to be a "radical" Christian is to be a "rooted" Christian.

The question that follows this is, "Rooted *in what?*" The answer is found in Galatians 5:22, 23 in what is commonly referred to as the "fruits of the Spirit." These nine "fruits" are the very foundations upon which living a radical Christian life is built.

We are representing love when we love without the expectation of anything in return. We have joy when we are in a right relationship with God. Peace is evident in our life when we have an inner calmness. We are patient when we endure in hope steadfastly. Kindness is our motto when we are doing good for others. Goodness is evident when we are living righteously and walking in the truth. Faithfulness is when we stay true to our word. Gentleness happens when our walk is filled with steps of humility. Self-control is our way of life when we resist our urges and live stronger than our impulses. We are fully alive when we are fruitful.

     Dear God, the evidence of You in my life is seen through my actions. May
I be rooted in You. I hunger to know You more and yield to Your desires. God,
may I lead today with kindness. May joy fill my thoughts. Help me be gentle
and humble. Guard my heart and keep my motives pure. I pray for Your will
to be done. May my life show the fruit of Your presence. Amen.

WEEK 37—DAY 3

Help Me Love the Unlovable

I say to you, love your enemies, bless those who curse you, do good to those who hate you,
and pray for those who spitefully use you and persecute you.

Matthew 5:44

Why on earth would someone not like you? You're a nice person, right? I'm sure you are, most days. The fact is, however, if you try to please everyone, you will fail—it's impossible to have everyone like you. Some people may not like you because they are jealous of you or because they are too proud. What are some reasons you don't like certain people? Maybe they lie, steal, or cheat. Perhaps they don't listen to you or they're rude to you. Receiving constructive support and criticism for the greater good is one thing, but being put down by someone who is hurtful and negative is another.

Jesus has serious things to say about how we ought to respond to people who hurt us: love them, bless them, do good to them, pray for them. But in practice, it's just plain hard to love people who do not like us! The reason for that is pride. We become too proud to love them unconditionally . . . which is likely to be very same reason they don't like us in the first place. Think about it. Do you want your pride to prompt you to perpetuate the cycle of refusing to give love, just because someone didn't love you? Jesus calls us to a different way of living. He leads us on a path of generous, abundant, unconditional, sacrificial, selfless love. He can make our proud hearts humble and fill us with His love so we can choose to bless others, whatever the situation.

What should you do about that "unlovable" person in your life who doesn't like you? Today, make the choice to be likable by having the kind of attitude you like being around. Some people may not like you; that's their choice. You need to love them through prayer, and trust that God has both of you on a path toward maturity and learning to be more likable.

Dear God, my heart can be fragile. In Your Word You say that above all else I should guard my heart (Proverbs 4:23). Protect me from those who want to tear me down and remove Your joy from my life, which is my strength. I need Your love for others inside me because I feel empty when I'm being attacked. Keep me strong and protected in Your arms of love. May my confidence and sense of acceptance come from You. Help me have uncondi-tional love for those who come against me. Amen.

TIM DETELLIS, ORLANDO, FL

WEEK 37—DAY 4

What Are Some Keys to Spiritual Growth?

---

*I beseech you therefore, brethren, by the mercies of God, that you present your bodies
a living sacrifice, holy, acceptable to God, which is your reasonable service. And do
not be conformed to this world, but be transformed by the renewing of your mind,
that you may prove what is that good and acceptable and perfect will of God.*

Romans 12:1, 2

Growing as a believer requires serving others. If you wanted to become a better leader, where could you learn about it? Attending a conference, reading a book, sitting under the teaching of a mentor? Sure, these things are helpful, but you only become a leader by *doing*. The same is true in your spiritual life. You can consume Scripture and listen to instruction, but your faith is put into action through the *doing* of the Word. That's the process of spiritual growth—listen, learn, do.

Here are two very practical ways you can grow spiritually: First, give something away. "God so loved the world that He gave" (John 3:16). We must give to grow spiritually. Why is this a process of spiritual growth? When you give, you must let go and have faith that God will replace what you have set free. Give something that involves a personal sacrifice, and give without an IOU attached. A gift is a gift, with no expectation for anything in return from the recipient.

Second, serve someone in need. The greatest gift you have is your time. Money can be replaced, but your time is a onetime gift that cannot be replenished. When you give of your time, your heart is attached at a deeper level—your actions become personal. If you just give with your money, you are outsourcing the help. When you put your hand to the project, you are directly involved.

Growing spiritually is a lifelong journey. As soon as we think that we have figured it all out, we have failed. May God's will be done in our lives not just daily but moment by moment.

 Dear God, You have made me not by accident but for Your will to be done. I am not a waste of Your time. Therefore, I want to be intentional about living each moment to make a difference. Open my eyes to see and my ears to hear what You are doing, and help me respond to those You place in front of me. My mission field is right where I'm standing. Today, I want to serve others and see You at work through my life. Amen.

WEEK 37—DAY 5

Reflection and Prayer

Do you want to be planted deep in God's Word? In what areas of your life do you need to reestablish a strong foundation for better growth?

_____

_____

_____

_____

_____

_____

_____

_____

_____

_____

List divine appointments that you have encountered this week. Thank God for those and write out a prayer for the individuals brought across your path.

_____

_____

_____

_____

_____

_____

_____

_____

_____

TIM DETELLIS, ORLANDO, FL

WEEK 38—DAY 1

What Is True Religion?

If anyone among you thinks he is religious, and does not bridle his tongue but deceives his own heart, this one's religion is useless. Pure and undefiled religion before God and the Father is this: to visit orphans and widows in their trouble, and to keep oneself unspotted from the world.

James 1:26, 27

You cannot read more than a few pages of the Bible without seeing God's heart for children, for orphans, and for the fatherless. God has defined what is pure or undefiled in His eyes as taking care of those who cannot take care of themselves.

Over and over and over in Scripture, God tells us of His great compassion for orphans, for the fatherless children. Psalm 68:5 says that God is "a father of the fatherless," and Psalm 27:10 says, "When my father and my mother forsake me, then the LORD will take care of me." In John 14:18 Jesus says, "I will not leave you orphans; I will come to you."

There are approximately 143 million orphans in the world today, with over 40 million of them in Africa. Every day 5,670 children become orphans—one every 13 seconds. Although 250,000 children are adopted every year, 14 million age out.

What is your part as a child of God in caring for those who cannot care for themselves? Are you called to foster parent, adopt, make a trip, help another family adopt, or start an orphan or widow care ministry at your church?

 Lord, please speak to my heart. How I long to be a part of what You are doing in the world! Please show me where You are at work and help me join You in it. Please show me what Your role for me in caring for orphans and widows is. Lord, it is my sincere desire to be part of what You call pure and undefiled. Amen.

ALEX HIMAYA, BROKEN ARROW, OK

WEEK 38—DAY 2

Dealing with Jealousy

Delight yourself also in the LORD, and He shall give you the desires of your heart.

Psalm 37:4

Sometimes I think jealousy should be spelled "jailousy" to help people realize that it's torture. What a prison it is to never feel content, satisfied, or fully delighted with your situation. It's sad to see people go there, and even sadder to see them stay. We all know people who are confined by jealousy, and if we are honest, we've made our own visits there from time to time. So what's the problem?

Desire. What we desire is very telling of the condition of our heart. What we long for forms our motives, which fuels our actions. It's easy for our desires to become self-gratifying rather than God-glorifying. How do we change our desires?

Delight. We change desire by changing that in which we find delight. "Delight yourself also in the LORD and He shall give you the desires of your heart." The word *delight* has the prefix *de*, which has several different meanings, including "completely." The word is saying, "Be completely in the light." When we are completely in the light of our Lord, our desires change. Instead of seeking material things, we seek spiritual things. We start desiring real purpose, meaning, wisdom, and truth. The best part is, He promises to give us those desires.

 Lord, thank You for Your patience with me. Help me not to allow jealousy to grow in my heart. May my desires be Your desires. I want to delight in You alone; I do not want to chase after things that don't matter. Help me make the decisions and changes in my life that reflect my belief in You and this promise from Your Word. In Jesus' name, Amen.

ALEX HIMAYA, BROKEN ARROW, OK

WEEK 38—DAY 3

Sharing What God Gives You

Let him labor, working with his hands what is good, that he may have something to
give him who has need. Let no corrupt word proceed out of your mouth,
but what is good for necessary edification, that it may impart grace to the hearers.

Ephesians 4:28, 29

In any sport, it is important to know how to win if you are going to compete in the game. In basketball, if you thought that holding the ball and not losing it was considered success, you would incur all sorts of trouble. You could be called for a five-second penalty, lose possession because of a shot clock, or frustrate your teammates by not passing the ball and making a basket.

I love that we serve a God who doesn't make things too complicated for us. All throughout Scripture, He tells us how to win. He is a God who wants us to be successful, victorious, and full of the abundant life that Jesus promises. In Ephesians 4:24 we are encouraged to put on our "new man." This new self in Christ Jesus is the only way to win, because the old self has completely missed the mark. Hebrews 11:6 says, "Without faith it is impossible to please Him." So how do we please Him? We place our faith and trust in Jesus, who is able to do more in us than we could ever do ourselves.

What does this new self look like? How do we know if we have scored? It is as we steward everything knowing that it all comes from Him. We take care of tangible needs and we use our influence to impart grace. There is nothing more exciting than when someone comes to a faith relationship in Jesus through the stewardship of what we uniquely have to give.

    Father, help me stick to the basics of the faith, knowing that the funda-
mentals are what help us win. I want to put on the new self in Jesus Christ
and never even look back to the old. Father, help me live out today this won-
derful victorious faith walk in Jesus Christ. Give me eyes to see where You
are working, and help me share what You have given me for the purpose of
helping others come to know You. Amen.

WEEK 38—DAY 4
Being Accountable

Each of us shall give account of himself to God. Therefore let us not judge one another anymore, but rather resolve this, not to put a stumbling block or a cause to fall in our brother's way.

Romans 14:12, 13

After my friend had major surgery, he went through physical therapy and conditioning to regain his strength and range of movement. He was fortunate to have a great trainer to work with him, who pushed him to achieve more than he thought possible. But on the very first day of training, he didn't feel that way.

During his initial session, his trainer told him to do pull-ups. My friend said, "You want me to *what*?" He couldn't believe his ears. He said, "You know I had surgery not too long ago, right? They cut right through the muscles in my back! Have you seen my scar? I don't know if I can do this. It's gonna hurt! Seriously, I don't think I have the strength. How about curls instead of pull-ups?" His trainer responded with, "Pull up, and quit your whining." And with that, my friend reached up and gripped the bar, prayed he wouldn't cry in front of his workout partners, closed his eyes, and started his ascent. As his feet came off the ground, the trainer placed his shoulder under the back of my friend's legs, pushing him up to achieve what he thought was impossible. His chin quickly passed over the bar again and again. The pain in his back was overwhelmed by the sense of accomplishment he felt inside. My friend recounts, "The unachievable became reality with the help of a friend; he shared his strength to increase mine."

You are held accountable for the opportunities God provides for you to add your strength to someone else's. What God has given you to share will be enough to help others achieve what they believed was impossible before you put your heart into their life. When you get the opportunity either to lift them up or help them down, consider sharing this message from Isaiah 40:29–31, "He gives power to the weak, and to those who have no might He increases strength. Even the youths shall faint and be weary, and the young men shall utterly fall, but those who wait on the LORD shall renew their strength; they shall mount up with wings like eagles, they shall run and not be weary, they shall walk and not faint."

Lord, I humble myself before You and ask You to use me to serve and help someone else. Give me a spirit of love and concern. Father, I ask You to hold me accountable to what You have called me to be and to do. Use me for Your honor and glory. Amen.

ALEX HIMAYA, BROKEN ARROW, OK

WEEK 38—DAY 5

Reflection and Prayer

Does jealousy have a foothold anywhere in your life? Ask God to help you overcome jealousy that might be keeping you from fully enjoying the blessings He has given you.

_____

_____

_____

_____

_____

_____

_____

What are some ares in your life that require more accountability? Write them down, and ask God to give you the humility and courage to seek an accountability partner.

_____

_____

_____

_____

_____

_____

_____

_____

WEEK 39—DAY 1

Share Your Faith

Go into all the world and preach the gospel to every creature.

Mark 16:15

Jesus holds every believer accountable for fulfilling the command in this verse. *Preach* means "to proclaim or share." Every person who knows Jesus Christ has a moral obligation to share the gospel, which is simply the Good News of salvation in Christ. Who are we to share this Good News with? "Every creature" certainly includes every single living person.

Christ instructs us to carry this out in the context of our daily lives. The Greek word translated as *go* in this verse could be translated, "as you are going." We are a "going" group of people—we live busy lives. Today we will have many things that will demand our attention, and in the midst of that busyness, we can miss our purpose. God gives us the opportunity to meet people in order to share the gospel we know. As you encounter people today, look for divine appointments.

We are commanded by our Lord to share the gospel with every living person. Faithfulness to Him means fulfilling His commandment. God's commission is very simple: as you go through each day, take advantage of opportunities to share the Good News of salvation in Christ with every person you encounter. Some people will be very hardened to the gospel, but there are others who will have a soft heart toward it. Sow seeds, and the Lord will honor you and His Word.

 Lord, make my heart sensitive to the opportunities around me to share the gospel with others. May I not only see the opportunities but also have the courage to seize them. I pray that the demands and distractions of this day will not prevent me from doing that which is most important. May I be faithful to fulfill my responsibility to You. I pray that my eyes would see how precious each and every person I encounter is to You. In Your matchless name, Amen.

CRAIG BOWERS, LOCUST GROVE, GA

Week 39—Day 2

How Does God Define Wealth?

Both riches and honor come from You, and You reign over all. In Your hand is power and might; in Your hand it is to make great and to give strength to all.

1 Chronicles 29:12

David offered a prayer of thanksgiving and blessing for the temple in 1 Chronicles 29:10–19. Today's verse is a key part of David's prayer, in which he acknowledges God as the true source of wealth and honor. Maybe you are asking why you are not "blessed" with great riches from God. Our verse today reminds us that true riches are not found in what we possess, but in who possesses us!

Since riches and honor come from God and you are a child of God, He has given you what is best for you! We humans tend to measure riches by how much we accumulate—if we haven't amassed a great deal of material goods, we think we are not blessed with riches. But we must adopt the biblical measurement of true riches. Knowing the Giver of every good and perfect gift is of far greater value than possessing the gifts that come from Him! David rejoiced, not simply because he could invest in God's work, but because his real joy came from being intimate with the God he served!

There are many things in life you can possess. They may be wonderful things that bring you joy. But you must remember that everything in this life that you possess can be taken from you. There is only one thing that cannot be taken from you—and that is the most valuable thing, the pearl of great price. It is the one thing that should cause you to rejoice more than anything, and that one thing is knowing Jesus Christ intimately, personally, eternally. The richest people in this life are those who have as their Father the Giver of every good and perfect gift.

Lord, may I remember that I am rich because You are my Father and You own everything. Knowing You is the greatest honor and richest blessing I could ever hope for in this life. As people all around me stockpile things that will one day rust and decay, may I seek to share with them the true riches of life—You. Lord, it is such an honor to share You with others. Thank You for giving me that opportunity. You have enriched my life with so many people and things, but the greatest of all these is knowing You. Amen.

WEEK 39—DAY 3

Communicate God's Truth to Others

Go therefore and make disciples of all the nations, baptizing them in the name of the Father and of the Son and of the Holy Spirit, teaching them to observe all things that I have commanded you; and lo, I am with you always, even to the end of the age.

Matthew 28:19, 20

In this concise statement, Jesus gives all of His followers their marching orders: make disciples! As a follower of Jesus, you are a disciple. You have submitted to Him, you have been transformed by Him, and you live by faith in Him. You have something in common with all other believers—Jesus has commissioned you to make others into disciples as well.

How do we go about fulfilling His commission? The first step in becoming a disciple is becoming a Christian. Therefore, the first step in making a disciple is to share the truth about Jesus with others. As you go through your day, you are to seek to share the gospel.

Once someone becomes a Christian, you are to share with them how to identify with Christ publicly through baptism. But we dare not stop there. Jesus instructs us to teach new believers to observe all the things He commanded. You are to teach them verbally and visibly what it means to be a follower of Christ. The best teaching tool you possess is your life; your conduct is to be a demonstration of discipleship.

Jesus promises that He will be with us throughout this process. He will grant us the grace to live for Him and the courage to be His witnesses. Fulfilling the Great Commission is more than just "winning people" to Christ. It is also about helping them develop into fully committed followers of Jesus. What a privilege we have been given in the Great Commission—taking part in the work of our holy God!

Thank You, Lord, for the joy of knowing You. Thank You for beginning a good work in me and for Your commitment to complete it. As I grow, may I seek to be faithful to fulfill Your Great Commission. May my life reflect an intense love for You. Reveal to me the areas of my life that have yet to be surrendered to Your lordship. Use me in the lives of other people. Grant me the courage to be transparent with those I seek to disciple so that they can see that none of us have arrived. In Your name, Amen.

CRAIG BOWERS, LOCUST GROVE, GA

Week 39—Day 4

Focus on the Word of God

Faith comes by hearing, and hearing by the word of God.

Romans 10:17

Faith is without question an essential part of knowing God. The Bible teaches that we are saved by grace through faith. Without faith it is impossible to please God. We read about the giants of faith in Hebrews 11. Since faith is an indispensable, crucial part of knowing God, how do we get it? This passage teaches us that faith comes by hearing the truth of God.

Our verse is an answer to five questions that immediately precede it. Beginning in verse 14, the rapid-fire questions go something like this: 1) How will people call on the Lord if they do not believe in Him? 2) How can they believe in Him when they have not heard about Him? 3) How will they hear about Him unless someone shares the truth about Him? 4) How can someone share unless they are commissioned to go? 5) Who will believe when someone does share? The answer: "Faith comes by hearing, and hearing by the word of God"! The greatest challenge of our day is not to get unbelievers to hear the gospel message, but to get believers to share the gospel message!

Your friends, coworkers, and neighbors will not believe in Jesus unless they know the truth about Jesus. As a believer, you have been commissioned to share the gospel with all people. The final question of the five is this: "Who will believe when someone does share?" We do not know who will believe and we are not responsible for how people will respond. We are responsible to share the truth. Throughout this day, will you seek opportunities to share Jesus with others?

 Lord Jesus, as I go through this day, I want to awaken faith in others. Help me share the truth of the gospel with others. I will leave the results of how people respond in Your hands. Help me remember that I have an instrumental role in bringing others to faith by sharing the truth about You with them. Thank You for giving us Your Word. Grant me a heart full of compassion for those who do not know You. In Your wonderful name, Amen.

WEEK 39—DAY 5
Reflection and Prayer

Based on the truths presented this week, how would you describe your responsibilities before God? What role do you have in the work God is doing in the world?

_____

_____

_____

_____

_____

_____

_____

_____

_____

_____

What can you begin to do today that will move you toward fulfilling these responsibilities?

_____

_____

_____

_____

_____

_____

_____

_____

_____

CRAIG BOWERS, LOCUST GROVE, GA

WEEK 40—DAY 1

How Can I Become a More Faithful Child of God?

He did not waver at the promise of God through unbelief, but was strengthened in faith, giving glory to God, and being fully convinced that what He had promised He was also able to perform.

Romans 4:20, 21

God promised Abraham that he would be the father of a great nation. After that initial promise, many long years passed by. As Abraham approached one hundred years of age and his wife closed in on ninety, they still no children. The prospects of God fulfilling His promise did not look good from a human perspective. Yet Abraham did not waver in his belief that God would show Himself true. In fact, the Scripture says that his faith grew stronger! In the midst of God's delay, Abraham's faith became more durable.

So what will it take for you to be a more faithful child of God? One way is to increase your understanding of the character of God. When others would have groaned and griped, Abraham gave glory to God because he knew the character of God. He was confident that God could do what He promised. To understand the character of God better, one needs to study the attributes of God. An attribute is whatever God has revealed as being true of Himself. God has revealed Himself in creation, in the Bible, and in the Person of Jesus Christ, His Son. Through these revelations one sees that God is eternal, holy, unchanging, righteous, faithful, all-powerful, gracious, just, merciful, loving, and much more. The more correct your concept of God, the more readily you will yield yourself to Him and submit to His authority.

As you review God's revelations, also remember God's faithfulness in the past. God had an impressive track record of faithfulness with Abraham. A quick review of fulfilled promises made it easier for Abraham to trust God in each new situation. As you journey through this day, join the psalmist in saying, "I will remember the works of the LORD" (Psalm 77:11). Take inventory of God's attributes and activities and be strengthened in your faith.

Lord, reveal more of Yourself to me today. Help me better understand who You are and praise You for Your holiness, righteousness, and mercy. Fill me with the knowledge of Your will in all spiritual wisdom and understanding. Give me the strength to serve You with all my heart. Help me not to waver in my trust in You. Allow me to bear fruit in every good work as I increase in my knowledge of You. Thank You for my salvation and for Your continuing faithfulness as a God who keeps His promises. Amen.

WEEK 40—DAY 2

What Should I Do During Times of Adversity?

You will prosper, if you take care to fulfill the statutes and judgments with which the LORD charged Moses concerning Israel. Be strong and of good courage; do not fear nor be dismayed.

1 Chronicles 22:13

David spoke wise words to his son Solomon before Solomon embarked on two assignments that were guaranteed to involve adversity—building the temple and ruling as king. David reminded him to follow the Lord's commands and to be strong and courageous. Moses similarly advised Joshua to "be strong and of good courage" as Joshua was about to walk into a similar challenge rife with adversity—leading the nation of Israel into the Promised Land (Deuteronomy 31:7). Following Moses' death the Lord spoke to Joshua and reiterated the command to "be strong and of good courage," instructing him also to obey His Word and to remember that He would be with him wherever he went (Joshua 1:6–9).

Though you are not leading multitudes into the Promised Land or reigning as a king, you do understand adversity. The same directions given to Solomon and Joshua to prepare them for challenges are applicable to you in whatever difficulty you will face. You are to be strong and courageous and continue moving forward in the midst of your adversity because God is faithful and will be there with you. Your strength and courage are based on His power. You are to live according to the principles of God, relying on His promises and resting in His power.

There are seasons when it is not easy to believe God is faithful. Friends fail you; your health deteriorates; your plans are thwarted; a fellow believer betrays you. In times like these, it is hard to harmonize God's dealings with His vows of love and protection. But always remember His steadfast love and faithfulness. Lamentations 3:24 says, "'The LORD is my portion,' says my soul, 'therefore I hope in Him!'" You need to wait on Him. He will, in His own time, demonstrate that He has neither forsaken nor deceived you. Great is His faithfulness in the midst of adversity!

Lord, I thank You for another day to live for You and serve You. I do not know what difficulties I may encounter this day, but I do know that You have already gone before me. Today I will live by Your principles as stated in Your Word. Help me be strong and courageous today. Remind me constantly of Your steadfast love and enduring faithfulness. May You be glorified in my response to the challenges of this day. Amen.

DR. DANNY WOOD, BIRMINGHAM, AL

Week 40—Day 3

What Role Does Obedience Play in a Mature Christian?

Daniel purposed in his heart that he would not defile himself with the portion of the king's delicacies, nor with the wine which he drank; therefore he requested of the chief of the eunuchs that he might not defile himself. Now God had brought Daniel into the favor and goodwill of the chief of the eunuchs.

Daniel 1:8, 9

In 605 BC King Nebuchadnezzar, the king of Babylon, captured Jerusalem and deported the best young people from Jerusalem to Babylon to train them in the ways of Babylonians. His desire was to change their thinking and their loyalty. He gave them new Babylonian names and placed them on the king's diet. Daniel took one look at the menu and knew right away that these foods violated the dietary laws given by God to Moses. So what was he to do? He was hundreds of miles from home in a new country, in a new job, with a new boss (not to mention a boss with serious anger issues!). Surely he did not want to rock the boat the first week on a new job ... did he?

Actually, a question like this does not revolve around the situation. The question is one of obedience. Period. Will you choose to be obedient to the Word of God, or will you choose to be disobedient? Daniel chose to follow God's Word. He was not belligerent, haughty, or playing the role of a martyr. The passage says God had given Daniel favor and goodwill with those in charge of the training program. Apparently these leaders had already noticed the godly qualities in Daniel and were impressed with his demeanor. With this favor, Daniel was able to suggest a ten-day test of his recommended diet. They agreed, and after ten days he was healthier than those on the king's diet. From that point forward, new menus were printed!

Daniel's step of obedience made a positive impact on the lives of others. His stand for God provided a platform that God would use to do even mightier works in the future. Today, start building a platform for God through your obedience.

 Lord, let me hide Your Word in my heart today that I might not sin against You. Bring to my mind Your commandments and Your teachings. Increase my knowledge of You and Your Word. I desire to be obedient, to walk in a manner worthy of You, and to be fully pleasing to You. Make me aware of stands that I need to make for You. Through my words and actions of obedience, allow me to begin building a platform that You can use to affect the lives of others. Amen.

WEEK 40—DAY 4

What Do You Do When You Are Faced with Trials?

---

*My brethren, count it all joy when you fall into various trials, knowing that
the testing of your faith produces patience. But let patience have its perfect work,
that you may be perfect and complete, lacking nothing.*

James 1:2–4

The issue raised in this verse is not *if* you face trials, but *when* you face trials. James has an interesting way of explaining the timing and types of trials. The word *fall* is the same word used in the parable of the Good Samaritan when Jesus said that the traveler "fell among thieves" (Luke 10:30). The trials that come into your life are unexpected and unwelcomed. These various trials are multifaceted and cover the whole gamut of life, including health issues, family problems, career setbacks, and persecution.

Yet in the midst of these trials you are to "count it all joy." You say, "That is not natural" . . . and you are right. It is supernatural! The godly response is one of joy because of the potential these trials have to produce something good in us. James says these trials can produce patience, an ability to endure. Through these trials God will refine and mature your faith and increase your capacity to bear a great burden, like a soldier carrying a heavy backpack. Effective soldiers must increase their capacity to travel long distances with heavy packs. They must build up their endurance. Likewise, the Christian life is not a short sprint, but a marathon, and God is building your faith capacity for the long run! Remember that God must work in you before He can work through you.

God desires for you to be complete, lacking in nothing, and this will only become a reality when your faith is tested in trials. The resulting endurance produces maturity and wholeness, and provides you with every trait needed for spiritual victory. With the prospect of these kinds of results, it is evident why you are to count it all joy when you face life's trials!

Lord, today, I want You to refine and mature my faith. Teach me patience and endurance as I depend on You. My great desire is to have the faith capacity to complete successfully the long run of this life of discipleship. If You need to use trials to accomplish Your purposes in my life, then I will respond with joy. Father, help me become complete, lacking in nothing. Provide me with what I need for spiritual victory. Make me a channel of Your blessings to others. Amen.

DR. DANNY WOOD, BIRMINGHAM, AL

WEEK 40—DAY 5

Reflection and Prayer

Make an inventory of some of God's fulfilled promises in your life. Be as specific as possible. Take time to thank God for His faithfulness in the past and the assurance of His faithfulness in the future.

_____

_____

_____

_____

_____

_____

_____

_____

Identify trials that you are presently encountering. How is God using them to increase your faith capacity? How can you respond more joyfully?

_____

_____

_____

_____

_____

_____

_____

_____

WEEK 41—DAY 1

Should I Tithe When I Am Struggling Financially?

"Bring all the tithes into the storehouse, that there may be food in My house, and try
Me now in this," says the LORD of hosts, "If I will not open for you the windows of heaven
and pour out for you such blessing that there will not be room enough to receive it . . .
All nations will call you blessed, for you will be a delightful land," says the LORD of hosts.

Malachi 3:10, 12

The thought of bringing God 10 percent of our income is challenging, especially in tough times. When evaluating our resources, we sometimes wonder how we will be able to address life's needs with the entire amount, much less with only 90 percent. If that's where life finds you today, the words of the prophet Malachi could cause you to feel like God is adding an unfair burden to your already almost unbearable load—as if He's levying a tax on being a Christian.

I think it might change our feelings dramatically if we could grasp one very exciting truth: God is not a charity case looking for donors; He's an entrepreneur looking for partners. By inviting us to tithe, He's giving us the opportunity to invest in the life-changing work He's accomplishing through His church, and also to enjoy huge returns. Place these two concepts side-by-side—your tenth and "the windows of heaven"—and you will realize something very important. God's not leading you into a deficit situation.

In the end, tithing is not about money; it's about faith. Scripture proclaims that the earth and everything in it already belongs to God, so it's certain He's not up in heaven sweating how He's going to get His hands on 10 percent of our income. He does, however, crave our trusting, childlike dependence on Him. And He so wants to show us His ability to multiply anything we release from our hands into His.

   Father, thank You for giving me the opportunity to invest in Your work. Help me trust You in this area of finances, especially when times are difficult, so that I don't miss out on the dividends to be gained for eternity. Amen.

MARK HOOVER, WICHITA, KS

Week 41—Day 2
There Is Redemption in Christ

Blessed be the God and Father of our Lord Jesus Christ, who has blessed us with
every spiritual blessing in the heavenly places in Christ, just as He chose us in Him before
the foundation of the world, that we should be holy and without blame before Him in love.

Ephesians 1:3, 4

These awesome words invite us to begin each day with praise and gratitude. Consider how many times some form of the word *bless* is used in verse 3. In the original language, the root of the word for *bless* is the idea of "good." Our Father has given us everything good, so doesn't it make sense that we should continually express good words, thoughts, and actions toward Him?

Verse 4 takes it to an even higher level by identifying two specific good gifts we've received because of Christ. First, we have been invited to experience redemption. We all know what it's like to suffer rejection. At various times we've been pushed away, abandoned, or rejected. God loves you so much that He never wants you to experience these things from Him. Jesus paid the ultimate price so that God could stretch His arms wide open and invite you into His family.

Secondly, God has plans for you. Before He even created the world, He was thinking about you and working out a plan to make you perfect in His sight. Of course, we know what it cost to execute that plan. The perfect Son of God took our sin on Himself so that His spotless record of righteousness could be inserted under our names. It's no wonder we're encouraged to begin each day with feelings of love toward our Father.

Father, there are no words to thank You adequately for the ultimate gift You've given to me in Your Son, Jesus Christ—atonement through His sacrificial death and glorious Resurrection. Thank You for inviting me into Your family and for the specific plans You have for my life, both here on earth and for eternity when I will live with You forever. Amen.

WEEK 41—DAY 3

The Spirit of Truth Is Our Inner Compass

The Spirit of truth, whom the world cannot receive, because it neither sees Him nor knows Him; but you know Him, for He dwells with you and will be in you.

John 14:17

It's been said that the deepest human fear is being left alone. If that's the case, how like our loving Lord to assure us it will never happen to God's children. Jesus spoke this message only hours before His arrest and subsequent crucifixion. He had to know the eleven guys who had accompanied Him for years would be prone to feel abandoned at His departure. These words were meant to assure them they wouldn't be.

Beyond that, Jesus insisted that it would actually be to their advantage for Him to leave them, for then the Holy Spirit would come and never leave. In Jesus, they were blessed to have God *with* them. In the Holy Spirit, they would be doubly blessed to have God forever *in* them. Nearly two thousand years later, the promise still holds true for you and me.

Consider what that means. God's presence inside us today helps us navigate a complicated world. Scripture tells us, "As many as are led by the Spirit of God, these are sons of God" (Romans 8:14). Part of the birthright of a Christian is the leading of the Holy Spirit. Think about it: never alone, and never directionless!

Jesus has one more comforting message in the words, "you know Him." Many mistakenly think of the Holy Spirit as an impersonal force. The Bible, though, frequently identifies Him as a Person, having personal traits. He is a Person you get to know better and better over the years that you spend following and communicating with Him, until finally, He ushers you into the very presence of Jesus.

 Father, it is difficult to understand how Your Holy Spirit actually dwells within me, but I'm so thankful for this truth! Thank You for Your constant presence in my life. May I be aware of Your presence with every thought, word, and action, and may Your Holy Spirit work through me today and every day for Your kingdom. Amen.

MARK HOOVER, WICHITA, KS

Week 41—Day 4

Grieving the Holy Spirit

Do not grieve the Holy Spirit of God, by whom you were sealed for the day of redemption.

Ephesians 4:30

Do you remember the last time you broke someone's heart with your words or actions? Wasn't it an awful feeling? It's especially difficult when you realize you've inflicted emotional suffering on someone you know cares deeply for you. Chances are, any such painful episode left you determined never again to break the heart of that parent, spouse, sibling, or friend. You just couldn't bear it.

Did you know that it's possible for us to hurt God's feelings? Today's scripture reminds us to be careful not to *grieve* the Holy Spirit of God. Notice that we're not cautioned about *angering* God in this passage, but *causing Him sorrow*.

Maybe we should pause to consider what it says about God that He can be grieved. First, it says He's gentle. We don't think of abrasive types being grieved; it's the tender-spirited. Secondly, He loves us. The prerequisite of grief is love. You can be angered by a total stranger, but to be grieved, you must first be invested emotionally. God has placed His heart at risk by loving you and me.

So how do we avoid causing God sorrow? I'm reminded of the early days of my marriage. After discovering quickly I could unintentionally offend my wife by not being in tune with her feelings, I knew I must become a student of them. I had to pay attention to the things that brought her joy and sorrow. I had to learn what mattered to her. Just so, we need to learn what matters to God.

Fortunately for us, the verses on either side of verse 30 tell us what we need to know. God is deeply concerned about the way we treat others. He notices our attitudes, our words, and our actions. They really matter to Him. When they're wrong, He suffers.

 Father, thank You for loving me so much that Your heart is vulnerable toward me. Guide me as I become a student of what matters to You, and change my heart so that my attitudes, words, and actions bring You joy, not sorrow. Amen.

Week 41—Day 5

Reflection and Prayer

Take some time to remember some examples of God's faithfulness to provide for you in the past. In gratitude for His past provision and confidence in the promise of His future blessing, what are some practical ways you can demonstrate your faith in God this week in the area of finances?

_____

_____

_____

_____

_____

_____

_____

_____

Consider your relationship to the Holy Spirit. Is He grieved over your attitudes, words, and actions? If so, remember that God is always ready to forgive and restore that sweet fellowship. Take some time to make things right with Him and enjoy His presence.

_____

_____

_____

_____

_____

_____

_____

_____

MARK HOOVER, WICHITA, KS

WEEK 42—DAY 1

How Does My Conscience Differ from the Guidance of the Holy Spirit?

God has revealed them to us through His Spirit. For the Spirit searches all things, yes, the deep things of God. For what man knows the things of a man except the spirit of the man which is in him? Even so no one knows the things of God except the Spirit of God. Now we have received, not the spirit of the world, but the Spirit who is from God, that we might know the things that have been freely given to us by God.

1 Corinthians 2:10–12

*P*astor, it is like God flipped a light on in my soul. A man who had recently become a Christian said these words, and shared a simple but profound comparison of the conscience and the Holy Spirit. He explained that his choices prior to salvation were based on the knowledge and evaluation of right and wrong, measuring the consequences of his decisions. His actions would be determined by what seemed right and rational to him. Satisfaction and regrets were based on feelings. This man had been acting according to his conscience.

But that viewpoint changed when he became a follower of Jesus and the Holy Spirit came to dwell in him. His decision-making process was completely different. Now when he made right choices, he felt God's pleasure and direction, and a renewed sense of purpose in life. When he chose sin, he felt conviction and uneasiness because he was displeasing God. Personal regrets became sorrow for sin against the holy God (John 16:8). Everyone is born with a conscience. Psalm 139:13 refers to the creation of one's "inward parts." It is the conduit in a person's soul that allows the Holy Spirit to work in the believer's life. While the conscience is aware, the Holy Spirit is alive. Through the Spirit's power, believers are taught (John 14:26), led (Romans 8:14), and strengthened (Romans 8:26; Ephesians 3:16).

As today's passage states, we can know more than surface facts about God. The Holy Spirit creates in us a hunger to know Him personally. He reveals mysteries and purposes. And, although there will always be things about God that are beyond our grasp to understand (Romans 11:33–36), the Spirit generates in us a passion to search for what we can comprehend. May we as believers never trust our conscience but fully depend upon the guidance of the Holy Spirit.

> *You desire for me to know the deep things of You, Lord. Create in me an insatiable desire to know who You are and what You are like. May I rely on the empowerment of the Holy Spirit's light to direct my paths. Thank You for desiring a pure relationship with me. Amen.*

WEEK 42—DAY 2

God Generously Provides to Those Who Give

Give, and it will be given to you: good measure, pressed down, shaken together, and running over will be put into your bosom. For with the same measure that you use, it will be measured back to you.

Luke 6:38

It happens almost every week. Out of nowhere someone in need will approach me. A car has broken down. A job has been lost. A family member is sick. The Holy Spirit will most often prompt me to help. So I will reach into my pocket and give. It is not always convenient. And sometimes I question the motives of those who may ask. But I know it is the Christlike thing to do.

The generosity God desires for us is not always financial. Perhaps a friend in crisis needs your time when your schedule is full. Or you are a vocalist, and plans for a leisurely day are interrupted when you are asked to sing for a funeral. Maybe God has called you to take a mission trip, but going would require giving up vacation time.

Today's passage simply says, "Give." But another principle follows this command. Jesus says blessings "will be measured back to you." Have you ever opened a package of chips, only to find it half empty? You are disappointed because you paid for it expecting a full bag of snacks. But God is generous and He fills our blessings bags to the brim! He rewards in abundance, often more than we could have expected.

God's measure of returned investments can look different than our standard. We tend to focus on material gain, but 2 Corinthians 9:10 speaks of "the fruits of your righteousness." Our heavenly Father may choose to bless our lives in a variety of ways. Salvation of loved ones. Answered prayer. Peace and protection. Extended good health. The list is endless.

Trust God when He says to give generously. He will do above all that we ask or imagine in return.

 Thank You, Father, for providing ways for me to give to those in need. You are our generous God, giving Your all in Jesus Christ. I have everything I need in You. Amen.

DR. TED TRAYLOR, PENSACOLA, FL

WEEK 42—DAY 3

Spiritual Shortsightedness in Giving

Do not overwork to be rich; because of your own understanding, cease! Will you set your eyes on that which is not? For riches certainly make themselves wings; they fly away like an eagle toward heaven.

Proverbs 23:4, 5

Years ago I visited a couple who had been attending our church. They lived in a gated community and their home was filled with fine furniture and collectibles from around the world. On the surface they had everything. But reality was a different picture.

The couple had become Christians during their childhood but had never made a commitment to live as fully devoted followers of Jesus. Their adult years were spent accumulating life's luxuries, but their possessions ended up managing them. A hurricane had destroyed their boat and beach home and it was taking months to make the repairs. Insurance rates had skyrocketed since the storm, causing additional expenses. The couple found themselves working harder just to keep up their lifestyle. There was no joy or peace in their lives. Exhausted and frustrated, they looked for an escape.

No material possession is meant to last forever. As today's passage says, "Riches certainly make themselves wings; they fly away like an eagle toward heaven." Tough economic times reinforce this lesson. Stocks crash, resulting in major financial loss and an uncertain future. Dream jobs can be here one day and gone the next. And what have we worked for?

The Bible does not state that possessions are negative things, but we are encouraged to evaluate our motives and goals in having things. Are they used to further kingdom work? Our investments should be made with eternal purposes in mind. Matthew 6:20 says, "Lay up for yourselves treasures in heaven, where neither moth nor rust destroys and where thieves do not break in and steal." Time and money are valuable kingdom resources, given to us by our Creator to glorify Him. May we always seek His plan for how we spend these resources each day.

 You are the Giver of all good things, Father. Thank You for trusting Your children to be stewards of the blessings You give. Help me know how I should invest in kingdom work in ways that spread the gospel. I praise Your name. Amen.

Does God Consider Loyalty an Important Trait?

*Ruth said: "Entreat me not to leave you, or to turn back from following after you;
for wherever you go, I will go; and wherever you lodge, I will lodge; your people shall
be my people, and your God, my God. Where you die, I will die, and there will I be
buried. The LORD do so to me, and more also, if anything but death parts you and me."*

Ruth 1:16, 17

Naomi's life had drastically changed. Her husband and two sons had died. She was living in Moab, which was a strange culture to her. And she had two daughters-in-law, Orpah and Ruth, who were grieving the loss of their husbands. When Naomi decided to return to Bethlehem, she released these young women to return to their homeland, where they would have a fresh start. Naomi was prepared to go alone.

Orpah chose to go back to Moab, but Ruth decided to remain by Naomi's side. Her choice was not easy. By returning home, Ruth would have a better opportunity to marry again. If she continued with Naomi, there were no guarantees of what her life would look like. But she put her own emotions and desires aside to take care of someone who needed her during difficult times. Ruth chose loyalty over convenience. Verses 16 and 17 convey the level of the commitment Ruth was making. She promised to walk alongside Naomi, to stay with her through death. She promised to live in a foreign land and abandon the god of the Moabites forever by worshiping and serving the one true God.

While loyalty is not specifically mentioned in this passage, the theme is evident. We see its importance to God because it parallels His commitment to His children. He is by our side (Deuteronomy 31:6; Joshua 1:9) and remains with us through challenging times (Isaiah 43:2; Hebrews 13:5).

We live in an age where relationships can dissolve at the first sign of inconvenience or offense. When followers of Christ exemplify loyalty by standing by people through tragedies, illnesses, and personal crises, we reflect His glory and are examples to the world of His faithfulness.

 Great is Your faithfulness, Lord. Teach me to be an example of Your loyalty and devotion by being the friend and family member who is present and available, no matter how tough things may get. You are that to me, and I am grateful. Amen.

WEEK 42—DAY 5

Reflection and Prayer

God's faithfulness and loyalty are mirrored in Ruth's devotion to Naomi. What example of this do you have in your life? Has someone shown exceptional commitment to you during a difficult time? Has God given you an opportunity to minister to a loved one when things got tough? What were the lessons you learned from these experiences?

_____

_____

_____

_____

_____

_____

_____

Read 2 Corinthians 9:6–15. What does God say about generosity? How will a person who gives freely and without conditions be blessed?

_____

_____

_____

_____

_____

_____

_____

WEEK 43—DAY 1

What Does the Bible Say About Leaving It All Behind?

As Jesus passed on from there, He saw a man named Matthew sitting at the tax office.
And He said to him, "Follow Me." So he arose and followed Him.

Matthew 9:9

*F*ollow Me. Only two simple words, and yet it was Jesus' favorite invitation challenge. The words are used more than a dozen times in the four Gospels as either a commandment from Jesus or a description of what it means to be His disciple. "Follow Me." This little command expresses very big expectations. It entails internal trust, because we don't know where He will lead us. It calls us to have a sense of urgency, because He is moving in the here and now, and His command to follow is always in the present tense. It is not a command to be obeyed later; it must be obeyed now. It invites us to a relationship, because as Christians we do not follow a mere ideology or a dusty rulebook. We follow a Person. And that Person claims the right to be our Leader. We are called to be His followers.

It also speaks to our external lifestyle. Giving up. Letting go. Moving on. He commands the lost person to turn from sin and be led home. He invites us to begin the discipleship journey by His side, no matter what the cost. In the scripture above, Matthew understood that following Jesus would cost him his comfortable lifestyle, his profitable job, and his established relationships. Yet he simply "arose and followed Him." What a picture of the breathtaking simplicity of our salvation! But for believers, isn't there a constant temptation? A desire to act as though following Jesus is something that we've already done? Nothing could be further from the truth! Dear friend, you aren't home yet. Your journey is continuing. So your obligation to follow Jesus is also continuing. He is leading you *toward* heaven. Today, what is He leading you *away* from?

Lord Jesus, I do not know all that waits for me along the journey in life. There are going to be bright days, to be sure, but there are also going to be dark days. There will be times when I am tempted to stop along the way because of some distraction or opportunity for disobedience. Some days, I may just be tired of it all. I am thankful that You will gently and constantly lead me on those days, and I am thankful for the home that waits at the end of the journey. I renew my personal commitment simply to follow You— wherever and at whatever cost. Amen.

DR. RICHARD POWELL, FORT MYERS, FL

Week 43—Day 2

What Is a Life That Counts?

There was a man named Zacchaeus who was a chief tax collector, and he was rich. And he sought to see who Jesus was, but could not because of the crowd, for he was of short stature. So he ran ahead and climbed up into a sycamore tree to see Him, for He was going to pass that way. And when Jesus came to the place, He looked up and saw him, and said to him, "Zacchaeus, make haste and come down, for today I must stay at your house." So he made haste and came down, and received Him joyfully.

Luke 19:2–6

Try this simple exercise: can you name both of your parents? Easy! How about all four of your grandparents? All eight of your great-grandparents? Unless your hobby is genealogy, it breaks down pretty quickly, doesn't it? Less than a century ago, your great-grandparents were in the prime of their lives. Don't you imagine that their lives mattered? Of course they did! Yet here we are today, and their names escape us. Time has moved on, and all that they were, all that they believed, and all that they accomplished is rapidly disappearing over the horizon.

And so it will be with you. Your kids know you. So do (or will) your grandchildren. But go just one more generation down your own family tree, and they probably won't even remember your name, let alone your life story.

So how do you intend to have a lasting significance? Look again at the scripture above, and I bet you'll see it. Other than Zacchaeus (and Matthew), how many first-century Jewish tax collectors can you name? Hundreds of them lived and died and completely faded away, but not Zacchaeus! We can see in this passage the very moment when his life started to matter in a way that would long outlive him. It was the moment that he came out of that tree and joyfully received Jesus. What will you do today to have a life that counts?

    Lord, I want today to matter, not just to me, but to You. I know that I cannot earn Your love, but I can bless Your heart. I can be pleasing to You. And I can receive Your love and leadership joyfully. Free me, my Savior, from the desire to "be somebody" for my own sake, and fix in my heart the desire to have a meaningful impact on my world for Your glory. Amen.

WEEK 43—DAY 3

What Was the Purpose of the Tithe of the Levites?

The LORD spoke to Moses, saying, "Speak thus to the Levites, and say to them: 'When you take from the children of Israel the tithes which I have given you from them as your inheritance, then you shall offer up a heave offering of it to the LORD, a tenth of the tithe.'"

Numbers 18:25, 26

It was the role of the Levites to stand before the people, day in and day out, and oversee the tithes and offerings that came into the temple. In many ways, they were the constant receivers of blessings from others, given in the name of the Lord. They lived a life of receiving.

While that was their assignment, don't you imagine that there was a very real risk there? There existed the awful possibility that the Levites would begin to see themselves as strictly those who *receive* blessings, not those who should be a part of *providing* blessings.

God established a safeguard for them in the verses above. Right in the heart of a chapter that describes how the Levites were well taken care of by the giving of others, the Lord reminds the Levites that they themselves must also give.

What about you and me? Are we not also the constant receivers of God's blessings? Surely your life is not without its fair share of struggles, but don't you agree that we have received far more from the Lord, and even from other people, than we have ever deserved? We face the same temptation the Levites must have faced: the temptation to see ourselves as those who get, not those called by God to give. That would have been a mistake for the Levites, and it's a mistake for us. Today, how can you turn God's blessings to you into blessings for others?

 Lord, I do not want this day to pass without stopping to say, "Thank You." You have given me far more than I have ever deserved. And quite often, Lord Jesus, You have done so through the love and generosity of other people. Thank You for those people. Now help me love and be generous to the people I encounter. Help me see that Your blessings given to me must be the basis of Your blessing others through me. Amen.

DR. RICHARD POWELL, FORT MYERS, FL

Week 43—Day 4

Adversity Is a Revealer of Our Strengths and Weaknesses

The Angel of the LORD appeared to him, and said to him, "The LORD is with you,
you mighty man of valor! . . . Go in this might of yours, and you shall
save Israel from the hand of the Midianites. Have I not sent you?"

Judges 6:12, 14

Threshing wheat, separating the good grain from the worthless chaff, was typically done outdoors. However, on the day the Angel of the Lord came to Gideon, Gideon was doing this dusty, nasty task inside the cramped confines of his father's winepress. Why? He was in hiding! He was trying to preserve at least some of his grain from the Midianite invaders. If you and I had evaluated Gideon that day, we might have called him a coward from a family of cowards in a nation of cowards. That's what he looked like . . . from the outside. But God knew better. In fact, Gideon was God's answer to the Midianite problem! God knew that inside Gideon was the potential to be a "mighty man of valor." It was just hidden.

At the risk of being too simplistic, let me ask, how do you get something deep inside to come out? Well, you squeeze! (I bet you've done it with toothpaste today!) How did the timid Gideon of Judges 6 become the brilliant strategist of Judges 7 and the seasoned leader of Judges 8? God squeezed him. Hard. God put him into impossible situations with overwhelming obstacles.

He will do the same thing to you. Remember, we as believers are never the objects of God's condemnation. Christ paid the penalty for our sins on the Cross. However, we will quite often be the objects of God's squeezing. As we endure the difficulties He allows or sends into our lives, we will see ourselves emerge with both our strengths and our weaknesses clearly demonstrated. It's then our responsibility to praise Him for our newly discovered strength and trust Him with our newly discovered weakness. Are you being squeezed today? May you quickly discover what the Lord is forcing out of you!

Lord, I don't have to like it, do I? Being squeezed is not any fun. But I know that You made me, saved me, and keep me for things beyond what I know I can handle. And so I know that You are going to have to show me things about myself that I have never seen. Thank You for loving me enough to want to see me grow. Thank You for caring about me, and seeing greatness even if, today, I have not been all that brave. Thank You for Your squeezing! Amen.

WEEK 43—DAY 5

Reflection and Prayer

The lives of Matthew and Zacchaeus were dramatically transformed when they met Jesus. How has your life been changed since you followed the Savior?

_____

_____

_____

_____

_____

_____

_____

_____

God calls us to see beyond the obvious, whether it's a matter of giving as well as receiving, or realizing that He sends trials in our lives to show us our potential and our weak spots. What has God shown you about yourself lately that was not plain to see?

_____

_____

_____

_____

_____

_____

_____

_____

_____

DR. RICHARD POWELL, FORT MYERS, FL

WEEK 44—DAY 1

The Unity of Our Faith

For the equipping of the saints for the work of ministry, for the edifying of the body of Christ, till we all come to the unity of the faith and of the knowledge of the Son of God, to a perfect man, to the measure of the stature of the fullness of Christ.

Ephesians 4:12, 13

When any group works together for a common goal, there is almost always a spirit of unity. That is true in a family, a business, a country, and it is true at church. Paul reminds us in this passage that the work of the church is done by the saints; every member has a role to play in serving our Lord. Every member has one or more spiritual gifts that can be used to move the church in the direction of God's will. When all of God's people are doing God's will, there is unity.

What is God's will for your life? What are your spiritual gifts? Have you found your place of service in our Lord's kingdom? People who serve God in the area of their giftedness enjoy coming to church and rarely complain. They are fulfilled in their walk with the Lord. The joy of service in the area of your calling will bless not only you but also the church where you worship. You have a unique part to play in God's master plan. Find it. Do it. God will bless you as well as His church.

Thank You, God, for gifting me to serve You. Help me today to recognize my gift and use it for Your glory. Help me bless my family, my friends, and my church as only I can through the presence of Your Holy Spirit in me. Amen.

Week 44—Day 2

The Road to Reconciliation

All things are of God, who has reconciled us to Himself through Jesus Christ, and has given us the ministry of reconciliation, that is, that God was in Christ reconciling the world to Himself, not imputing their trespasses to them, and has committed to us the word of reconciliation.

2 Corinthians 5:18, 19

Have you ever had the feeling that you are living your life in a way that is less than what God had in mind for you? There is a word for that in the Bible: *sin*. We often minimize our sin by thinking, *Everybody does it*, or, *I am as good as he or she is*. But sin is against God and it is no small thing. In fact, the Bible teaches that sin is so bad that the penalty for it can only be removed by blood—and not by just any blood. It has to be holy blood, Christ's blood.

A boy who came into his house wearing muddy shoes one day could not resist jumping on his parents' feather bed. Just as he started to jump, his mother walked in and caught him. She was about to spank him when his big brother came in the room. He had seen the whole thing. He walked over to their mother and said, "Let me take this one for him." Then he bent over the bed and took his little brother's punishment. Christ took our punishment on the Cross. Our sin debt was big, but His sacrifice was bigger still.

 Dear Jesus, I am a sinner. I have broken Your laws over and over again. Please have mercy on me and forgive my sins. I surrender my life to You now and forever. Thank You for loving me. Thank You for dying for me on the Cross. Thank You for hearing my prayer. Amen.

PAUL BROOKS, RAYTOWN, MO

WEEK 44—DAY 3

How Can I Cope with Feelings of Loneliness?

*At my first defense no one stood with me, but all forsook me. May it not be charged against them.
But the Lord stood with me and strengthened me, so that the message might be preached fully
through me, and that all the Gentiles might hear. Also I was delivered out of the mouth of the lion.*

2 Timothy 4:16, 17

Loneliness is a serious problem, and it is as old as creation. After God created the world and said everything was good, He said something very different. "It is not good that man should be alone" (Genesis 2:18). If God said loneliness is not good, it is not good!

Paul certainly felt alone in a Roman prison awaiting execution. But he wrote, "The Lord stood with me." God was his source of strength and comfort in the loneliness of that Roman jail. I remember a woman who lost her husband a few years ago. I saw her afterward and asked how she was handling the loneliness of her empty house. She said, "Oh pastor, I have a new husband!" I said, "You do?" "Yes," she replied, "The Lord is my husband. Haven't you read Isaiah 54?" She was referring to verse 5, which says, "Your Maker is your husband, the LORD of hosts is His name." Intimacy with God can bring us a sense of peace in our moments of loneliness that cannot be matched by anything or anyone else.

When Elijah suffered from loneliness, God did two things. First, He made His presence and power very real to Elijah. Then God told him to go back to work. The second part of overcoming loneliness is to find and do the will of God for your life. Worship the Lord and bless others through your work! Doing so will bless you.

 Oh Father, fill my loneliness with Your presence. Help me turn my focus from my hurt to Your Holy Spirit who lives in me. I know how much You love me; help me receive Your love. Help me discover Your purpose for my life and then fulfill it. Amen.

WEEK 44—DAY 4

The Call to Be Generous

You know the grace of our Lord Jesus Christ, that though He was rich, yet for your sakes He became poor, that you through His poverty might become rich.

2 Corinthians 8:9

Few passages of Scripture better express the heart of the gospel than this one. Christ was rich beyond anything we can imagine. Not only did He own the universe and everything in it—He reigned over heaven, enjoying power and glory and praise as its King. But His love for us caused Him to set aside His vast wealth and power, and to live as we do, so that we might one day become heirs to His kingdom. He gave up heaven so He could give up His life for us. Amazing love!

The apostle Peter wrote, "To this you were called, because Christ also suffered for us, leaving us an example, that you should follow His steps" (1 Peter 2:21). Generosity began with Jesus. Now He expects us to follow in His steps and give. We are not asked literally to suffer on a cross, but we are asked to share what He has given us.

Have you ever noticed that the most famous verse in the Bible talks about giving? "God so loved the world that He gave His only begotten Son, that whoever believes in Him should not perish but have everlasting life" (John 3:16). It is the nature of God to give. It is the nature of Christ-followers to give. Sometimes greed gets the best of us, but when we give, we follow in the steps of our Lord and that always brings out the best in us.

 Thank You, God, for giving Your Son Jesus Christ as a sacrifice for my sins. Help me become a generous person, just as You are. When I am tempted to be greedy, help me remember the unspeakable gift of salvation. I love You and I want to be like You. Amen.

PAUL BROOKS, RAYTOWN, MO

WEEK 44—DAY 5

Reflection and Prayer

We have been reconciled to God through Christ's death on the Cross. If you have confessed your sins to God and surrendered your life to Christ, write out your testimony below and read it to someone this week.

_____

_____

_____

_____

_____

_____

_____

_____

_____

God has said that loneliness is "not good." Write about loneliness you have experienced. List some specific steps you have taken or plan to take to help overcome this loneliness.

_____

_____

_____

_____

_____

_____

_____

_____

_____

WEEK 45—DAY 1
What Does God Expect from Us?

*Someone will say, "You have faith, and I have works." Show me your faith
without your works, and I will show you my faith by my works.*

James 2:18

The Bible tells us that it is impossible to please God without faith (Hebrews 11:6). Faith is the essence of Christianity; we are saved by it. It is a simple yet powerful truth. Some followers dilute the fullness of faith by deemphasizing the necessity of works. But faith includes action; Scripture tells us that faith without works is dead (James 2:26).

John Calvin once wrote, "We are justified by faith alone, but the faith that justifies is never alone." Real faith is always rooted in our obedience to the Lord. The people at the church in Antioch were the first to be called Christians—and they were called this because of the way they lived, as followers of Christ's example. We're called to do the same, to live out our faith for others to see. By so doing, we offer the world a tangible and relatable model of what faith in Christ is all about.

So what does God expect from us? He expects us to have faith, which Hebrews 11:1 describes as "the substance of things hoped for, the evidence of things not seen." We are to believe that God's kingdom is a present reality because Christ's Resurrection made it possible. Our faith is meant to reveal the rule of God's kingdom as He works to reconcile and restore every part of creation according to His plan.

   Father God, thank You for providing the only possible solution to the chaotic effects of sin in our life—Your Son on the Cross. Thank You for releasing us from the power of sin. I now want to use my freedom to live fully for You. May I be able to declare with James that I can show my faith by my works. Amen.

DR. PETER CHIN, SOUTH KOREA

WEEK 45—DAY 2
Hold On to God

Commit your way to the LORD, trust also in Him, and He shall bring it to pass.
He shall bring forth your righteousness as the light, and your justice as the noonday.

Psalm 37:5, 6

It's easy to declare God to be trustworthy and faithful when things are going well. Believing in His goodness during life's darkest circumstances, however, is extremely difficult. This is why the psalmist urged the believer to keep holding on to God. Your dark night will pass and enduring it will produce an even stronger faith, one that will help you through even the most perplexing and gut-wrenching moments of life. In the midst of our darkest despair, our soul can find security in the fact that God is all-knowing, all-powerful, and all-loving. What makes God's nature so incredible is that all of His attributes are made available to us! This is why we can entrust our lives to Him. He knows what we can handle, and His purposes are good.

Children obsessed with candy may at first resent their parents for disposing of all the sweets in the house. After all the temper tantrums and pleading, the child may even feel betrayed. But as the parents lovingly continue to provide a healthy diet, the child will realize that his or her parents are doing what's best. The child becomes healthier because of their actions.

Brothers and sisters, like the child, we are limited in our knowledge, and that prevents us from knowing what is best for us now and for the future. We may want to blame God for seeming so distant from our troubles. But rest assured, He knows what's going on in our lives and has a plan in place. He certainly knows what is best for us and offers all the resources we need to receive His best. If you learn to hold on to God, you will experience His faithfulness in such a way that your trust in Him will be like your trust that the sun will rise every day.

   Father God, in my darkest of moments, help me trust in You. When I feel furthest from You, help me trust You are near. Even when I feel like giving up, never let me go. Help me persevere and endure as You refine my faith. Amen.

Week 45—Day 3

What Role Does Satan Play in Our Adversity?

Be sober, be vigilant; because your adversary the devil walks about like a roaring lion,
seeking whom he may devour. Resist him, steadfast in the faith, knowing
that the same sufferings are experienced by your brotherhood in the world.

1 Peter 5:8, 9

One of the tactics Satan uses to lead people astray is convincing them that he doesn't exist at all. We as believers are perhaps most at risk for spiritual attacks when we neglect to deal with, or even acknowledge, the spiritual forces at work in our life. In moments of adversity, many Christians acknowledge that Satan plays a role, but sometimes we neglect to take it as seriously as we should and fail to work at finding strategic ways to deal with the problem.

Elijah believed that setting up a face-off between God and four hundred fifty priests of Baal would quell the adversity and loneliness he was feeling as God's only prophet. Although God proved Himself to be God through the miraculous fire from heaven that burned the sacrifice, this made things worse for Elijah. Jezebel declared that she would do everything in her power to kill him. As he fled, he felt betrayed by God and just wanted to give up. The weight of Elijah's adversity was wearing him down and not even the experience of running faster than a chariot could help him recover his hope. Satan's strategy was to force Elijah to focus on his circumstances and problems, rather than seeing the spiritual forces at work. To overcome his despair, he needed to spend time with God to become spiritually strengthened (1 Kings 18:16—19:18).

When describing Satan as a "roaring lion," Peter was probably illustrating Satan's fierce desire to tear people away from God. Satan operates in a stealthy and cunning way. When we are suffering, we must remain prayerful and not neglect our time with God. When we are in prayer, we will see that we don't suffer alone. Not only is God with us, but like Elijah, we have fellow brothers and sisters around the world who are standing their ground alongside us.

Father God, even in my most difficult moments, help me remember that
You are always with me and that I'm not fighting alone. Keep me from being
distracted from Your presence by Satan. Help me take my relationship with
You seriously through all adversity. Amen.

DR. PETER CHIN, SOUTH KOREA

Week 45—Day 4
Where Is God When I Am in Pain?

To you it has been granted on behalf of Christ, not only to believe in Him, but also to suffer for His sake.

Philippians 1:29

Simply put, believing involves pain. If that's hard to digest, just think about any other passion you currently pursue in your life. You'll notice that everything worth pursuing involves pain. For example, an athlete desiring to win a gold medal intentionally endures physical and emotional pain and pushes her body to the limit. No successful athlete is surprised or deterred by pain. Neither do they come to training expecting their coach to do all the training in their stead. However, they do expect their coach to know their limits and customize their workouts to help them reach their potential without giving them more than they can bear.

In the same way, we should come to faith expecting pain. Pain is a natural part of our spiritual growth and life in general. We decided to follow Jesus because we believed in His kingdom and everything it represents. The pain we experience in this world indicates that there are broken things that need to be fixed. It's a screaming reminder that something isn't right and demands attention.

Our heavenly Father hears all of our pains—even the silent ones. He is more than just a coach; He is our Creator. He knows every part of us intimately and promises never to leave us alone. He not only fights alongside us but also goes before us, trailblazing the difficult paths we need to traverse. Sometimes our pain gets so loud that it convinces us that God has abandoned us. So we ask, "Where is God when we hurt the most?"

The Cross gives us that answer. Like a lamb before its shearers, Jesus was silent. Jesus was silent because He was dying for our sin on the Cross, taking on our guilty verdict. Sin is what caused every form of pain in the world. He saw our pain, went before us, and brought down the power of sin in our life through His own perfect life, death, and Resurrection.

So where is God when you are in pain? Just look to the Cross and find your answer.

Father God, sometimes it's really hard for me to feel Your presence when I'm in pain. I feel abandoned and alone. Thank You that this is not actually the case. You are always with me and that same power that conquered death lives in me. Help me trust in You more! Amen.

WEEK 45—DAY 5

Reflection and Prayer

Can you describe how your faith is displayed through works so people can see it in your home, workplace, school, or community?

_____

_____

_____

_____

_____

_____

_____

_____

Try to remember a difficult circumstance in your life that challenged your relationship with God. Can you recall how you got through it and what new insight you gained about God through the experience?

_____

_____

_____

_____

_____

_____

_____

_____

DR. PETER CHIN, SOUTH KOREA

WEEK 46—DAY 1

God Uses Adversity

The Lord will not cast off forever. Though He causes grief, yet He will show compassion according to the multitude of His mercies. For He does not afflict willingly, nor grieve the children of men.

Lamentations 3:31–33

The more storms we have weathered, the more careworn we become. In fact, all of us have had storms. Let's call it baggage. For some it's dysfunctional family baggage; for others it's religious baggage. Some of us have deep wounds inflicted upon us by others. Some of us may even have self-inflicted pain. We all carry our pain differently—using our baggage as an excuse for everything that is wrong in our lives, or hiding our baggage in silence and shame. But have you ever thought about how God views our baggage? The good news is that God can use our "storm stories."

In October 1991 a "perfect storm"—so called because it was three storms combining in one location into one storm—created an almost apocalyptic situation in the Atlantic Ocean. Sometimes the storms in our life seem bigger than anything we have ever experienced because they seem to pile up on top of one another. But God never wastes an experience, no matter how horrific. Wondering *how* God can use our storms for His glory is a shared perplexity among all believers. In grappling with the hard questions of life, it is crucial to keep in mind that our human tendency is to see things from the wrong perspective. We cannot comprehend an infinite God with our finite minds. If we attempt to measure God from a human perspective, all our thinking will be out of whack. And we will sin against Him when we think of things that are unbefitting to His glory. We must ask Him to show us His perspective through His Word and by His Spirit, and commit to having faith in His goodness, power, and wisdom, even when we don't understand His ways.

Praise God that He gives His people beauty for ashes, joy for mourning, and praise for heaviness, (Isaiah 61:3). Praise Him that He gives us so much to look forward to, so we can say with Paul, "I consider that the sufferings of this present time are not worthy to be compared with the glory which shall be revealed in us" (Romans 8:18).

 Lord, I realize the risk of greater intimacy with You includes getting more rain on my earthly parade. But I do look forward to seeing how Your greater glory will be shown through my life one day. Amen.

WEEK 46—DAY 2

Is There Strength in Weakness?

Concerning this thing I pleaded with the Lord three times that it might depart from me. And
He said to me, "My grace is sufficient for you, for My strength is made perfect in weakness." Therefore
most gladly I will rather boast in my infirmities, that the power of Christ may rest upon me.

2 Corinthians 12:8, 9

I admire how vulnerable the apostle Paul was with the people he led. Paul saw his power as originating in his weakness, not his own personal strength. His weakness was made strong through Christ's power. Notice the smallest word in the Lord's assurance to Paul—*is*. His sufficiency in the present tense reveals the constant availability of divine grace. The last time I went golfing, I experienced a pretty lucky bounce on one hole, and then the next hole, and, unbelievably, also on the third hole. One of my playing partners commented, "Even God's grace should be running out on you." There is a much deeper lesson here. Paul said that while God would not remove his "thorn" as he had hoped, God would constantly supply him with grace to endure it. God's grace was not going to run out.

Sometimes we think we are stuck with a certain hardship because we just aren't learning the lesson God wants us to learn. But the truth is that when we are totally out of answers, confidence, and strength, we are in the position to be most effective for Him. The hardships of physical suffering, mental anguish, disappointment, and failure can serve as a divine juicer that squeezes out the impurities of our lives. God's power flows most freely through pure channels.

No one in the kingdom of God is too weak to experience God's power, but many are too confident in their own strength. If you want God's power, it can only be obtained on God's terms. In Paul's case, that included his piercing thorn. But he realized that his persecution meant God's presence. The more grief he had, the more grace he received! The more grace he received, the more of God he had!

   Spirit of God, thank You for the grace You carry into my life. I admit I am
not the quickest to recognize Your sovereignty, Father. I do believe that You are
at work in the situations of my life. Instead of pining away for a better tomor-
row, help me, Lord, to rest in Your presence. Rid my soul of its deepest ditches
and highest hurdles that separate me from fully trusting You. I want to stop
trying to find a way out and start trusting Your way. In Jesus' name, Amen.

DR. GLYNN STONE, LONGVIEW, TX

WEEK 46—DAY 3

How Do I Handle a Difficult Trial Not of My Own Doing?

In this you greatly rejoice, though now for a little while, if need be, you have been grieved by
various trials, that the genuineness of your faith, being much more precious than gold that perishes,
though it is tested by fire, may be found to praise, honor, and glory at the revelation of Jesus Christ.

1 Peter 1:6, 7

Recently my four-year-old son asked, "Is it yesterday yet?" Knowing the context, I understood his question. His excitement about things coming up the following day had motivated him to ask if yesterday was in the past yet. An entertaining dialogue ensued, with our seven-year-old son trying to explain time to his younger brother.

It has rightly been observed that "even a broken clock is right twice a day." When we are experiencing hardships that really aren't our fault, what surfaces as most important is the urgency of clearing our own name. But even if your speech is right, your spirit can still be wrong.

Unless we connect time with eternity, we will live as if time is always working against us. But since God created time, it can be your friend. Expectations about the future affect present decisions. If you lose sight of your eternal blessings, all you will see is your present buffetings. Time is either for us or against us.

James states Peter's perspective as a blessing: "Count it all joy when you fall into various trials, knowing that the testing of your faith produces patience. But let patience have its perfect work, that you may be perfect and complete, lacking nothing" (James 1:2–4). Having lived a few years longer than my children, I can appreciate their struggles with time and the blessings of being time-tested.

Father, my recent ambitions have been focused on temporal situations. I
ask for Your forgiveness. I want to live with balance. As You said at creation,
I want to declare at the end of the day that it was good. You know my day;
You even know my minutes. Help me to live the next five minutes for You.
I need You, Father, more than I need "Father Time." Help me, Jesus. Amen.

Week 46—Day 4

Dependence on God Is the Answer to Trouble

I will be glad and rejoice in Your mercy, for You have considered my trouble; You have known my soul in adversities, and have not shut me up into the hand of the enemy; You have set my feet in a wide place.

Psalm 31:7, 8

David is one of the greatest examples of trusting in God's promises. He saw God's control, sensed God's presence, and stood secure knowing God had set his feet on solid ground. It's been said that you can never lose your footing when you are on your knees. Take this moment to position yourself in a posture of submission to our holy God.

God is absolutely resolved to do whatever it takes to make us holy, not least of which includes using difficulties for our good and His glory. Since He knows our natural reaction to difficulty is to question, God gives us over seven thousand promises in the Bible. Every promise from God is like a gift card waiting to be cashed (although, they never run out of equity!). Suffering is a beautiful hermeneutic; it makes the Word of God come to life. When God speaks, it is always purposeful. When God gives you a promise, it is not there for you simply to linger over and cling to; it is there to *respond* to. Promises are meant to lead us to obedience!

When Joseph's brothers asked him to forgive their mistreatment of him, Joseph declared, "You meant evil against me; but God meant it for good, in order to bring it about as it is this day, to save many people" (Genesis 50:20). In describing the promises of empowerment that God gave to Joseph, Charles Spurgeon said, "He was not to use the promise as a couch upon which his indolence might luxuriate, but as a girdle wherewith to gird up his loins for future activity." God's promises are prods, not pillows.

We should never end our time in Scripture or in prayer with a sentiment of emotional cuddliness. God encourages us in order to motivate us, not to make us feel warm and fuzzy. The only way we can be courageous like Joseph or David in handling the storms of life and living victoriously is to trust God at His word by acting on His Word.

Father, Your ways are certainly beyond my limited understanding. I admit that I am tempted to think I can live independently. More than wanting to impress You, I want to need You. As Your Spirit shows Your promises to me, help me use the encouragement to become more effective for Your purposes. Amen.

DR. GLYNN STONE, LONGVIEW, TX

WEEK 46—DAY 5

Reflection and Prayer

As you ponder recent difficulties in your life through the lens of God's grace, take a moment to record past storms and the specific Bible verses that God used to encourage you through those seasons of hardship.

_____

_____

_____

_____

_____

_____

_____

_____

_____

_____

Like King David, can you recognize God's control in a recent tragedy? Can you feel God's power over a present temptation? Can you sense God's grace in the testing of your faith?

_____

_____

_____

_____

_____

_____

_____

_____

_____

_____

WEEK 47—DAY 1

Prayer Is the Pathway to Deliverance

Brethren, pray for us, that the word of the Lord may run swiftly and be glorified, just as it is with you, and that we may be delivered from unreasonable and wicked men; for not all have faith.

2 Thessalonians 3:1, 2

We live in a day when the Bible is doubted and mocked by some, and simply ignored by most. Yet we know the power of Scripture because it has been life for us! How do we ensure that the ministry of the gospel and the Word of God move forward in difficult times? According to the apostle Paul, it is prayer that makes the difference.

Writing to people who had been truly and miraculously transformed by the Word, Paul pleads for them to pray for God's Word to "run swiftly and be glorified" and for Paul and his ministry team to "be delivered" from evil, faithless men. In essence, Paul is telling us how to pray.

We must pray for God's Word to spread, to be cast like seed across the many kinds of soil, to be delivered and preached to a whole generation of people. To pray this way is to pray for the nations to hear, for people to be sent, and for hearts to be prepared. It is putting our entire trust in God to bring change to our world through His powerful Word.

If you study the revivals that have occurred in history, the common denominator to them all is astonishing. It is not preaching or worship that bring revival, although they are present. It is *prayer* that brings revival fires to us. It is *prayer* that Paul appeals to believers to practice.

Are you praying for the Word of God to run swiftly? To be glorified? Are you praying for those who deliver God's Word to you? To others? To the nations? May God send revival, and may it begin with our prayer.

    Lord Jesus, Your Word is amazing and powerful. Thank You for delivering it to us faithfully. I ask You today to make it run swiftly through the nations and be glorified by the messengers. Deliver those who bring the Word, ensuring that they can complete their task. Lord, send revival, and let it begin in me. Amen.

JOHN MEADOR, EULESS, TX

WEEK 47—DAY 2

Is Fasting Good for Us?

I sat down and wept, and mourned for many days; I was fasting and praying before the God of heaven.

Nehemiah 1:4

In a world of fast food, instant gratification, and getting things our way, fasting has not been a topic in great demand. I am rarely asked about this biblical practice. However, Scripture gives us account after account of fasting! Moses, Nehemiah, Isaiah, Jesus, and many others give us vivid pictures of this spiritual discipline.

Nehemiah, understanding the huge task of rebuilding the walls of the Jerusalem and realizing the call of God on his life to lead the rebuilding effort, could do nothing else *but* fast. He first sat down, wept, and mourned, which most likely was his immediate human response to the unthinkable condition of Israel and his personal grief over its destruction. He was personally moved. He also began doing something. He began fasting and praying.

What do you do when you don't know what to do? Consider doing what Nehemiah did. By fasting, Nehemiah ceased focusing on himself and his daily needs, and began seeking God's answer to the tragedy of a fallen Jerusalem. By fasting, he redirected his attention to something that needed his attention. He did not just go on about his day; he stopped, he fasted, and he prayed.

Is fasting good for us? If you ask Nehemiah, you're going to get a positive answer. In fasting and prayer, Nehemiah heard God speak to him about his responsibility, he realized his call, he received a plan, and he was given courage to obey. God did the miraculous—but only after Nehemiah fasted and prayed.

The most surprising part of Nehemiah's story is not the rapid progress or overwhelming victory of this task. It is that no one else had the courage to attempt this for over one hundred years, and then one man fasted and prayed. Many times I've been led to fast and pray, and every single one of those times have been life-changing. Fasting *is* good for us!

Today, Father, in Jesus' name, I ask You to show me the power of prayer and the power of fasting. Help me know that You can and will speak to listening people today, and that You still use people in these times as You used Nehemiah in the past. Whatever I face, You have the answer. Teach me to listen through fasting and prayer. In Your holy name, Amen.

WEEK 47—DAY 3
We Are Called to Encourage One Another

*Let us consider one another in order to stir up love and good works, not forsaking
the assembling of ourselves together, as is the manner of some,
but exhorting one another, and so much the more as you see the Day approaching.*

Hebrews 10:24, 25

Encouragement is one of the most needed ministries today! There are so many things that tear us down, discourage us, and beat us up in life. Encouragement is at times the missing ministry in the church. How many have fallen and not had the courage to get up and run the race of the Christian life with endurance because of a lack of encouragement? How many times have you needed an encouraging word?

Hebrews 10:24, 25 calls every one of us to be an encourager! What does it mean to encourage? The word *exhort* in the verses above has an incredibly clear and simple meaning in the original language. It means "to call out to from alongside." To exhort or encourage someone is to shout to a fellow runner in the race of life, "You can do this, and I'm running with you!"

When do we do this, and how? Today's verses give us all we need to know. First, we need to "consider one another." Look around you, and you'll see fellow travelers who are hurting. Consider what they need. Consider what they are going through.

Second, we are to "stir up love and good works" in their lives. Encouragement is not a ministry that we do from time to time—it is a way of life. It affects how we look at life and who we look at when we run!

Third, we must stay connected with one another, "not forsaking the assembling of ourselves together." The church gathering should be the most encouraging time of our week, where we gather with others who love us, run the race with us, and believe that God has an incredible plan for us all! Who are you encouraging today? Who are you thinking of, and how will you urge them forward?

   Lord, Your Holy Spirit is my constant encouragement. I thank You for never leaving or forsaking me, and I want to be the same kind of encouragement to others. Help me look beyond myself and see others in this race. Help me have Your insight and wisdom as to how to encourage them, and let my words be words of ministry and help. In Jesus' mighty name, Amen.

JOHN MEADOR, EULESS, TX

Week 47—Day 4
The Making of an Encourager

Comfort each other and edify one another, just as you also are doing . . . Warn those who are unruly, comfort the fainthearted, uphold the weak, be patient with all.

1 Thessalonians 5:11, 14

The Bible speaks so much about encouraging others that we should pay special attention to the need that must be present for it. Statistics of those who seem to drop out of the Christian life and no longer gather in churches to worship are alarming. Some statistics tell us that 80 percent of teenagers never engage with the church or practice their faith when they leave the encouragement and accountability of home!

Practicing our faith was never intended to be solely a biological family phenomenon. Our biological family should help us form our faith and urge us to live it out daily, and the church is intended to nurture faith further. The Christian life is ultimately a *faith family phenomenon*. As brothers and sisters, and as spiritual mothers and fathers, we are to encourage those who follow Christ.

Paul uses key words to urge us to do this: *warn, comfort, uphold, be patient.* When we warn the unruly, we truly help them, and we affirm God's moral standards to those who don't want to give in to sin and rebellion. When we take a stand, we encourage righteousness and faithfulness. Comforting the hurting is obviously needed. Upholding and allowing people to lean on us during tough times is a great form of encouragement.

Here are three key questions we must ask to see whether we are serving as good members of the family of faith: Are we looking to help others follow Christ in our daily conversations and in our relationships? Do we get together with others to "get" or to "give"? Are we investing in others so that Christ may be lived out in them? Some of the greatest people I've ever known appeared for only a short time, spoke words of encouragement to me, and then disappeared. And yet, without those words, my life might have been disappointingly different. Thank God for the encourager!

 Heavenly Father, thank You for giving me words of encouragement through loving people. You know just what I need exactly when I need it, and You know just who to send. My prayer today is that I can be an encouragement to others just as others have been to me. In Jesus' name, Amen.

Week 47—Day 5

Reflection and Prayer

If the response to a lost and hurting world depended on my practice of prayer and fasting, how would this world fare? Of course, it doesn't all depend on you, but you've been called to shoulder the burden of prayer and fasting. What do you need to change to be faithful?

_____

_____

_____

_____

_____

_____

_____

_____

_____

After being challenged to be an encourager, are you seeing the needs of others in a more discerning way than you have before? Do you know who it is you are to encourage and what it is you are to say? Write out your plan of action for being an encourager.

_____

_____

_____

_____

_____

_____

_____

_____

_____

WEEK 48—DAY 1
The Need for Christian Friendship

Jonathan said to David, "Go in peace, since we have both sworn in the name of the LORD, saying, 'May the LORD be between you and me, and between your descendants and my descendants, forever.'" So he arose and departed, and Jonathan went into the city.

1 Samuel 20:42

Probably everyone who knows this story has desired to have a friend like David had in Jonathan. It seems in our modern, consumer-oriented, throwaway world, people often just use one another until they are both used up, and then their friendship is easily thrown away. David and Jonathan's friendship, however, was a covenant friendship. A covenant was made with signs, sacrifices, and an oath that sealed a relationship with promises of blessings for obedience and curses for disobedience. The expression of love and friendship between Jonathan and David paints one of the most beautiful portraits of a covenant in Scripture.

In our day of agreements, contracts, and casual acquaintances, we have very little understanding of covenants. Agreements and contracts simply say, "I will until you don't, then I will not." Covenants say, "I will, even when you cannot." A covenant friendship puts the Lord *between you and your friend*. Ecclesiastes 4:12 says, "A threefold cord is not quickly broken." Our friendships would be different if we could always remember that the Lord is between friends.

Earlier in the story, Jonathan had stripped himself of his most prized possessions. He laid aside his robe, his garments, his sword, his bow, and his belt. The sign for the covenant was simply that he "took off the robe that was on him and gave it to David" (1 Samuel 18:4). This is what love always does; it strips itself for the sake of its object.

Our Lord stood up in heaven and stripped Himself. He "made Himself of no reputation [emptied Himself], taking the form of a bondservant" (Philippians 2:7). He walked among us and called us friends, saying, "Greater love has no one than this, than to lay down one's life for his friends" (John 15:13).

 Heavenly Father, help me be more like Your Son and the example of Jonathan, willing to lay down some things in my own life to be a real friend. Help me see my friends through my relationship with You. Amen.

WEEK 48—DAY 2

How to Behave Like a Christian

Let love be without hypocrisy. Abhor what is evil. Cling to what is good. Be kindly affectionate to one another with brotherly love, in honor giving preference to one another; not lagging in diligence, fervent in spirit, serving the Lord.

Romans 12:9–11

It seems that since God made humans in His own image, humans have been "returning the favor" by making God into an image that best represents their own personality. Have you ever noticed that mean people seem to have a mean god, while judgmental people have a judgmental god, and lazy people have a carefree god? There are many of these kinds of people who justify their character and actions by creating God in their image, thereby nullifying the truth of Scripture. Scripture commands us to conform to His image, but we are busy conforming God to our image.

When people meet you today, what kind of god will you represent? Will they see a loving and merciful God, patient and full of grace? Will they see a God who is willing to serve, preferring to serve rather than to be served? Remember, our God washed feet! I don't know of any other gods that would do that. Many times it is our own unyielding personalities that become hindrances for the world to see Jesus—who lives in us! They cannot see Him; they just see a non-conformed personality.

The Bible clearly teaches that we are to be Christlike. The best way to behave like a Christian is to yield ourselves to what Scripture teaches us about Christ. When we become followers of Jesus, and His Spirit takes up residence in us, we have access to His divine nature. Conforming to His image will manifest itself in loving others, abhorring evil, and holding tightly to good things. It will prompt us to extend kindness and experience sweeter friendships as we truly prefer that our friends be blessed more than ourselves. We will find ourselves on a mission, diligent about the Father's business as we serve the Lord every day.

Dear Jesus, help me represent You well to everyone I meet today. May others know that You are real by my actions and attitude. Teach me how to be more like You. Please empower me to love the unlovable, be kind to the unfriendly, and be merciful and gracious to those who may not know You. And above all, help me speak the truth in love. Amen.

ROY MACK, MCDONOUGH, GA

WEEK 48—DAY 3

The Value of Godly Counsel

The LORD sent Nathan to David. And he came to him, and said to him:
"There were two men in one city, one rich and the other poor."

2 Samuel 12:1

Have you ever had a friend who confronted you about a questionable action? If so, thank God for that friend. It has been said that sin causes temporary insanity. Only an insane person would be involved in the actions that David was involved in, and knowing the consequences, continue in them. Arguably, David had broken 90 percent of the Ten Commandments, and his soul was sinking faster than the Titanic. Nathan noticed David's countenance had fallen. During this time in David's life, he was without joy. He lost his desire for worshiping and walking with God. He was a man most miserable, indifferent to the things of God.

David was having sleepless nights. He could see his sin written across the ceiling of his room as he tossed in bed. He could see his sin written across the walls in the palace. He could see it in his supper plate as he lost his appetite. He saw it in the faces of his counselors as they conducted the business of the kingdom. He was living a lie but he couldn't escape the truth.

Nathan told David a parable that mirrored David's life. It disarmed David and allowed him to hear the story of his life with his guard down. David, who was the judge and jury of Israel, heard his own case, found himself guilty, and sentenced himself to death.

Then came the words of Nathan that will stand as long as time. He said to David, "You are the man!" (2 Samuel 12:7). In this instance, the wisdom of Proverbs 27:6 comes to mind: "Faithful are the wounds of a friend." Literally stated, the one who loves you will bruise you, and those lingering wounds will be faithful to heal you. Nathan's words of counsel were tough, but trustworthy; they ended the insanity of David's sin.

 Dear Lord, thank You for the friends who love me enough to wound
me with the truth. Thank You that they are courageous enough to risk our
very friendship to free my soul from the grip of sin. Help me be that kind
of friend, who will speak up when I see my friends snared in Satan's traps.
Help me value authentic friendship for the treasure that it truly is. Amen.

WEEK 48—DAY 4
The Result of Sin

David said to Nathan, "I have sinned against the LORD." And Nathan said to David, "The LORD also has put away your sin; you shall not die. However, because by this deed you have given great occasion to the enemies of the LORD to blaspheme, the child also who is born to you shall surely die."

2 Samuel 12:13, 14

Here David acknowledged his sin; we can also read his confession in Psalm 51. His sin had been forgiven. The result of his sin, however, would be far-reaching. David would experience a horrible wage for his sin, just as Romans 6:23 says, "The wages of sin is death." James reiterates that message in the first chapter of his epistle: "When desire has conceived, it gives birth to sin; and sin, when it is full-grown, brings forth death" (James 1:15). Only God can know when sin and its consequences are finished. David's sin included lust, lies, and adultery; and sin was not finished. David had Uriah murdered, and sin was not finished. The child died, and sin was not finished. Civil war broke out, and sin was not finished. David's enemies blasphemed God, and still sin was not finished.

If David could have seen the result of his sin when he looked upon Bathsheba, he would have fallen on his knees at that very moment. However, David didn't consider the consequences and it took the confrontation of a friend for David to acknowledge his sin.

God "put away" his sin and removed it as far as the East is from the West, but the wage of that sin would have a lifelong impact. Maybe you struggle with the results of sin. God is not punishing you for your sins. God punished Jesus in our place at the Cross; we have been made right with Him. But we still need God's grace and mercy to handle the ongoing results of our sin. After you confess your sins, you can ask Him for His help. He will create in you a clean heart and a steadfast spirit; He will restore to you the joy of your salvation (Psalm 51:10, 12).

Dear Jesus, help me, by Your grace, to deal with the consequences of my past sins and know that I am truly forgiven. Allow me to know the joy of Your salvation with a clean heart. Give me strength to withstand the temptations of Satan and give me Your eyes to see the traps Satan has for me. When I am tempted, help me understand that the wages of sin are always death, and to count the costs. Please help me turn from sin and run to You. Amen.

ROY MACK, MCDONOUGH, GA

WEEK 48—DAY 5

Reflection and Prayer

How would you view difficult relationships differently if Jesus were at the center of them? Would your attitude change? Would you show more mercy and grace because of Jesus?

_____

_____

_____

_____

_____

_____

_____

_____

_____

_____

Do you represent the true character of Christ to the people in your life? Is the fruit of the Spirit evidenced in your actions and words?

_____

_____

_____

_____

_____

_____

_____

_____

_____

_____

Week 49—Day 1

Faith Casts Out Fear

He arose and rebuked the wind, and said to the sea, "Peace, be still!" And the wind ceased and there was a great calm. But He said to them, "Why are you so fearful? How is it that you have no faith?"

Mark 4:39, 40

*D*o not be afraid. It's the most common command in the Bible. Maybe God knew we would need to hear it over and over. "Do not be afraid." Circumstances overwhelm us. The future frightens us. We struggle with the fear of uncertainty, the fear of others, the fear of failure, the fear of death. God knew we would struggle with fear, that it would paralyze us, and so He comes to reassure us. "Trust Me, and you do not need to be afraid."

It seems almost strange that Jesus would ask the disciples, "Why are you so fearful?" After all, they were in the midst of a storm. It was night, the wind was howling, and the waves were crashing over the boat. The prospect of being capsized and swallowed into the raging sea would frighten even the most courageous.

But Jesus connected their fear to the absence of faith. Little faith, big fear; big faith, little fear. It isn't abnormal to have fears. But when our faith grows, our fears diminish. When we put our trust in Christ, why would we need to fear? Fear of the future? He has all things under control. Fear of others? If He accepts us, who can condemn us? Fear of unmet needs? If He will take care of the flowers of the field, He will also take care of us. Fear of death? He has defeated death and given us the promise of eternal life that no one can take away.

Jesus proved He could calm the wind and the sea with just a word. Is anything too hard for Him? No. He can be trusted. When you do put your trust in Him—when you *really* trust Him—fears begin to vanish. If He can bring peace to a raging sea, then He can also bring peace to a troubled heart.

God, remind me that You are in control. Forgive me for failing to trust Your gracious provision. Forgive me for focusing on the wind and the waves around me and forgetting that You control them all. Speak Your truth into my life and bring the peace that only trusting You can bring. I do trust You. Amen.

WILLY RICE, CLEARWATER, FL

Week 49—Day 2

How Can God Allow Suffering in a Believer's Life?

O Lord, to You I cry out; for fire has devoured the open pastures,
and a flame has burned all the trees of the field.

Joel 1:19

Suffering happens. It happens to believers and unbelievers, the faithful and the unfaithful. God never promises to protect us from all suffering. Sometimes the unthinkable happens, our world caves in, and we wonder, "Where is God?" If you've ever asked that question, you're in good company. Plenty of people have asked the same question, "Where is God when I hurt?"

When our world falls apart we want to know, "Why?" The fire devours the fields, the flame burns the trees. We're left staring at scorched earth and asking the hard questions. Sometimes the answers just don't seem to come—at least not the answers we want. But maybe when we cry out to God, we will find the answers we need.

We find that trouble doesn't mean that God has abandoned us. In our suffering, He is closer than ever. After all, He is the God who suffered for us. He knows what it's like to lose a Son . . . ever heard of a God like that? We know that He has a plan bigger than our heartache. We hear His promise to work all things for our good. Our faith grows, not because we have all the answers, but because we learn to trust Him no matter what.

The big question isn't, "Why?" but, "What now?" With or without God, we will experience a share of suffering. With or without God, there will still be questions. But without God, there is no hope and no purpose in our pain. With God, there is hope for a better tomorrow, and a confidence that He is working through our suffering to accomplish His eternal plan. Even when the field is scorched, we can face tomorrow with hope and confidence because tomorrow belongs to Him. We don't have to understand to trust, and trusting Him is the key to moving forward.

 Father, when trouble comes, help me to trust You. Remind me that You have a purpose in all things even when I can't see it. Assure me that no matter what I feel, You have not abandoned me or forgotten me. Just as Your eye is on the sparrow, You are watching me. I am so grateful. I know You are there and I know You will never leave me. Amen.

Week 49—Day 3

How Can I Be Restored?

Before I was afflicted I went astray, but now I keep Your word.
You are good, and do good; teach me Your statutes.

Psalm 119:67, 68

We have all gone astray. The Bible says it and we have all proven it. But God draws His children back home and measures out loving discipline, for He disciplines *those He loves*. Our weary, empty heart draws us back to Him like a thirsty person longs for water. Affliction and difficulty can be the very rod that brings us home; it can be a sign of His love. His conviction can be a reminder that He will never let us go.

When we come home to Him, we come home to His commands. We come home to truth. We realize anew that His Word guides us into green pastures. He is good and, therefore, His Word is good. His Word is given to bring us to that place of blessed obedience where we can enjoy the good things of the Lord.

When we come back to Him, we have a new passion to know and obey His Word. Every spiritual renewal that is genuine and lasting draws us back into His Word. Will you seek His wisdom daily? Will you follow His loving guidance? The faithful follower of Christ will value God's Word, seek His guidance on a daily basis, and know His blessings in the process. Are you committed to learning and following His statutes? Does your daily schedule show that it is a priority?

Make a new commitment to listen to His voice every day. Renew your passion for His truth and His commands. Ask Him to guide your steps today and experience that joy of walking with Him.

 Father, forgive me for the times I have gone astray. I acknowledge my sin, and I want to turn away from it and follow in Your paths. Thank You for never giving up on me. Thank You for the conviction of Your Holy Spirit and for the times You have lovingly disciplined me. Thank You for never letting me go. I am grateful for Your Word; it is powerful and true. With Your help, I want to apply it to my life and walk with You today. Amen.

Week 49—Day 4
Serve God with Abandon Like Titus

To Titus, a true son in our common faith: Grace, mercy, and peace from
God the Father and the Lord Jesus Christ our Savior.

Titus 1:4

Someone told you. Maybe it was a parent, friend, leader, family member or acquaintance. Someone brought the message of grace and truth into your life. The baton of faith landed in your hand and, by His grace, you took it and began the journey of faith. Aren't you grateful for that someone?

Faith is indeed a journey. It is more like a marathon than a sprint. It is a long journey that begins with faith; then as our faith grows, so does our knowledge, love, and obedience. We grow up into fully devoted followers of Christ and in time, we understand God's purpose. He has saved us to carry the message to others. He has saved us to serve His purpose.

Paul carried the message to Titus. Paul taught and trained him, and Titus grew into spiritual maturity. He was a true son in the faith. In time, Titus also accepted his leadership post. He heard his calling to help point others to God. He too would come to serve God by teaching others all the things he had learned. And the journey of faith continues.

Who brought the message to you? Who are you bringing the message to? Who nurtured you and helped you grow in the faith? Who are you helping to grow so that one day they will become leaders and teachers of others? The journey continues. The work goes on. The baton of faith must be handed off to the next generation. For now, it is in our hands. But we must be reminded that He has blessed us in order to be a blessing. He has saved us to serve. He has called us to call others.

 Thank You, God, for those who brought the truth to me. Thank You for the message that was faithfully delivered. I can never repay what has been given to me. Where would I be without Your grace and forgiveness in my life? Help me carry on by growing in You and fulfilling Your purpose for my life. You have work for me to do. There are others You have brought into my path. Help me have a contagious influence and use me to pass the faith along. Amen.

Week 49—Day 5

Reflection and Prayer

What fear is most paralyzing to you right now? In what way would total trust in the Lord diminish your fear? Name your fear. Write it down and tell God why it paralyzes you. Now write out which character trait or promise of God best addresses that fear. Ask God to help you trust Him completely.

_____

_____

_____

_____

_____

_____

_____

_____

Think about those who most influenced you to receive Christ and then grow spiritually. Write their names and consider sending a note or making a call to express your thanks. If they have already gone to be with the Lord, write out what you would say to them if you could.

_____

_____

_____

_____

_____

_____

_____

_____

WILLY RICE, CLEARWATER, FL

WEEK 50—DAY 1

Glory Only in the Lord

You see your calling, brethren, that not many wise according to the flesh, not many mighty, not many noble, are called. But God has chosen the foolish things of the world to put to shame the wise, and God has chosen the weak things of the world to put to shame the things which are mighty; and the base things of the world and the things which are despised God has chosen, and the things which are not, to bring to nothing the things that are, that no flesh should glory in His presence.

1 Corinthians 1:26–29

We tend to deify the honorable people we read about in Scripture. We forget that Paul said he was the chief of sinners, yet God used him to spread His Word to the world. Peter was a rough and tough fisherman who cut off a soldier's ear and denied Christ, but God used him to preach to multitudes. David was not even considered by his own family to be worthy of kingship, but God called him a man after His own heart. Many times we deify others to excuse ourselves from service to the Lord.

God still uses ordinary people to achieve extraordinary things. He has given you a special design with unique gifts and has made you His child! He wants to use you. The question is: will you allow yourself to be used? In our flesh, we always want to come up with excuses for why we cannot serve God. We say we're not smart enough or good enough. But 1 Corinthians 1 should put to rest all of our excuses.

God does not call the mighty, noble, or wise. He wants our lives to show the touch of the King. In other words, He makes the weak mighty; He makes the common noble; He makes the foolish wise. God equips those He calls. He transforms the hearts of ordinary people to impact this lost and dying world.

God loves us and has a purpose for us; we just need to submit to His will and be obedient to His voice. Get busy using the time, talents, and treasures He has given you to make a difference where He has placed you.

 Thank You, Lord Jesus, that I am fearfully and wonderfully made. Thank You for making me unique. Help me identify my gifts and be motivated by Your Holy Spirit to use them for Your kingdom. Help me be sensitive to Your voice and obey You. Amen.

Christians Should Expect and Be Prepared for Suffering

Beloved, do not think it strange concerning the fiery trial which is to try you, as though some strange thing happened to you; but rejoice to the extent that you partake of Christ's sufferings, that when His glory is revealed, you may also be glad with exceeding joy. If you are reproached for the name of Christ, blessed are you, for the Spirit of glory and of God rests upon you. On their part He is blasphemed, but on your part He is glorified.

1 Peter 4:12–14

Every time I return from an overseas mission trip, it seems like my house is bigger, my car runs smoother, and my food tastes better. In other words, I have a deeper appreciation for everything.

I've noticed that one of the biggest differences between the church overseas and the American church is that Americans do not understand true sacrifice. In other countries, believers are regularly martyred for their stance. Most people in America never bother to take a stand for Jesus out of fear of rejection or a lawsuit. In Africa, many walk for miles to worship. They stay as long as they can, lingering long after the service. In America, one of the most dangerous places to be is the back door of a church at noon on Sunday morning because of the stampede to the local restaurant. We've become leisure junkies. We get paid and then run to the steak house and the movie theater, but we're too worn out to come to God's house.

When others mock you for being a strong Christian, it may be because they don't understand the Christian faith, or because you expose their sinful condition. Many people say they don't go to church because they don't want to go to church with hypocrites. I tell them, "You go to the ball field, the bank, and the store with us. You might as well come to church with us." The bottom line is that none of us are living 100 percent of what we know 100 percent of the time, which qualifies us all as hypocrites.

When was the last time you suffered for your faith? When was the last time someone noticed your faith? Is your Bible visible? Do you take a stand for Christ daily? Christians say they are willing to die for Christ, yet so many are not willing to live for Him.

 Dear Lord Jesus, help me pray for my Christian brothers and sisters who are suffering and remember the family members of those martyred for Your name's sake. Lord, help me be bold and courageous, and not waiver in the face of adversity. Amen.

Week 50—Day 3

Work for the Lord Is Not in Vain

*My beloved brethren, be steadfast, immovable, always abounding in the
work of the Lord, knowing that your labor is not in vain in the Lord.*

1 Corinthians 15:58

There is a big difference between doing things out of duty and doing things out of desire or delight. Many times in ministry and Christian service, we do things out of duty only to realize later that we received a bigger blessing than the people to whom we ministered. God never ministers *through* you without ministering *to* you.

It all comes down to His touch and His presence. We stand in great need of a touch from the Holy One. Most of us need an attitude adjustment. We don't have to go to church; we get to go to church. We don't have to give; we get to give. We don't have to serve; we get to serve. We don't have to praise; we get to praise.

I remember when my oldest daughter started playing recreational league sports. My wife kindly reminded me not to embarrass our daughter by losing my composure during the games. I responded, "Honey, I'm a preacher. Don't worry about me." For the first two minutes of her first game, I was good— quiet and poised. Then, all of a sudden, something came over me. It was like I was possessed. I jumped up and started screaming at my daughter to get in the game, grab the ball, and be aggressive. We are passionate about those we love! So we also ought to be passionate about the Lord because we love Him.

Our motivation to labor for Christ should come from a desire to please Him because we love Him. We can never repay Christ for Calvary. If He is our King and Lord, we should cheerfully serve Him in big and small deeds, knowing it is not in vain. What you do makes a difference in the lives of others. Be relentless and immovable in your service to the Lord.

 *Lord, thank You for this life You have given me. Help me approach this
day as a precious gift. Help me remember that what I do matters and that
others are affected by my actions. Help me add something of value to all
of those around me today. Help me be steadfast and immovable. Help me
make a difference for Your name's sake, understanding that abounding in
Your work is never in vain. Amen.*

Week 50—Day 4

Everyone Can Make a Difference

He who has pity on the poor lends to the Lord, and He will pay back what he has given.

Proverbs 19:17

Do you have a generous heart concerning the needy? I remember sitting in a restaurant with a group of men when God spoke to my heart, telling me to witness to a lady and her son in a nearby booth. As I got up to go to her, God clearly told me to give her one hundred dollars also. I'm an evangelist, so witnessing to her was the easy part for me, but giving her that kind of money was a different story. However, I obediently gave her the money. Within weeks, three different people came up to me and gave me one hundred dollars. Now, I'm not suggesting that you should give money away so that God will bless you back, but I am challenging you to listen to God and be obedient.

Many believers say they want to do great things for God, but God looks for those willing to do the little things. We must practice our faith daily, learning and relearning what we thought we already knew. Being a Christian is much more difficult than becoming a Christian. Being a daily disciple of the Lord means submitting over and over to His will, not ours. Sometimes we have to overcome obstacles. Sometimes we need to recognize that we are the obstacle. We need to recommit our lives to Him daily, placing ourselves in His hand to shape, mold, and use us as He sees fit.

One day a man came into my office and said, "You know, I believe the one greatest question the Lord will ask us when we get to heaven is, 'What did you do with this life that I gave to you?'" Each day is a gift. Be grateful, and show your gratitude by using every day for the Lord's service.

 Precious Jesus, thank You for Your love and generosity. Lord, reshape me as You see fit. Help me surrender my will to Yours and keep me from being an obstacle to Your kingdom. Help me trust You as You guide me, and help me be sensitive to Your direction. May I see those around me in need today and meet their needs cheerfully. Thank You for this wonderful day You have given me; help me live it in a way that is pleasing to You. Amen.

WEEK 50—DAY 5

Reflection and Prayer

I've heard it said that a rut is just a grave with the ends knocked out. Are you truly living your life for Jesus, or are you in a religious rut? Are you living or existing? In what areas are you willing to recommit to the Lord?

_____

_____

_____

_____

_____

_____

_____

Has there been a moment when you admitted you were a sinner in need of a savior, and then recognized that Jesus is that Savior? In other words, are you truly saved? Have you reached out and taken the nail-scarred hand of Jesus? How has your life changed since then?

_____

_____

_____

_____

_____

_____

_____

_____

Week 51—Day 1

Get Ready, He Is Coming Again

He said to me, "These words are faithful and true." And the Lord God of the holy prophets sent
His angel to show His servants the things which must shortly take place. "Behold, I am coming
quickly! Blessed is he who keeps the words of the prophecy of this book"... He who testifies
to these things says, "Surely I am coming quickly." Amen. Even so, come, Lord Jesus!

Revelation 22:6, 7, 20

A grandmother was house-sitting and taking care of her grandsons while her daughter and son-in-law were away on an anniversary trip. She made sure the first day was filled with activities for the five- and seven-year-old boys. She took them to the park, played board games and read books with them, and fixed their favorite dessert at dinner. Even so, when bedtime came, she could hear the older boy crying in his bedroom. As she came in to check on him, the boy said, "Grandmommy, I'm home, so how come I'm still homesick?"

His predicament is easy for us to understand. Home is not so much about a place as it is about relationships. When we are with the people we love and need most, we feel at home. That's why followers of Christ should live with a certain homesickness for Jesus. That desire to be home with the Lord moved John to write: "Even so, come, Lord Jesus!" The earliest believers would often end their prayers with that same plea.

Praise the Lord, Jesus is coming!

The Lord speaks of His return in the present tense: "I *am* coming." With each passing day, His return grows nearer and nearer. He also says that His return comes suddenly and unexpectedly: "I am coming *quickly*." It will be too late to get ready for His coming when Jesus comes. Our coming Lord calls us to live with expectancy and preparation each day.

  Dear Lord Jesus, I thank You that You are coming soon. I ask for the fill-
ing of Your Holy Spirit so that I can live a holy and obedient life today. Give
me a hunger and a thirst for You and a deep homesickness for You alone.
Then, by Your mighty power, fill my hunger, quench my thirst, and satisfy
my heart with Your wonderful presence. "Even so, come, Lord Jesus!" Amen.

DR. STEPHEN RUMMAGE, BRANDON, FL

Week 51—Day 2

Total Surrender Is the Beginning

One came and said to Him, "Good Teacher, what good thing shall I do that I may have eternal life?"

Matthew 19:16

We often call him the rich young ruler. He was all of these things. Though young, he had established himself as a leader in the Jewish community and had become quite wealthy. Besides that, he was morally upstanding, keeping God's commandments from his youth. His concern for spiritual matters inspired him to run to Jesus, kneel at His feet, and ask the world's most important question: "How can I have eternal life?"

The Lord's love moved Him to tell the rich young ruler the one thing he lacked: "If you want to be perfect, go, sell what you have and give to the poor, and you will have treasure in heaven; and come, follow Me" (Matthew 19:21). With laser insight, Jesus looked into the heart of the young man and identified the one thing that kept him from surrendering and following.

The rich young ruler came to the right Person at the right time with the right question, and he got the right answer. His promising beginning makes the ending of the story all the more heartbreaking: "When the young man heard that saying, he went away sorrowful, for he had great possessions" (Matthew 19:22).

Imagine the scene as the young man got up from his knees and turned his back on Jesus. He had come face-to-face with the Son of God, he had been offered eternal life from the very lips of Jesus, and yet he walked away unhappy and unsaved. Why? Because he refused to surrender. The tragic account of the rich young ruler reminds us of a simple but profound reality: if we are not following Jesus on terms of total surrender, then we are not following Jesus at all.

Dear Lord Jesus, show me what You are calling me to surrender so that I can follow You fully and closely. By Your grace, empower me to lay aside habitual sins, ungodly attitudes, and selfish desires. May my plans, my possessions, my dreams, my thoughts, and my actions be totally surrendered to You, for You alone are my Lord and Master, and seeking Your kingdom is my greatest joy. In Your name and power I pray. Amen.

WEEK 51—DAY 3

Serve God on His Terms

It happened as they journeyed on the road, that someone said to Him, "Lord,
I will follow You wherever You go." And Jesus said to him, "Foxes have holes
and birds of the air have nests, but the Son of Man has nowhere to lay His head."
Then He said to another, "Follow Me." But he said, "Lord, let me first go and bury my father."

Luke 9:57–59

We serve God on His terms, and His terms require a surrendered life. In Luke 9:57–62 a number of people expressed an interest in following Jesus, but none of them seemed willing to surrender to Him. Giving up a home, disappointing a family, or being rejected seemed to be higher prices than they were willing to pay.

When you began to follow Jesus Christ, you came to Him on terms of total surrender. You brought Him the ruins and regrets of your old sinful life, as well as your plans and hopes for the future. You said, "Lord, here is my life, I give it to You." As you grow in Christ, He will show you other areas of surrender to which He is calling you.

Imagine that you have a beautiful chess set in your home. Your friend is an avid chess player, so you decide to give the set to him as a gift. You wrap each pawn, knight, bishop, rook, king, and queen, package everything in a box, and carry the set to your friend's house. You hand it to him and say, "I'm so glad for you to have this." Then, a few weeks later, while you are dusting the bookcase where you once kept the chess set, you discover one piece hidden behind a book. Here's the question: do you take your friend the last piece, or do you leave him with an incomplete chess set? The answer is simple. If you truly gave him your chess set, the missing piece already belongs to him.

In the same way, if you have truly given Jesus your life, then every part of you already belongs to Him. As He shows you new areas of surrender, give those pieces of your life to Him.

  Dear Lord Jesus, I want my life to be completely Yours. Forgive me for attempting to follow You on my own terms rather than seeking and surrendering to You. Reveal to me areas of my life that I need to submit to Your lordship today. Give me Your grace that I might trust every piece of my life to Your care and leadership. I praise You that You are more than worthy of all my life, my service, and my praise. To You be glory. Amen.

DR. STEPHEN RUMMAGE, BRANDON, FL

WEEK 51—DAY 4

The Cost of Discipleship

When He had called the people to Himself, with His disciples also, He said to them, "Whoever desires to come after Me, let him deny himself, and take up his cross, and follow Me. For whoever desires to save his life will lose it, but whoever loses his life for My sake and the gospel's will save it. For what will it profit a man if he gains the whole world, and loses his own soul?"

Mark 8:34–36

With flames raging behind her, Tracinda Foxe held her newborn son out of the third-floor window of her Bronx apartment, trying to get air into his tiny lungs. The fire was getting hotter and her baby's only chance of survival was for Tracinda to drop him from the window. She prayed, "God, please save my son." Then, she let him go. The one-month-old fell thirty feet through freezing air and, miraculously, landed safely in the arms of a man who, oddly enough, played catcher for the local baseball team!

Just as that baby lived because his mother let him go, we will find true life in Jesus Christ when we surrender to the cost of discipleship. By faith, we let go of ourselves and entrust ourselves completely to Him. The same Lord Jesus who saved us is also able to take our surrendered lives and transform them for His kingdom and glory.

In today's passage, Jesus places everything in the world on a balance. He piles up all the world's money, education, power, pleasure, achievement, and glory on one side until the scales are groaning under the weight. Then, just one soul is placed on the other side of the scales. Instantly, the one soul tips the scales. Your soul is infinitely more valuable than the combined treasures of the entire universe!

That's why it's so important for your soul to be saved. Jesus says that our souls are saved when we lose our lives for His sake. This means denying ourselves—saying no to our own desires and will. It means taking up our cross—dying to our old lives. It means following Jesus—totally surrendering to His lordship. Growing in our faith in Christ requires that we completely entrust all that we are to all that Jesus is.

 Dear Lord Jesus, I trust You with my eternal soul. Because You have saved my soul from sin and given me Your gift of eternal life, I desire to follow You with all that I am. Please deliver me from half-hearted discipleship. By Your grace and through Your Holy Spirit, empower me to obey You, honor You, and glorify You in my words, thoughts, and actions today. Amen.

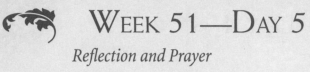

WEEK 51—DAY 5

Reflection and Prayer

What are some areas in your life that you would be ashamed of if Jesus were to come today? As you journal, ask for the Lord's deliverance from those sins, weaknesses, and misplaced priorities.

_____

_____

_____

_____

_____

_____

_____

_____

_____

In what ways do you need to say no to yourself as the dominating force in your life? What is the "one thing" that is keeping you from fully following Jesus?

_____

_____

_____

_____

_____

_____

_____

_____

_____

DR. STEPHEN RUMMAGE, BRANDON, FL

WEEK 52—DAY 1

Discipleship Begins with Caring for One Another

A new commandment I give to you, that you love one another; as I have loved you, that you also love one another. By this all will know that you are My disciples, if you have love for one another.

John 13:34, 35

It has been said that people do not care how much you know until they know how much you care. Just before Jesus gave this command in John 13, He had mentioned to His disciples that He would be leaving very soon. It was in that context that He shared what would be expected of His followers after His departure—they were to love one another. That was a challenge in itself, but then He added, "as I have loved you." We are called to love each other just like Jesus loved us. When the Lord Jesus spoke of love, He spoke of *agape* love, supreme and sacrificial. It was supreme in that no one ever loved like Jesus; He was willing to love even though the object of His love did not merit such love. It was sacrificial in that He was willing to give His all for the object of His love.

This is the same love that the apostle Paul told husbands they were to exhibit for their wives. We husbands are to love our wives to the point that we would give ourselves for them.

Jesus made a demand that is not possible for us to fulfill apart from His divine nature being imparted to us in the Person of the Holy Spirit. "The fruit of the Spirit is love, joy, peace, longsuffering, kindness, goodness, faithfulness, gentleness, self-control" (Galatians 5:22, 23). As we believers yield ourselves to Christ as surrendered vessels, He fills us with His presence. He loves through us and we serve Him with His gifts, just as Romans 5:5 says: "The love of God has been poured out in our hearts by the Holy Spirit who was given to us."

The Lord Jesus has given us not only an impossible demand but also an incredible opportunity. When we allow Him to love through us, the world recognizes that Christ is still alive. After all, Jesus said that people will know we are His disciples by our love (John 15:35). To know means to experience firsthand. What a privilege we have been given in displaying His love by His presence in us.

 Lord Jesus, may You be seen in me today through a life of surrender, service, and singleness of purpose—having Your love on display in my life. In Christ's name, Amen.

WEEK 52—DAY 2
Bearing Fruit Is a Lifestyle

If you abide in Me, and My words abide in you, you will ask what you desire, and it shall be done for you. By this My Father is glorified, that you bear much fruit; so you will be My disciples.

John 15:7, 8

I have never known much about farming. When I was a child and a teenager, I worked in the tobacco fields of eastern North Carolina. I believe that it was through those experiences that I developed the work ethic I possess today.

The first church the Lord called me to pastor was Lavonia Baptist Church, just outside Gaffney, South Carolina. Those were some of the greatest days of my life. I made friends in that community who have loved and cared for my family through the last thirty-five years. While serving there, I was encouraged to plant my very first garden. Wow, did I have lots to learn! I needed, and was blessed to receive, much help in planting, weeding, and caring for my first garden.

One thing that I will never forget is my neighbor planting potatoes. To this city dweller, the potato seed looked almost like the full-grown potato itself. I learned that the potato seed would remain only a seed until it died. Then, it had the ability to reproduce itself several times over. Jesus spoke of this truth in John 12:24: "Unless a grain of wheat falls into the ground and dies, it remains alone; but if it dies, it produces much grain."

This is so true in the life of the believer today. Unless we die to ourselves, our ambitions, and our desires, we will abide alone. It is God's will that we bear fruit. In order for that to happen, we must be in Him; we must stay around Him and remain in Him. We must obey His Word and desire His purpose for our lives. Then, the characteristics of the Almighty will be evident for others to see in our lives. His name will be made great and His glory will be on display! May we be faithful and fruitful in His service.

 Lord Jesus, I view this world as Your field of service. May I be a faithful farmer that prays and works the field of harvest today, for Christ's sake. In His name, Amen.

DR. JOHNNY HUNT, WOODSTOCK, GA

WEEK 52—DAY 3
Jesus Is Our Model

He poured water into a basin and began to wash the disciples' feet,
and to wipe them with the towel with which He was girded.

John 13:5

In the first century, it was a custom in the Middle East to wash the feet of your guests before inviting them into your home. With the dusty roads, the sandaled feet made things a little dirty, to say the least.

Jesus took this custom to a whole new level of service when He, the Son of God, was willing to stoop to wash His disciples' feet. It was a beautiful act of love and humility. He also taught His disciples about salvation and sanctification through foot washing. He told Peter that those who have relied on Him for salvation are "completely clean" (John 13:10). When He drew us by His love, we repented of our sin. He gave us the gift of salvation, imparting His righteousness to us; this act of complete cleansing never needs to be repeated. I am grateful for that! He also reminded Peter that as we continue to live in this world, we sometimes stumble and make sinful choices; as a result, our feet get a little dirty. Therefore, we need cleansing on a regular basis. He cleanses us through our daily confession and washes our feet as we repent. This is His process of setting us apart, the progression of sanctification.

When Jesus washed His disciples' feet, He commanded them to wash each other's feet. Our Lord never asks us to do anything that He has not already done Himself. He gave much exhortation, but it was balanced with much exemplification. Remember, Jesus "did not come to be served, but to serve, and to give His life a ransom for many" (Matthew 20:28).

Jesus was a man on a mission who knew who He was, where He came from, and where He was going (John 13:3). He was the picture of security; He could do what He did because He knew who He was. We share in that security when we are found in Him and follow Him, which includes humbly serving others.

    Lord Jesus, You came, lived, and died for us. We are grateful that the grave could not hold You and that You rose again. Through Your resurrected power, allow me to live as You lived in service to others and bring glory to Your name. In Jesus' name, Amen.

WEEK 52—DAY 4
Being a Disciple Is a Privilege

He who loves his life will lose it, and he who hates his life in this world will keep it for eternal life. If anyone serves Me, let him follow Me; and where I am, there My servant will be also. If anyone serves Me, him My Father will honor.

John 12:25, 26

Jesus seemed to teach paradoxical truths constantly. You must lose to win; you must give up to gain; you must die to live. Time and time again He spoke of the high cost of discipleship. The subject appears repeatedly throughout all four Gospels, and it comes up in today's passage. Jesus said that if you love your life—which carries the connotation of wishing to hold on to it—you will lose it. What exactly does this mean for us?

First, Jesus calls us to come to Him; we respond in faith and experience our initial surrender in the new birth. Then He says, "If anyone serves Me, let him follow Me." He also says, "If anyone desires to come after Me, let him deny himself, and take up his cross, and follow Me" (Matthew 16:24). We are not to take up His Cross, but our cross. This is a call to loyal obedience that is not just for now, but for a lifetime. True discipleship is saying no to ourselves and submitting to the lordship of Christ, and having that become our pattern of life (John 8:31; 1 John 2:6).

Jesus calls us to come to Him and to the end of ourselves to become so desirous of Him and His righteousness that we will make any sacrifice for Him. Hymn writer Thomas Shepherd put it this way: "Must Jesus bear the cross alone, and all the world go free? No, there's a cross for everyone, and there's a cross for me." We are called to live His life and not settle for ours.

As we surrender to His call to discipleship, Jesus promises to be there with us. What could be more reassuring than His presence? He also promises that the Father will honor us for our service. Indeed, He is to be praised!

 Lord Jesus, I am privileged to wear Your name. May my commitment to being a disciple honor Your great name, for Your greater glory. For Christ's sake, Amen.

DR. JOHNNY HUNT, WOODSTOCK, GA

WEEK 52—DAY 5

Reflection and Prayer

As you examine your journey with Christ, which of your characteristics most clearly display that you are a true disciple? What steps can you take to nurture those characteristics?

_____

_____

_____

_____

_____

_____

_____

_____

_____

A disciple of Jesus is a learner, a follower, and an obedient believer. In what ways are you growing as a disciple?

_____

_____

_____

_____

_____

_____

_____

_____

_____

CONTRIBUTORS

Tim Anderson . . . . Clements Baptist Church; Athens, AL . . . . Week 29

Craig Bowers. . . . . First Baptist Church; Locust Grove, GA . . . . Week 39

Kie Bowman. . . . . Hyde Park Baptist Church; Austin, TX . . . . Week 20

Paul Brooks. . . . . First Baptist Church; Raytown, MO . . . . Week 44

Dr. Peter Chin . . . . Global Mission Church; South Korea . . . . Week 45

Jeff Crook . . . . Blackshear Place Baptist Church; Flowery Branch, GA . . . . Week 33

Tim DeTellis . . . . New Missions; Orlando, FL . . . . Week 37

Chris Dixon. . . . . Liberty Baptist Church; Dublin, GA . . . . Week 27

Dr. Adam Dooley . . . . Dauphin Way Baptist Church; Mobile, AL . . . . Week 11

Tim Dowdy. . . . . Eagle's Landing First Baptist Church; McDonough, GA. . . . . Week 30

Dr. Grant Ethridge . . . . Liberty Baptist Church; Hampton, VA . . . . Week 13

Dr. Ronnie Floyd. . . . . Cross Church; Northwest Arkansas. . . . . Week 18

Brian Fossett. . . . . Brian Fossett Ministries; Dalton, GA . . . . Week 50

Jerry Gillis. . . . . The Chapel at Crosspoint; Getzville, NY. . . . . Week 5

Mike Hamlet. . . . . First Baptist Church North Spartanburg; Spartanburg, SC . . . . Week 21

Junior Hill . . . . Junior Hill Ministries; Hartselle, AL . . . . Week 10

Alex Himaya. . . . . The Church at Battle Creek; Broken Arrow, OK . . . . Week 38

Mark Hoover. . . . . New Spring Church; Wichita, KS . . . . Week 41

Dr. Johnny Hunt . . . . First Baptist Church; Woodstock, GA . . . . Weeks 1, 52

Norman Hunt. . . . . Hopewell Baptist Church; Canton, GA . . . . Week 8

Marty Jacumin. . . . . Bay Leaf Baptist Church; Raleigh, NC. . . . . Week 6

Bobby Joiner. . . . . Chaplain for NewSong; Leesburg, GA. . . . . Week 35

Dr. Richard Mark Lee . . . . . First Baptist Church; McKinney, TX . . . . Week 25

Dr. Michael Lewis . . . . First Baptist Church; Plant City, FL . . . . Week 19

Roy Mack . . . . Pinecrest Baptist Church; McDonough, GA . . . . Week 48

John Meador . . . . First Baptist Church; Euless, TX . . . . Week 47

Dr. Dwayne Mercer . . . . First Baptist Church; Oviedo, FL . . . . Week 28

Dr. James Merritt . . . . Cross Pointe Church; Duluth, GA . . . . Week 32

Dennis Nunn . . . . Every Believer a Witness Ministries, Dallas, GA . . . . Week 9

Jim Perdue . . . . Crosspointe Baptist Church, Millington, TN . . . . Week 34

Bob Pitman . . . . Bob Pitman Ministries; Muscle Shoals, AL . . . . Week 3

Vance Pitman . . . . Hope Baptist Church; Las Vegas, NV . . . . Week 31

Dr. Richard Powell . . . . McGregor Baptist Church; Fort Myers, FL . . . . Week 43

Paul Purvis . . . . First Baptist Church, Temple Terrace, FL . . . . Week 16

Willy Rice . . . . Calvary Baptist Church; Clearwater, FL . . . . Week 49

Dr. R. Philip Roberts . . . . . . Midwestern Baptist Theological Seminary; Kansas City, MO . . . . . Week 15

Dr. Stephen Rummage . . . . . Bell Shoals Baptist Church; Brandon, FL . . . . Week 51

Jeff Schreve . . . . First Baptist Church; Texarkana, TX . . . . Week 12

Dan Spencer . . . . First Baptist Church; Thomasville, GA . . . . Week 36

Dr. Glynn Stone . . . . Mobberly Baptist Church; Longview, TX . . . . Week 46

Matt Surber . . . . The Fellowship at Two Rivers; Nashville, TN . . . . Week 2

Allan Taylor . . . . First Baptist Church; Woodstock, GA . . . . Week 4

Arden Taylor . . . . Along the Journey; Gray, TN . . . . Week 26

Eric Thomas . . . . First Baptist Church; Norfolk, VA . . . . Week 14

Dr. Ted Traylor . . . . Olive Baptist Church; Pensacola, FL . . . . Week 42

Phil Waldrep . . . . Phil Waldrep Ministries; Trinity, AL . . . . Week 23

Jerry Walls . . . . Southside Baptist Church; Warner Robins, GA . . . . Week 22

Rick White . . . . The People's Church; Franklin, TN . . . . Week 17

Mike Whitson . . . . First Baptist Church; Indian Trail, NC . . . . Week 7

Dr. Danny Wood . . . . Shades Mountain Baptist Church; Birmingham, AL . . . . Week 40

Dr. Rob Zinn . . . . Immanuel Baptist Church, Highland, CA . . . . Week 24

Scripture Index

Scripture	Week/Day	Page
Genesis 39:2, 3	Week 11, Day 1	52
Genesis 39:20	Week 35, Day 2	173
Genesis 46:3, 4	Week 22, Day 3	109
Exodus 3:3–5	Week 30, Day 1	147
Exodus 31:18	Week 8, Day 3	39
Leviticus 25:17	Week 6, Day 3	29
Numbers 14:8, 9	Week 21, Day 1	102
Numbers 18:25, 26	Week 43, Day 3	214
Deuteronomy 4:32, 35	Week 28, Day 3	139
Deuteronomy 4:39, 40	Week 28, Day 4	140
Deuteronomy 6:6	Week 14, Day 3	69
Deuteronomy 19:19, 20	Week 6, Day 4	30
Joshua 1:6	Week 11, Day 4	55
Joshua 3:8	Week 14, Day 2	68
Joshua 7:7	Week 23, Day 2	113
Joshua 7:10, 13	Week 27, Day 3	134
Joshua 14:7, 8	Week 27, Day 4	135
Judges 6:6	Week 26, Day 3	129
Judges 6:12, 14	Week 43, Day 4	215
Ruth 1:16, 17	Week 42, Day 4	210
1 Samuel 3:8–10	Week 29, Day 1	142
1 Samuel 12:22	Week 4, Day 3	19
1 Samuel 18:7, 8	Week 17, Day 2	83
1 Samuel 20:42	Week 48, Day 1	237
2 Samuel 7:29	Week 8, Day 2	38
2 Samuel 12:1	Week 48, Day 3	239

2 Samuel 12:13 .... Week 33, Day 3................................... 164

2 Samuel 12:13, 14 .... Week 48, Day 4................................... 240

1 Kings 3:5............................. Week 17, Day 3.................................... 84

1 Kings 19:11, 12...................... Week 3, Day 1 12

2 Kings 4:1, 2 .... Week 23, Day 4................................... 115

1 Chronicles 22:13..................... Week 40, Day 2................................... 198

1 Chronicles 28:9...................... Week 5, Day 2 23

1 Chronicles 29:12..................... Week 39, Day 2................................... 193

2 Chronicles 2:12...................... Week 15, Day 3.................................... 74

Nehemiah 1:4 .... Week 47, Day 2................................... 233

Nehemiah 1:5, 6........................ Week 18, Day 1.................................... 87

Esther 4:16............................. Week 31, Day 2................................... 153

Job 19:25–27 .... Week 36, Day 3................................... 179

Job 42:7, 9, 10......................... Week 24, Day 1................................... 117

Job 42:12, 13 .... Week 24, Day 2................................... 118

Psalm 4:6–8............................ Week 24, Day 4................................... 120

Psalm 23:1 .... Week 1, Day 1 2

Psalm 23:3 .... Week 1, Day 2 3

Psalm 23:2, 3 .... Week 1, Day 3 4

Psalm 23:2, 3 .... Week 4, Day 2 18

Psalm 23:4 .... Week 1, Day 4 5

Psalm 25:4, 5 .... Week 26, Day 1................................... 127

Psalm 27:14 .... Week 14, Day 4.................................... 70

Psalm 31:7, 8 .... Week 46, Day 4................................... 230

Psalm 32:5, 6 .... Week 34, Day 2................................... 168

Psalm 37:4 .... Week 38, Day 2................................... 188

Psalm 37:5, 6 .... Week 45, Day 2................................... 223

Psalm 46:1–3........................... Week 26, Day 4................................... 130

Psalm 46:10 .... Week 27, Day 1................................... 132

Psalm 79:13 .... Week 13, Day 2.................................... 63

Psalm 81:10 .... Week 27, Day 2................................... 133

Psalm 119:67, 68 .... Week 49, Day 3................................... 244

Psalm 139:1–4 . . . . Week 28, Day 1 137

Psalm 139:13, 14 . . . . Week 28, Day 2 138

Psalm 150:1, 2, 6 . . . . Week 3, Day 3 14

Proverbs 2:1, 2, 4, 5 . . . . Week 8, Day 4 40

Proverbs 2:6, 7 . . . . Week 9, Day 1 42

Proverbs 3:5, 6 . . . . Week 29, Day 2 143

Proverbs 13:10 . . . . Week 10, Day 4 50

Proverbs 14:10 . . . . Week 19, Day 4 95

Proverbs 16:18 . . . . Week 31, Day 3 154

Proverbs 19:17 . . . . Week 50, Day 4 250

Proverbs 23:4, 5 . . . . Week 42, Day 3 209

Ecclesiastes 2:26 . . . . Week 2, Day 1 7

Ecclesiastes 9:10 . . . . Week 12, Day 1 57

Ecclesiastes 11:6 . . . . Week 11, Day 3 54

Song of Solomon 2:4 . . . . Week 2, Day 2 8

Song of Solomon 5:16 . . . . Week 2, Day 3 9

Isaiah 26:3 . . . . Week 26, Day 2 128

Isaiah 30:21 . . . . Week 4, Day 4 20

Isaiah 40:31 . . . . Week 12, Day 2 58

Isaiah 55:3 . . . . Week 10, Day 2 48

Isaiah 64:4 . . . . Week 29, Day 3 144

Isaiah 64:9 . . . . Week 14, Day 1 67

Jeremiah 1:6–8 . . . . Week 11, Day 2 53

Jeremiah 2:13 . . . . Week 3, Day 4 15

Jeremiah 15:19, 20 . . . . Week 31, Day 1 152

Jeremiah 18:4–6 . . . . Week 29, Day 4 145

Jeremiah 22:21 . . . . Week 15, Day 2 73

Jeremiah 29:11 . . . . Week 36, Day 1 177

Jeremiah 33:3 . . . . Week 19, Day 1 92

Jeremiah 42:1–3 . . . . Week 5, Day 3 24

Lamentations 3:22, 23 . . . . Week 22, Day 4 110

Lamentations 3:31–33 . . . . Week 46, Day 1 227

Lamentations 3:40 .... Week 21, Day 2 103

Ezekiel 22:30 .... Week 20, Day 1 97

Daniel 1:8, 9 .... Week 40, Day 3 199

Daniel 4:30, 31 .... Week 16, Day 4 80

Daniel 6:10, 11 .... Week 33, Day 4 165

Daniel 6:16 .... Week 36, Day 2 178

Daniel 9:3, 4 .... Week 18, Day 3 89

Hosea 2:19 .... Week 2, Day 4 10

Hosea 3:4, 5 .... Week 34, Day 4 170

Hosea 6:6 .... Week 4, Day 1 17

Joel 1:19 .... Week 49, Day 2 243

Joel 2:12, 13 .... Week 32, Day 1 157

Joel 2:17, 19 .... Week 32, Day 2 158

Amos 6:3, 7 .... Week 35, Day 4 175

Jonah 3:1–4 .... Week 32, Day 4 160

Habakkuk 3:17, 18 .... Week 7, Day 2 33

Zephaniah 3:17 .... Week 35, Day 3 174

Haggai 2:4 .... Week 12, Day 3 59

Malachi 3:10, 12 .... Week 41, Day 1 202

Matthew 1:20 .... Week 6, Day 2 28

Matthew 5:44 .... Week 37, Day 3 184

Matthew 6:8 .... Week 20, Day 4 100

Matthew 6:25, 26 .... Week 21, Day 4 105

Matthew 6:31, 33 .... Week 23, Day 1 112

Matthew 6:33, 34 .... Week 22, Day 1 107

Matthew 9:9 .... Week 43, Day 1 212

Matthew 16:19 .... Week 8, Day 1 37

Matthew 19:16 .... Week 51, Day 2 253

Matthew 28:19, 20 .... Week 39, Day 3 194

Mark 3:35 .... Week 13, Day 3 64

Mark 4:39, 40 .... Week 49, Day 1 242

Mark 8:34–36 .... Week 51, Day 4 255

Mark 16:15.............................Week 39, Day 1....................................192
Luke 6:38 ....Week 42, Day 2....................................208
Luke 9:57–59..........................Week 51, Day 3....................................254
Luke 19:2–6...........................Week 43, Day 2....................................213
Luke 24:38 ....Week 19, Day 2.....................................93
John 8:31, 32 ....Week 13, Day 4.....................................65
John 12:25, 26 ....Week 52, Day 4....................................260
John 13:5 ....Week 52, Day 3....................................259
John 13:34, 35 ....Week 52, Day 1....................................257
John 14:17 ....Week 41, Day 3....................................204
John 15:7, 8 ....Week 52, Day 2....................................258
John 16:13 ....Week 15, Day 1.....................................72
Acts 2:4..............................Week 12, Day 4.....................................60
Acts 9:3–5 ....Week 32, Day 3....................................159
Romans 3:24 .... Week 9, Day 2 43
Romans 4:20, 21 ....Week 40, Day 1....................................197
Romans 7:18–20.......................Week 33, Day 1....................................162
Romans 7:22–25.......................Week 33, Day 2....................................163
Romans 8:1, 2 ....Week 31, Day 4....................................155
Romans 8:29 .... Week 7, Day 3 34
Romans 10:17 ....Week 39, Day 4....................................195
Romans 12:1, 2 ....Week 37, Day 4....................................185
Romans 12:9–11.......................Week 48, Day 2....................................238
Romans 14:12, 13 ....Week 38, Day 4....................................190
1 Corinthians 1:26–29 ....Week 50, Day 1....................................247
1 Corinthians 2:9.................... Week 9, Day 3 44
1 Corinthians 2:10–12 ....Week 42, Day 1....................................207
1 Corinthians 6:9, 11.................Week 25, Day 4....................................125
1 Corinthians 10:13 .... Week 6, Day 1 27
1 Corinthians 13:4–7 ....Week 30, Day 3....................................149
1 Corinthians 13:8–10 ....Week 30, Day 4....................................150
1 Corinthians 13:12, 13 ....Week 25, Day 3....................................124

1 Corinthians 15:58 .... Week 50, Day 3.................................249

2 Corinthians 1:3, 4...................... Week 25, Day 1.................................122

2 Corinthians 5:18, 19................... Week 44, Day 2.................................218

2 Corinthians 8:9........................ Week 44, Day 4.................................220

2 Corinthians 9:10, 11................... Week 24, Day 3.................................119

2 Corinthians 12:8, 9.................... Week 46, Day 2.................................228

2 Corinthians 12:9....................... Week 37, Day 1.................................182

Galatians 2:20 .... Week 21, Day 3.................................104

Galatians 5:22, 23 .... Week 37, Day 2.................................183

Galatians 6:1 .... Week 36, Day 4.................................180

Galatians 6:2 .... Week 5, Day 1 .... .22

Ephesians 1:3, 4........................ Week 41, Day 2.................................203

Ephesians 2:10......................... Week 9, Day 4 .... .45

Ephesians 4:12, 13...................... Week 44, Day 1.................................217

Ephesians 4:28, 29...................... Week 38, Day 3.................................189

Ephesians 4:30......................... Week 41, Day 4.................................205

Ephesians 4:31, 32...................... Week 5, Day 4 .... .25

Ephesians 6:5, 6........................ Week 15, Day 4................................. .75

Philippians 1:29 .... Week 45, Day 4.................................225

Philippians 3:13, 14 .... Week 16, Day 3................................. .79

Philippians 4:6, 7...................... Week 34, Day 3.................................169

Philippians 4:19 .... Week 16, Day 2................................. .78

Colossians 1:9, 12 .... Week 17, Day 4................................. .85

Colossians 2:6, 7 .... Week 20, Day 2................................. .98

Colossians 3:23 .... Week 13, Day 1................................. .62

1 Thessalonians 5:11, 14 .... Week 47, Day 4.................................235

1 Thessalonians 5:17 .... Week 18, Day 4................................. .90

2 Thessalonians 3:1, 2 .... Week 47, Day 1.................................232

2 Thessalonians 3:5 .... Week 30, Day 2.................................148

1 Timothy 6:7 .... Week 23, Day 3.................................114

2 Timothy 1:7 .... Week 19, Day 3................................. .94

2 Timothy 3:16, 17 .... Week 7, Day 4 .... .35

2 Timothy 4:16, 17 .... Week 44, Day 3.................................... 219

Titus 1:4 .... Week 49, Day 4.................................... 245

Hebrews 3:1 .... Week 25, Day 2.................................... 123

Hebrews 4:15, 16 .... Week 34, Day 1.................................... 167

Hebrews 6:11 .... Week 20, Day 3..................................... 99

Hebrews 10:23......................... Week 10, Day 1..................................... 47

Hebrews 10:24, 25 .... Week 47, Day 3.................................... 234

James 1:2–4 .... Week 40, Day 4.................................... 200

James 1:26, 27 .... Week 38, Day 1.................................... 187

James 2:18 .... Week 45, Day 1.................................... 222

James 4:3 .... Week 22, Day 2.................................... 108

James 4:8 .... Week 10, Day 3..................................... 49

James 5:15, 16 .... Week 18, Day 2..................................... 88

1 Peter 1:6, 7.......................... Week 46, Day 3.................................... 229

1 Peter 4:12–14 .... Week 50, Day 2.................................... 248

1 Peter 5:5 .... Week 17, Day 1..................................... 82

1 Peter 5:8, 9.......................... Week 45, Day 3.................................... 224

1 John 1:9............................. Week 3, Day 2 13

Revelation 18:23 .... Week 7, Day 1 32

Revelation 20:10 .... Week 35, Day 1.................................... 172

Revelation 22:12 .... Week 16, Day 1..................................... 77

Revelation 22:6, 7, 20 .... Week 51, Day 1.................................... 252

Prayer Journal

Keeping and praying through a prayer journal every day has been a very productive thing for me and has helped me tremendously in my daily time with the Lord. We need a focused and reverent time of prayer with the Lord every day, and it needs to be without interruption as much as possible.

I started this practice for several reasons. First, I want to be involved in the ministry of intercession at a high level. Many times people would stop me and say, "Pastor Johnny, would you pray for me?" I would respond that I would do so and I did so one time or two and then forgot. I wanted to pray continually for those folks until they saw God do something. Second, during my time with the Lord, I find that if I do not have a guide to keep me on course, my mind will wander. My journal keeps me focused on what and who I am praying for.

My prayer is that this little tool will help you develop a more fruitful time with the Lord, and that you will see Him do great and mighty things as a result of your prayers. I will give you some topics to follow and then some suggestions for how to pray. This list is certainly not exhaustive and you will want to add much more to each item as the Lord directs you. I am excited about what the Lord will do in and through you for His honor and glory. I pray this new journey will take you to new heights in your relationship with the Lord Jesus. We *need* to talk to Him, and He desires to hear more from us. Let's commit together to take our prayer life to a whole new level. We will be the ones to receive the greatest benefit from it.

Prayer is not much of a priority for many people today, but it should be the most important appointment we have each day. Remember, prayer happens when we depend upon God. However, the opposite is also true. Prayerlessness happens when we depend upon ourselves. Our dependency needs to be firmly rooted in Him. So, whatever else you do each day, pray, pray, pray.

Dr. Johnny M. Hunt
Pastor, First Baptist Church of Woodstock
Woodstock, Georgia

 # CONFESSION

It is important that we begin our time with the Lord with a time of confession. As we do, we should acknowledge our need for the Lord—that we are absolutely inadequate and nothing apart from Him.

John 15:5—I am the vine, you are the branches. He who abides in Me, and I in him, bears much fruit; for without Me you can do nothing.

Write out a prayer here and tell the Lord how dependent you are on Him today and every day.

_____

_____

_____

_____

_____

1 John 1:9— "If we confess our sins, He is faithful and just to forgive us our sins and to cleanse us from all unrighteousness."

Luke 11:4— "Forgive us our sins."

Psalm 139:23, 24— "Search me, O God, and know my heart; try me, and know my anxieties; and see if there is any wicked way in me, and lead me in the way everlasting."

Proverbs 28:13— "Whoever confesses and forsakes [his sins] will have mercy."

_____

_____

_____

_____

_____

Pray that you will see your sins in view of God's holiness and that you will be as offended and grieved as God is about them.

List sins of omission.

_____

_____

_____

_____

_____

_____

_____

_____

List sins of commission.

_____

_____

_____

_____

_____

_____

_____

_____

_____

_____

_____

_____

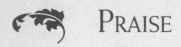 PRAISE

We have so much for which to praise the Lord. So much of our time with the Lord often is, "Gimme, gimme, gimme." We need to stop and praise Him for His goodness and His graciousness to us.

Psalm 22:23—"You who fear the Lord, praise Him!"

Psalm 67:3—"Let the peoples praise You, O God; let all the peoples praise You."

Psalm 145:10—"All Your works shall praise You, O Lord, and Your saints shall bless You."

Praise Him for who He is: He is holy (1 Peter 1:16, Revelation 20:6). He is merciful (Psalm 23:6; 103:8; 106:1). He is kind. He is righteous.

Express your gratitude.

_____

_____

_____

_____

Praise Him for His works: He saved us, and He sustains us and spares us from this wicked world.

Express your gratitude.

_____

_____

_____

_____

_____

_____

_____

Praise Him for who you are: You are His new creation.

2 Corinthians 5:17—"If anyone is in Christ, he is a new creation; old things have passed away; behold, all things have become new."

Express your gratitude.

_____

_____

_____

_____

_____

_____

_____

_____

List other things for which you want to praise Him.

_____

_____

_____

_____

_____

_____

_____

_____

_____

_____

 # THANKSGIVING

We need to have a time of thanksgiving to God for His goodness to us. We will never be able to thank Him enough for all His blessings!

1 Thessalonians 5:18—"In everything give thanks; for this is the will of God in Christ Jesus for you."

Ephesians 5:20—"Giving thanks always for all things to God the Father in the name of our Lord Jesus Christ."

Thank Him for His faithfulness to you.

_____

_____

_____

_____

_____

Thank Him for the mountaintop experiences He has given you.

_____

_____

_____

_____

_____

_____

_____

_____

_____

Thank Him for the valley experiences He has brought you through, or that you may be in now.

_____

_____

_____

_____

_____

Thank Him for blessing you physically, emotionally, financially, and spiritually in abundance.

_____

_____

_____

_____

_____

_____

Thank Him for the material things of life He has provided for you.

_____

_____

_____

_____

_____

_____

Thank Him for the finances He has entrusted to you.

Thank Him for shelter, food, and clothes.

Thank Him for your health and the health of your family members.

List other things you are thankful for (church, friends, God's guidance, etc.).

Submission and Surrender

James 4:7—"Submit [surrender] to God. Resist the devil and he will flee from you."

We need to surrender and submit everything to the Lord daily in order for Him to use us. Here are some suggestions. Try to add more of your own.

Surrender my mind
Surrender my will
Surrender my emotions
Surrender my spirit
Surrender my motives
Surrender my goals
Surrender my family

Surrender my body
Surrender my attitude
Surrender my tongue
Surrender my thought life
Surrender my dreams
Surrender my past, present, and future
Surrender my career

_____

_____

_____

_____

_____

_____

_____

_____

_____

_____

We should pray that we will be controlled, consumed, and anointed by the Holy Spirit of God today.

Ask the Lord to help you decrease so that He may increase. Submit yourself to Him and commit your day to Him. Ask Him to guide your every step today.

_____

_____

_____

_____

_____

# INTERCESSION

What a wonderful privilege and responsibility the body of Christ has to intercede on behalf of others. This should be a high and holy time daily when you are privileged to participate in this blessed ministry.

Samuel said in 1 Samuel 12:23, "Far be it from me that I should sin against the LORD in ceasing to pray for you." He understood it! First Timothy 2:1 says, "I exhort first of all that supplications, prayers, intercessions, and giving of thanks be made for all men." Ephesians 6:18 reads, "Praying always . . . in the Spirit . . . for all the saints."

God help us to be faithful intercessors!

Intercede for family members.

_____

_____

_____

_____

_____

_____

Intercede for the senior pastor of your church.

_____

_____

_____

_____

_____

_____

Intercede for church and church leadership.

_____

_____

_____

_____

_____

_____

_____

_____

Intercede for friends.

_____

_____

_____

_____

_____

_____

_____

_____

_____

_____

_____

Urgent Prayer Requests

Philippians 4:6—"In everything by prayer and supplication, with thanksgiving let your requests be made known to God."

In this area, I list all the requests that did not fit in any of the other areas. If someone has asked me to pray for them, I list their names and needs in this section and call them out before the Lord daily. These requests may come from family members, friends, or people I do not know, and they may be physical, emotional, spiritual, or financial in nature.

When I hear that God has answered the prayers I am praying on this list, I mark through the request with a red pen. The red mark indicates that God heard and answered my prayers. It serves as a great reminder and motivation to keep on praying, because God answers prayer. There is nothing too small or too big to list here. God is concerned about anything that concerns us.

Physical needs

_____

_____

_____

_____

_____

_____

_____

_____

_____

_____

_____

_____

Emotional and financial needs

_____

_____

_____

_____

_____

_____

_____

_____

_____

Spiritual needs

_____

_____

_____

_____

_____

_____

_____

_____

_____

_____

_____

SPECIAL FOCUS PRAYERS

There is one final thing I want to suggest. You may want to designate particular days of the week to focus on specific issues. For instance, on Sundays, you may want to focus on praying for missionaries, and on Mondays, you may want to focus on praying for your immediate family members. You may not need to develop this section if all your prayer requests are covered in other areas of your daily journal. Even if they are, you may still like to try this approach.

On Sunday, my focus will be _____

On Monday, my focus will be _____

On Tuesday, my focus will be _____

On Wednesday, my focus will be _____

On Thursday, my focus will be _____

On Friday, my focus will be _____

On Saturday, my focus will be _____

You may want to develop a separate page for each day.

Discipleship Moments

Discipleship Moments

Discipleship Moments

DISCIPLESHIP MOMENTS

Discipleship Moments

Discipleship Moments

Discipleship Moments

DISCIPLESHIP MOMENTS

DISCIPLESHIP MOMENTS

DISCIPLESHIP MOMENTS